Food, Society,
and Environment

Food, Society, and Environment

CHARLES L. HARPER
Creighton University

BRYAN F. LE BEAU
University of Missouri at Kansas City

Prentice
Hall

Upper Saddle River, New Jersey 07458

Library of Congress Catalog-in-Publication Data

Harper, Charles L.
    Food, society, and environment / Charles L. Harper, Bryan F. Le Beau.
      p. cm.
    Includes bibliographical references and index.
    ISBN 0-13-030566-9 (pbk.)
    1. Gastronomy.   2. Food habits.   I. Le Beau, Bryan F., (date)   II. Title.

TX631 .H367 2003
641'.01'3—dc21

                                  2002017094

AVP, Publisher: Nancy Roberts
Senior Acquisitions Editor: Chris DeJohn
Editorial Assistant: Christina Scalia
Editorial/production supervision and interior design: Mary Araneo
Marketing Manager: Amy Speckman
Marketing Assistant: Anne Marie Fritzky
Prepress and Manufacturing Buyer: Mary Ann Gloriande
Photo Permission Coordinator: Nancy Seise
Cover Art Director: Jayne Conte
Cover Designer: Bruce Kenselaar

This book was set in 10/12 New Baskerville by A & A Publishing Services, Inc., and was printed and bound by Courier Companies, Inc. The cover was printed by Phoenix Color Corp.

© 2003 by Pearson Education, Inc.
Upper Saddle River, New Jersey 07458

Printed in the United States of America

10 9 8 7 6 5 4 3 2 1

ISBN 0-13-030566-9

Pearson Education LTD., London
Pearson Education Australia PTY, Limited, Sydney
Pearson Education Singapore, Pte. Ltd
Pearson Education North Asia Ltd, Hong Kong
Pearson Education Canada, Ltd., Toronto
Pearson Educación de Mexico, S.A. de C.V.
Pearson Education — Japan, Tokyo
Pearson Education Malaysia, Pte. Ltd
Pearson Education, Upper Saddle River, New Jersey

To Anne and Chris,
whose love sustains us
when food is not enough

Contents

Preface

The title *Food, Society, and Environment* came from conversation. When people asked us "what is your book about?" that's exactly what we told them—mentioning a bit about how we treated the three terms as important qualifiers. Our book is addressed to two kinds of readers. First, to those who find food issues fascinating because they relate to such universal and basic human concerns, and particularly those who may appreciate the insights of the humanities and social sciences "about food." Second, to those in educational settings—students and faculty—for whom food issues are important because they relate to other human concerns. As an early reviewer of our project said: "Food is a topic critically important to many fields, but one which often slips through the cracks of conventional analysis." Specialized food scholars will find little new in this book, though we hope to have accurately incorporated some of their important findings and insights. As we explain in the following introduction, rather than a very specialized approach, we attempt to discuss the important links between food issues from different perspectives and areas of scholarship, insights, and perspectives.

That is indeed a challenge—but one that we found fascinating and engaging. It also extended a long-standing friendship and collegial relationship. Given our intended readers, we have written in an informal style, because we think that reading should be more like a conversation between authors and their readers.

We thank the College of Arts and Sciences of Creighton University for providing sabbatical leaves, which provided the time and resources making our project possible. In particular, we thank Prentice Hall Publisher Nancy Roberts, who decided to publish the work, and also Chris DeJohn, Sharon Chambliss, and Christina Scalia, and all of the Prentice Hall staff who supported its development. We thank the following Prentice Hall reviewers for their suggestions and comments: David Kozak, Fort Lewis College; Amy Bentley, New York University; Harold C. Furr, University of Connecticut; Ken Albala, University of the Pacific. We thank our academic colleagues and students, who encouraged us, as well as suffered us while it was being completed. Last but not the least, we thank our wives Anne and Chris, who both encouraged and suffered us individually through this and other projects over the years.

We are interested in your insights and responses, and encourage you to contact us if you wish.

Charles Harper
charper@creighton.edu
Bryan Le Beau
LeBeau@umkc.edu

INTRODUCTION

Food as a Human Value and Problem

Consider how Americans are bombarded with messages about food. Stroll down the aisle of any supermarket and you will see all manner of foods claiming "reduced fat," "low calorie," and "low cholesterol." Flip through magazines and you will find advice about how to eat to lose weight, have more energy, enhance your physical performance and sexual attractiveness, and prevent diseases. Here's a sample of such headlines we found: "Eat all you want and burn fat 24 hours a day....Lose 25 lbs. by Thanksgiving....Creamy shakes that zap anxiety....New eggs lower cholesterol....Cure winter depression by eating more complex carbohydrates, taking vitamin B supplements, and St. Johns' wort....New anti-cancer miracle meals, quick and delicious, you'll like them....Eat right to prevent arthritis and cardiovascular disease....Broccoli, the miracle food that will prevent cancer....Garlic (capsules) promote cardiovascular health....A diet and exercise plan to banish your bulging belly, butt, and thighs....Vitamins that make you smarter." We could go on and on, but you get the idea.

How valid are these claims? Undoubtedly some are, but others are false or deliberately misleading. Such media messages raise concerns about health fraud and food quackery. For instance, in 1970 and again in 1989 General Nutrition Inc. (GNC), the largest retailer of nutritional supplements in the United States, was charged with making unsubstantiated claims for a number of nutritional products, including supplements touted as fat melters, muscle builders, and energy boosters. In 1994 the Federal Trade Commission (FTC) alleged that GNC continued making spurious claims for over 40 products, in spite of FTC orders not to do so. GNC agreed to pay a $2.4 million fine—the largest civil penalty for violating an advertising order in the FTC's history.[1]

Food concerns do not end with misleading claims and quackery; there are also controversies about how food is produced, processed, and transported. Popular and scientific concerns relate to the uses of pesticides, herbicides, growth hormones, antibiotics in producing food, or about the health consequences of the multitude of chemical additives, preservatives, shelf-life extenders, flavor enhancers, and coloring agents in many of our foods. In the United States a vigorous "health food" movement promotes natural and organic foods, free of such additives in production and processing. Organic foods comprise a small part of America's total food budget, but they are the fastest growing retail food sector. Strong concerns exist about the health and ecological impacts of genetically modified foods, though that is by no means a new phenomenon.

Concerns go beyond personal well-being, and include how food is sold or distributed by companies whose money influences political policies and raises controversies as to conflicts of interest. For instance, in 1999 public interest groups resigned from a U.S. Federal Government advisory panel about food safety, because, they alleged, "The pesticide industry and agribusiness lobbyists and their allies...hijacked the process."[2] Because food is such an important human concern, it often becomes a bargaining chip or weapon in political struggles around the world.

Other food controversies surround the environmental consequences of modern agriculture. In 2000 a report released by the International Food Policy Research Institute (affiliated with the United Nations) reported that 40 percent of the world's farmland was *seriously degraded* by soil erosion, loss of organic matter, compaction, pollutant chemical penetration, nutrient depletion, and excess salinity.[3] With the growth of crop irrigation since the 1950s, many of the world's rivers are being drawn down, and collectively farmers are overpumping groundwater, causing aquifer depletion and falling groundwater tables around the world. In the United States, for example, agricultural and municipal use has reduced the Colorado River to a trickle as it empties into the Gulf of Mexico. Similarly, the Ogallala Aquifer that underlies the

---

FOOD SELF-INVENTORY

Here's an interesting and easy activity that will engage you with food in a personal way. Keep track of what you eat at different times for a week, or at least several days to get a good "sample" of your own eating behavior. You may be surprised about yourself, and you can use this in the next chapter when we discuss healthy diets. Also, to the extent you can, think about where the food came from, and how it got produced and delivered to you.

Great Plains from Texas to the Dakotas is being rapidly depleted to support dry-land agriculture. The water supply that remains is being polluted with agricultural and industrial chemicals such as pesticides, nitrates, and petrochemicals. Indeed, a worldwide water crisis looms, which bodes ill for increasing food supplies to satisfy a growing world population.[4]

Malnutrition remains a problem in the United States, as well as around the world. *Famine* is commonly associated with natural disasters such as prolonged droughts and hurricanes (such as in Bangladesh, Guatemala, and Mozambique) or civil wars and political violence (such as in Ethiopia, Somalia, Rwanda, and Sierra Leone). These result in gruesome media images of starving children and often stimulate heroic global relief efforts. Chronic and persistent malnutrition among those who don't have enough to eat to support health and well-being is a more widespread problem than famine, however, even though it gets less media attention. Furthermore, not all malnutrition is caused by not having enough to eat, and not all is found in poor countries, the United States being a case in point.

The U.S. pharmaceutical industry spends billions of dollars to find a weight loss drug for those who are overnourished and overweight, conditions that result in life-threatening personal health problems along with large private and public health costs. At the same time, another segment of America suffers from not enough to eat and lives in food-insecure families. They are overproportionately women and children.[5] Such hunger in the midst of general economic prosperity and recent government budget-cutting policies has resulted in a pervasive network of private charitable organizations that collect and distribute food. But this network is inadequate for the need. In 1997 and 1998 studies by the Conference of Mayors in thirty U.S. cities reported increasing needs for emergency food. Nevertheless, in about half of those cities people were turned away because food supplies were inadequate.[6]

Why do we mention these issues? Only to emphasize that we live in a world permeated by information, messages, and concerns about food of many kinds on many different levels. Messages and concerns come from our friends and relatives, the media, businesses, a multitude of experts and professionals, and from officials charged with protecting public interests. Indeed, insuring the adequacy and nutritiousness of food for you and the world's people is among the most basic and elemental human needs underlying all others. Thus, questions about food connect us to seemingly endless layers of scientific, historical, cultural, social, economic, environmental, political, ethical, and social justice issues and controversies.

PEELING THE FOOD ONION

Asking questions about food is like peeling an onion. With each layer you peel away there are different meanings and problems. Many reflect the issues we mentioned. Consider just a few:

A QUESTION

"Tell me what you eat, and I will tell you what you are," claims Anthelme Bril-
lot-Savarin (1755–1826) French politician and gourmet, author of *Physiology of
taste*.[7] Think about this old and familiar saying. In what sense do you think it is
true, misleading, or false?

- To begin with the obvious, food is basic to every individual's health and
well-being. The metabolic truism "you are what you eat" means that the
dietary adequacy of food shapes your individual characteristics, human
potential, illnesses, and life span.
- Because food is so universally important, eating provides settings for
social bonding and cultural meaning among all people. To eat with others is always a social event with diverse symbolic meanings. It is a universal basis for defining human identity, social solidarity, and the
boundaries of group affiliation. Age and gender are defined in terms of
appropriate food. Food preparation and eating styles (cuisines) are an
important basis of national, ethnic, and other forms of human affiliation. Food symbolizes important beliefs of the world's religions, and all
have rituals and taboos involving eating and food.
- Unequal access to food, both in America and around the world, means
that there is malnutrition among the poor, along with the diseases of
overindulgence and unhealthy diets among the affluent classes. Food, in
other words, is related to social class and global inequalities.
- Eating and food shapes the history of nations and the world. The discovery of new food and its spread and control have shaped the growth
and decline of civilizations, the exploration of the world, and the dominance or dependence of groups and nations. Conventional history is
written about politics, famous people, and "big events." It could just as
easily emphasize the historical significance of spices, potatoes, crop and
animal hybrids, canning and freezing techniques, irrigation and fertil-
ization, or convenience foods.
- Human food production has the greatest measurable impact on the
earth's biophysical environment, and every agricultural resource system
(such as fertile soil, pastureland, surface and groundwater, and ocean
fisheries) is now measurably degraded and under unprecedented stress.
- Even with today's huge world population (6 billion and still growing),
there is enough food produced to adequately feed (in theory) every
man, woman, and child now alive. But after steadily growing since the
1940s, evidence suggests that per capita food production leveled off in
the 1990s.[9]
- The possession of food is a political resource (sometimes a weapon),
and rights about owning the resources to produce food (like land) or

---

THE UNDERNOURISHED AND OVERNOURISHED

In a large desert tent in war-torn Sudan, doctors and nurses from an aid agency are hard at work hovering over starving children administering high-calorie biscuits and sugar water in an effort to revive them. The children traveled from miles away, mostly on foot, and all of them are emaciated, with skin stretched tightly across their bones, and with stomachs that, ironically, are distended from a calorie and protein deficiency, known as "kwashiorkor," that disturbs the water balance of the abdomen.

Half a world away, patients arrive at the cardiac ward of Mt. Sinai hospital in Manhattan, often complaining of chest pains. Doctors prepare some for open-heart surgery, schedule others for angioplasties to open clogged arteries, and administer anticlotting medication to others. Like the Sudanese children, many of them also have swollen abdomens—in this case from too much food. Many New Yorkers will survive, unlike many Sudanese children, only to return later with similar symptoms. The Sudanese children, like many in poor nations, live in the midst of a civil war and are victimized by not having enough food, particularly not enough protein, to support normal health and growth. The New Yorkers, like many affluent people everywhere, are victimized by the proliferation of high-calorie, high-fat foods that are widely available, heavily advertised, and served in huge portions. This has become what Yale psychologist Kelly Brownell calls a "toxic food environment," in which sweets and fats increasingly crowd out nutritionally complete foods providing essential vitamins and minerals. For instance, one fifth of the "vegetables" eaten today in the United States are French fries and potato chips.[8]

---

controlling the distribution of food within a population are always potent political, legal, and social justice issues.

These layers of meaning can be analyzed separately, but they are very much interconnected in reality. Food is really a *system* of different dimensions—and each is a vast topic by itself. Each could form a book and, indeed, each does have a huge published body of writing, research, and commentary from a variety of scholarly, sociocultural, moral and ethical perspectives. A thorough depth analysis of these issues (or any one of them) is certainly beyond the scope of a single short book, but that is not our purpose. Ours is at once more modest and more ambitious.

WHAT YOU CAN EXPECT: OUR FOCUS, SCOPE, AND ORGANIZATION

Rather than being definitive about any particular aspect of food, our book is a broad overview that illustrates several important dimensions of the food system and how they are connected. We integrate work in nutritional sciences with more general perspectives of the social sciences and humanities (one of us is a sociologist, the other a historian). It is not primarily a book about sociology, history, political science, anthropology, environmental studies, philosophy, or ethics, but it is rather about a topic critically important to them all, and one that often slips through the cracks of conventional analyses.

Our book is an introduction to food issues for North American readers, but we think that to understand the contemporary American food system and its problems requires some understanding of the world history of food and eating. To understand the North American situation, you need some understanding of the circumstances that surround the production and distribution of food around the world today. This is particularly true in a globalizing era in which trade, culture, and politics increasingly connect people around the world—people who share a common environment and planetary resource base. You can envision the "shape" of the book by thinking of an hourglass. The shape is dictated by the subject—food in North America—but it requires historical and contemporary contexts beyond the borders of any single nation.

We begin with a broad historical account and then focus more narrowly and specifically on the food system in the United States. Then we move to issues about the ownership and control of food (political economy), and then to environmental and population issues that relate to the production and adequacy of the food supply. These important issues of the twenty-first century are national, but also tied to international circumstances. We end by discussing some social justice issues surrounding food and nutrition raised by these discussions and a summary of conclusions about food and nutrition that our discussion generates.

Chapter One begins with an important prologue about the *biological baseline* of food, using information from anthropology and nutrition science. Chapter Two discusses one of the profound transitions in human history: the prehistoric beginnings of the transition from hunting and gathering (or foraging) to agriculture, and its resulting transformations of human life. We discuss the historical background of food, farming, and eating in the ancient and medieval world, including attitudes toward the land, the "civilizing process" that affected eating habits toward the late Middle Ages, and the worldwide exchange of foods around the world during the "Age of Exploration." We illustrate the powerful role of food in shaping history and politics, and we discuss how food and eating are cultural constructions, as well as how food preferences became powerful ways of symbolizing the sacred, good and evil, social belonging or exclusion, and taboos.

Chapter Three narrows to focus on food in America from the middle of the nineteenth to the middle of the twentieth centuries. We begin by focusing on the "big transitions" of this period, the industrial revolution in America, along with the shift from largely self-sufficient farms to commercial ones selling foods as commodities. Those historical transitions involved improvements in agricultural technology, transportation, the growth of the corporate econ-

---

"STANDARD AMERICAN MEALS"

By the 1920s a standard American meal included a breakfast that might have eggs, cereal, fruit, toast, and coffee; a light lunch of a sandwich and soup or salad; and a substantial dinner with meat as a central entrée, potatoes and vegetable side dishes, and dessert of cake, pie, or ice cream.[10]

---

omy, and the influx of immigrants. Here we will discuss the growth of food corporations and particular food technologies like canning, refrigeration, and freezing. We will note the emergence of Nutrition as a scientific field providing research and public policy about nutrition, and the growing involvement of state and federal government in food production, distribution, and safety. We will note the influence of the "big events" of the twentieth century: two world wars separated by the great depression, continuing diversity of cuisines, and an emerging cultural notion of "standard American meals"—on food and eating.

Chapter Four focuses on the political economy of the American food system from the 1950s to contemporary times, which requires connecting American events to those abroad. This is where our "hourglass" begins to expand once more, after three chapters of narrowing. We begin by discussing what some call a "second agricultural revolution" beginning in the 1950s, whereby the continued application of scientific agronomy, genetics, and irrigation produced dramatic increases in agricultural productivity. These included the diffusion of hybrid animals and crops, agrochemical inputs, irrigation and—more recently and controversially—genetically modified animals and crops. Second, we note the emergence, particularly since the 1970s, of the world market economy and trade in agricultural commodities, along with important multilateral treaties and organizations (such as NAFTA and the WTO). Third, we discuss the growing economic concentration in land ownership and in the production and marketing of foodstuffs, resulting in huge food oligopolies[11] that control the buying and selling of most food in the United States and around the world. This trend has been connected to the continuing decline in small farms, a process that began in the 1890s.

In Chapter Five we continue to explore the consequences of the growth of modern industrial agriculture. We turn in more depth to the social meaning of eating with others and to the relationship between eating, cuisines, and the social order in contemporary America. We also chronicle the increasing commodification and corporatization of food and eating in the United States (what has been termed the "McDonaldization" of society[12]) and a decline in home-cooked meals.

Chapter Six elaborates on some of these themes with reference to environment and population issues. We address the measurable impact of intensive agriculture on the degradation of soil and water, and the reduction of genetic diversity that accompanies the worldwide diffusion of monoculture farming and selected hybrids of animals and crops. Here we underline the irony of recent times: Increasing food production at the expense of unsustainable use of environmental resources to support growing abundance. We will discuss various strategies suggested to address this dilemma, including political-economic and biotechnical strategies. Second, we address the dilemma of an increasing food supply with continuing malnutrition, both in America and around the world. Overwhelming evidence suggests that it is not an inadequate total food supply that causes malnutrition, but rather poverty and unequal access to food, or lack of food entitlements, that produce malnutrition. We will explore the causes of these.

These chapters provide context for Chapter Seven, which discusses the highly contested, troublesome, and problematic—yet crucial—issues of food, ethics, and justice. Among many possibilities, we focus on a supremely important issue raised in previous chapters: Why do we have malnutrition and hunger amidst a world of plenty? We note several ethical and justice perspectives as they relate to food, here meaning the virtues and limits of efforts to address problems of hunger. The chapter then applies them to how the United States has and continues to deal with hunger by public programs and charitable efforts. Similarly, we discuss world hunger in terms of the ethical dimensions of the trade-and-aid programs that address the problem.

Food is an important human value that generates an extensive set of issues on many levels—many more issues than we can explore in depth or even enumerate in this single volume. Thus, we provide a list of further readings at the end of each chapter.

CHAPTER 1

The Biological Base

Food, Humans, and Well-Being

In the Introduction we said that thinking about food was like peeling an onion, with different layers of insights and issues. We begin with this prologue about the *biological baseline* because it is certainly the most salient layer of meaning of the "food onion." Like all other living things, humans are physiological beings that require nutrients for energy, growth, and body maintenance. Most mammals have diets limited to one category of food—either plant or animal—and often limited to only a few items within that category. Cattle eat grass, chipmunks eat seeds, hyenas eat mostly carrion, and monkeys and apes, human's closest primate relatives, usually eat plant foods in natural settings. Humans, on the other hand, can utilize a wider range of foods than most other species. Our teeth include the cutting incisors of rodents, the grinding molars and premolars of herbivores, and the pointed canines of carnivores. Our digestive system includes long gut with gastric juices that convert complex starch molecules to simpler sugar ones, pepsin that digests proteins, and pancreatic bile that emulsifies fats so they can be absorbed. This anatomical and physiological complexity means that humans are omnivores who can eat both plant and animal foods. Most are omnivores, but some humans survive as mostly plant eaters while others eat mostly meat.

Regardless of the incredible variety of human cuisines, our bodies process each meal in the same way. No matter how elegant or simple, everything digestible is converted to chemicals to be *metabolized*—that is, combined with oxygen and releasing heat to provide energy, which is measured in calo-

---

DIFFERENT HUMAN CUISINES

Eskimos eat mostly meat, but even the most northern Eskimos manage to eat plants in small amounts—mainly roots, berries, and buds from willow thickets on the tundra, supplemented by the fermented stomach contents of the plant-eating animals they hunt (like Caribou), which they consider a delicacy. They are healthy also because they consume nearly all parts of the animals they kill, including the internal organs that furnish the entire range of vitamins and minerals they need. The traditional Eskimo diet was healthy—healthier in some ways than the average North American diet. But as they became "civilized" they began to show dietary deficiencies. At the opposite extreme are those who consume plants almost exclusively. Some do so by choice, some because they cannot afford meat, and some because neither wild nor domesticated animals are plentiful where they live. Most vegetarians-by-choice eat some animal products like milk, butter, cheese, and eggs, and even in small amounts these contribute valuable nutrients. But many people in the world are vegetarians by necessity. The typical rural peasant of Gambia in West Africa consumes cereal (rice, millet, sorghum, and maize), as well as nuts, beans, and fruit. They do not prefer that diet and will readily eat meat products and fish at the rare times they can get them. The result of such a low protein diet is a variety of dietary deficiency diseases, particularly evident during the "hungry season," those months each year after the previous harvest has been eaten and before new fields begin to produce.[1]

---

ries. A calorie (really a kilocalorie) is the amount of energy it takes to raise the temperature of one kilogram of water one degree Celsius. Caloric energy is essential for "stoking the body's furnace" but, as we all know, when excess calories are not used up, they are stored as compounds that make us fat. Food produces energy and serves two other physiological functions. It builds and maintains body tissues and regulates important body processes. Some foods are particularly nutritious because they perform all three of these physiological roles, while others mainly contribute to energy.

FOOD AND NUTRIENTS

Food has six different kinds of chemicals, or *nutrients*, essential for these three functions. Carbohydrates, proteins, and fats are *macronutrients* that provide the body with energy and "building blocks." Vitamins and minerals, or *micronutrients*, are necessary in only small amounts as catalysts to make other important bodily processes take place. The sixth nutrient is *water*, the essential medium of life for all of the body's structures and processes. Once food has been chewed or swallowed and passes through the esophagus into the stomach, most must be broken down before it can be absorbed into the bloodstream through the pores of the stomach and intestinal walls. Only water, a simple sugar (glucose), alcohol, and some inorganic salts can be absorbed directly. Chewing, stomach gastric juices, and the physical actions of the gastrointestinal tract must break everything else down. The carbohydrates from the fiber in some plant foods go through the stomach wall essentially unchanged, but other kinds of carbohydrates (e.g., starch) are broken down into simpler sugars (e.g., glucose). Proteins are broken down into amino acids, and fats become smaller molecules such as fatty acids and glycerol.[2]

Carbohydrates primarily provide our bodies with energy, and all contain carbon, hydrogen, and oxygen in complex molecules. By using solar energy, green plants manufacture carbohydrates from atmospheric carbon dioxide and water. *Simple carbohydrates* include naturally occurring sugars in fresh fruits, some vegetables, milk, and refined sweeteners like corn sugar and cane sugar. *Complex carbohydrates* include starch and fiber. Starches make up a large part of the world's food supply, mainly as breads and pasta. Staple foods like corn, rice, manioc, taro, potatoes, wheat, and other cereal grains are rich in complex carbohydrates. They must be digested to simple carbohydrates (sugars) to be metabolized into energy. The only carbohydrates that do not come from plants are lactose (or milk sugar) from the milk of mammals, and glycogen, found in the liver and muscle of animals. Glycogen is not a major source of energy. It is made and stored by the liver and muscle tissues. It is energy "in storage" and released only in times of high physical stress and food deprivation.[3]

Fats (or lipids) are the body's chief storage form for caloric energy. Important food sources for fats include meat, milk, poultry, eggs, nuts, and the various seed oils (e.g., corn, olive, sunflower, soybean, and others). Like carbohydrates, they are composed of carbon, hydrogen, and oxygen, but in different combinations. Whenever you eat, you store some fat, and within a few hours after a meal, you take the fat out of storage and use it for energy until the next meal. Excesses of carbohydrates and proteins can be converted into fats, but the reverse is not true. Unlike carbohydrates and proteins, fats can be stored in practically unlimited amounts. There are several forms of lipids, of which cholesterol is the most widely known because of its association with cardiovascular disease. But we don't eat much cholesterol; it is manufactured in the body from the main form of fat we eat (triglycerides). The kinds of fats most associated with cardiovascular disease are "saturated fats" from animals (e.g., beef and pork) rather than "unsaturated fats" from some kinds of vegetable oils, but scientific evidence about the connection between diet and cardiovascular disease is complex. Fats from some fish, and even some kinds of cholesterol actually seem to protect people from cardiovascular disease.

Proteins are critical for building and repairing living tissue. They are part of every cell in your body, and about 20 percent of your total body weight. Proteins are large molecules of carbon, hydrogen, oxygen, and nitrogen, that are made of building blocks called amino acids. Your body needs over twenty of

---

CHOLESTEROL AND FATS

The underlying cause of heart disease is hardening of the arteries (atherosclerosis) caused by a build up of cholesterol-containing plaque in the artery walls in and near the heart. But only some cholesterol does this, those with low-density lipoprotein—LDL. Other kinds, those with high-density lipoprotein—HDL—actually remove cholesterol from the arteries and carry it back to the liver for recycling or disposal. While there is controversy about how to increase HDLs, researchers recently concluded that substituting saturated fats with unsaturated fats—particularly monounsaturated fats—would do this most effectively. Sources of *saturated fats* include all animal meats, butter, cheese, coconut oil, cream, lard, whole milk, hydrogenated oils, and stick margarine. Sources of monounsaturated fats include canola oil, peanuts and peanut butter, olives, and poultry. Sources of *polyunsaturated fats* include almonds, corn oil, fish, cottonseed oil, liquid/soft margarine, mayonnaise, pecans, safflower oil, sesame oil, soybean oil, sunflower oil. Particularly good sources of *omega-3 fats* include canola oil, ocean fish, shellfish, soybeans/tofu, walnuts, flax seed, and wheat germ.[4]

---

these amino acids. Some carbohydrates, fats, and amino acids are nonessential because the body can manufacture them from proteins or other raw materials. On the other hand, eight amino acids are *essential nutrients* because they cannot be synthesized by the body by other nitrogen-containing compounds, and must be supplied—preformed—by the diet. Meat, milk, and dairy products are rich in complete proteins that have all essential amino acids. These essential amino acids are isoleucine, leucine, lysine, methionine, phenylalanine, threonine, tryptophan, and valine. Most protein from plant and vegetable sources is incomplete, lacking in one or more essential amino acids. But you can get complete amino acids and protein by eating the right combinations of vegetables that compensate for their respective deficiencies. For instance, corn and soybeans, or beans and rice eaten in combination will provide complete proteins.

Water comprises about 65 percent of body weight, and is probably second only to oxygen in its immediate importance to your body. All body processes, including its metabolic reactions, require the presence of water. You can go without food for months, while your body digests its muscles and other tissues. But without water for only a few days, you begin to lose body mass and feel weak and ill. The typical person requires several quarts of water a day, and water is obtained not only from drinking fluids, but also from practically all fruits and vegetables. Chronic lack of water (dehydration) causes the body not to be able to efficiently absorb and metabolize what nutrients it has. Dehydration is, in fact, one of the world's largest sources of infant malnutrition and death, particularly in poor developing nations. It is typically caused by diarrhea from impure drinking water. In fact, the nutritional status of the world has been enhanced in the last several decades by increasing access to pure water in poorer nations of the world and promoting cheap and effective *Oral rehydration therapy* (ORT) to children afflicted with diarrhea. ORT, promoted by UNICEF, uses a solution of water and salts administered to children to enable them to retain body fluids.

Minerals are inorganic compounds that occur naturally in the earth's crust that are important to a healthy diet, although the exact function of some is unclear. While all minerals are micronutrients, there are *major minerals* required in the largest quantities—calcium, sodium, and potassium—and *trace minerals*, such as iodine, iron, zinc, and selenium, required in minute amounts. *Major minerals* include calcium, phosphorus, magnesium, sodium, chloride, potassium, and sulfur. *Trace minerals* include iodine, iron, zinc, copper, fluoride, selenium, chromium, molybdenum, manganese, and cobalt. In fact, the function of some (silicon, vanadium, and nickel) is so unclear to nutrition science, that researchers are not sure whether they perform any necessary function, or whether their presence is dietary happenstance. The function of others, however, is well understood, along with deficiency symptoms and toxicity symptoms, when too much is ingested. Calcium (found in milk and milk products, small fish, yogurt, legumes and some green vegetables) is the principal mineral that builds bones and teeth and allows normal muscle contractions. Its deficiency leads to stunted growth in children and bone loss (osteoporosis) in adults, but it has no known toxicity symptoms. However, calcium can be injurious, if not toxic at high intake levels. Sodium (found in salt, soy sauce, and many processed, canned, or boxed foods) helps the body maintain normal acid and fluid balance. Sodium deficiency produces muscle cramps and mental apathy, but too much sodium contributes to high blood pressure.

THE VALUE OF SALT

Meat eaters get enough sodium without adding salt, unlike plant-eating vegetarians, who require additional salt. This explains why historically salt (sodium chloride) was a valuable commodity in the ancient world, among people who didn't have much meat. Etymologically, our word salary derives from the Latin word for salt, because soldiers of the Roman Army required, and were entitled to, a salt ration. Evolutionary biologists speculate that humans in Africa evolved and transmitted a high capacity to retain salt, that was adaptive for maintaining body fluids in hot climates. In the contemporary United States, where most dietitions believe our food is often too salt rich, retaining salt may lose its adaptiveness. Indeed, African Americans exhibit exceptionally high rates of hypertension (high blood pressure).

EVOLUTION AND VITAMIN C

Curiously, humans, most primates, and guinea pigs are the only mammals that require dietary sources of vitamin C. Other mammals are able to synthesize it from glucose. Scientists hypothesized that millions of years ago a genetic mutation altered the enzyme responsible for the synthesis. Fortunately, it was not a lethal mutation, because humans and the other affected species are able to get generous quantities from plant sources in the environment. Others suggested that this mutation might have been advantageous, since it freed glucose to be used by the body for energy.[7]

Vitamins are organic compounds necessary in very small amounts for the growth and maintenance of life. As essential nutrients, they cannot be synthesized by the body and must be supplied by the diet. Vitamins come in two different categories. *Fat-soluble vitamins* include vitamins A, D, E, and K, are generally found in the fats of foods, and are absorbed from the diet with the aid of other fats and liver bile. Once in the bloodstream, they are "escorted" to body cells by proteins, since they are not soluble in water. Fat- soluble vitamins can be stored by the body, so they need not be consumed daily. Megadoses of fat-soluble vitamins can build up to toxic levels and cause undesirable side effects. Up to a year's supply of vitamin A can be stored by the body, mainly in the liver. If you stop eating food with vitamin A, deficiency symptoms will not appear until after your stores are depleted. Then, however, the symptoms are severe and include blindness and reduced resistance to infections. Rarely seen in the United States or Canada, vitamin A deficiency is a severe public health problem in developing nations, where millions of children suffer from blindness and other consequences. Toxicity from the buildup of vitamin A is not common, but includes symptoms of joint pain, irritability and fatigue, headaches, nausea, and liver damage.[5] *Water-soluble vitamins* include eight B vitamins (the B-complex family) and vitamin C. They are found in the watery parts of food cells, such as those in green vegetables and orange juice. In the body they act as *coenzymes* that assist enzymes in doing their metabolic work.[6] Since the body excretes water-soluble vitamins if blood levels rise too high, the body cannot store them, and they rarely reach toxic levels in the body. On the other hand, they must be in the foods you eat almost daily. They are also rather fragile, meaning that while water-soluble vitamins are naturally present in many foods, they can be washed out or destroyed during food storage, processing, and preparation. In sum, while many of us take vitamin and mineral supplements as some medical and nutritional experts recommend, excesses of either can be wasteful or even dangerous. Eating a varied and balanced diet can provide enough vitamins to maintain good health.

NUTRITIONAL SCIENCE, RECOMMENDED INTAKES, AND FOOD PYRAMIDS

Interest in food and well-being is surely as old as human beings. The earliest known nutrition record is Ebers papyrus, an Egyptian medical treatise from 1500 B.C.E. It recommended eating roast liver to cure night blindness long before it was known that it is caused by lack of vitamin A, and that liver is a good source of vitamin A. In 400 B.C.E. Hippocrates, known as the father of modern medicine, taught that health was related to diet. He recognized what we now know as *scurvy*, caused by lack of vitamin C, resulted in bleeding gums, tooth loss, and even death. Scurvy was the scourge of armies, sailors, and other travelers forced to do without vitamin C-rich foods for weeks on end. Its cure was not known until the sixteenth century, when a beverage of spruce needles or oranges and lemons was recommended; by the early 1800s British navy sailors were dubbed "limeys" because they were required to drink lemon or lime juice daily.

A deficiency disease called *rickets* dates back to Roman times, when children frequently suffered skeletal deformities. It became so common in England that it was know as "English disease." By the 1800s eating cod liver oil was recognized as its cure. Crusty black skin patches were symptoms of another deficiency disease called *pellagra*, from Italian words meaning sour skin. It was long thought fatal. In 1730 a Spanish physician observed that people who developed the disease were mostly poor people with limited diets of mainly corn and little meat, and they could be helped by changing their diets. Physicians then knew how to cure these diseases, before they discovered that they were caused by deficiencies of vitamins C (scurvy), D (rickets), and niacin— one of the B-complex vitamins (pellegra). Similarly, people have long been aware that too little food does not sustain life, and that too much makes a person overweight. But they only recently recognized grave health consequences of being too heavy.

The seventeenth century marked the beginnings of modern science and the scientific method. By the nineteenth century physicians knew that certain foods cured a number of deficiency diseases without knowing exactly why. Only in the middle of the nineteenth century did the science of chemistry develop to the point where foods could be analyzed; chemists discovered that foods consisted of carbohydrates, proteins, and fats, along with minerals and water, which they assumed to be a complete diet.[8] A way to precisely measure caloric energy was discovered by the 1880s. In the early twentieth century, nutritional scientists discovered the substances, now called vitamins, needed in minute quantities to prevent disease and maintain health. In 1912 Dr. Casimir Funk called them *vitamines* because they were originally thought to be amino acids. The name was shortened to vitamins when it was discovered that some were not.[9] Scientists then began to study precisely how much of what nutrients were needed by the human body. Our point is that nutrition is old as a human concern, but young as a scientific field of study.

Fruits and vegetables are rich sources of vitamins and minerals. Many people are replacing such healthy foods with high-fat diets.

To make things easier for people to understand the complex findings of nutritional scientists, governments began to publish guidelines about how much of different kinds of nutrients to eat for a healthy diet. A committee of experts appointed by the National Academy of Sciences published the first guidelines, which became known as Recommended Daily Allowances (RDAs) in the United States, in 1941. RDAs are meant as *average* recommendations for populations rather than for particular individuals, whose needs may differ. Such recommendations are examined frequently (but seldom change appreciably) to reflect advances in scientific knowledge. To provide a standardized benchmark for people's nutritional needs, the U.S. Government devised the Dietary Reference Intakes (DRIs), which are used in the United States and Canada. The DRI estimates the nutritional needs of healthy people and includes different recommendations based on age and gender. It is calculated as a composite of different values like the measure of Adequate Intake (AI), RDAs, and Tolerable Upper Intake Levels (UL). The DRI represents a major shift in thinking about nutrition guidelines, from the emphasis on nutritional deficiencies in order to prevent chronic diseases to the widespread recognition that there can be risks with very high intakes of nutrients. See Table 1.1 for Daily Recommended Intakes used on food Labels (Daily Values).

Because there are many different nutrients, foods having different nutrient content, and people with different needs, governments began to establish

TABLE 1.1 Daily Values (DV) Used on Food Labels[a]

Daily Reference Values (DRVs)[b]		Reference Daily Intakes (RDI)			
Food Component	Amount	Nutrient	Amount	Nutrient	Amount
protein[c]	50 g	Thiamin	1.5 mg	Calcium	1,000 mg
fat	65 g[d]	Riboflavin	1.7 mg	Iron	18 mg
saturated fat	20 g	Niacin	20 mg	Zinc	15 mg
cholesterol	300 mg[e]	Biotin	300 mcg[f]	Iodine	150 mcg
total carbohydrate	300 g	Pantothenic Acid	10 mg	Copper	2 mg
fiber	25 g	Vitamin B6	2 mg	Chromium	120 mcg
sodium	2,400 mg	Folate	400 mcg[f]	Selenium	70 mcg
potassium	3,500 mg	Vitmin B12	6 mcg	Molybdenum	75 mcg
		Vitamin C	60 mg	Manganese	2 mg
		Vitamin A	5,000 IU[g]	Chloride	3,400 mg
		Vitamin D	400 IU[g]	Magnesium	400 mg
		Vitamin E	30 IU[g]	Phosphorus	1 g
		Vitamin K	80 mcg		

[a]Based on 2,000 calories a day for adults and children over 4 years old.
[b]Formerly the U.S. RDA, based on National Academy of Aciences' 1968 Recommended Dietary Allowances.
[c]DRV for protein does not apply to certain populations; Reference Daily intake (RDI) for protein has been established for these groups: children 1 to 4 years: 16 g; infants under 1 year: 14 g; pregnant

women: 60 g; nursing mothers: 65 g.
[d](g) grams
[e](mg) milligrams
[f](mcg) micrograms
[g]Equivalent values for the three RDI nutrients expressed as IU are: Vitamin A, 900 RE (assumes a mixture of 40% retinol and 60% beta-carotene); vitamin D, 10 mcg; vitamin E, 20 mg.

SOURCE: Adapted from Boyle, M. (2000). *Personal Nutrition* 4th Ed; and National Academy of Sciences (1997-2000). *Dietary Reference Intake Series.* Washington, DC: National Academy Press.

food guides that busy individuals could use without the complexities of such tables. In 1958 the U.S. Department of Agriculture (USDA) recommended that people eat foods daily from the *basic four* food groups (milk, meat, vegetables and cereals, bread and pasta), which was updated in 1989 to a *five group* plan reflecting new knowledge. In 1992 the USDA and the Department of Health and Human Services (HHS) jointly produced a graphic *Food Guide Pyramid* that reflected newer research and incorporated the five group plan to serve as a nutrition educational tool. It suggests eating larger amounts of foods at the base and smaller amounts as one moves up the pyramid. At the base are foods high in carbohydrates and low in fats, including breads, cereals, rice, and pasta (6–11 daily servings). Above these are fruits (3–5 daily servings) and vegetables (2–4 daily servings) that supply vitamins, minerals, and fiber. Protein foods are at the next level, including milk, yogurt, and cheese (2–3 daily servings) and meat, fish, beans, and eggs (2–3 daily servings). In addition to protein, these supply other minerals like calcium, but are often high in fat. At the tip of the pyramid are fats, oils, and sugars. They are not considered a separate food group because they provide extra calories but lit-

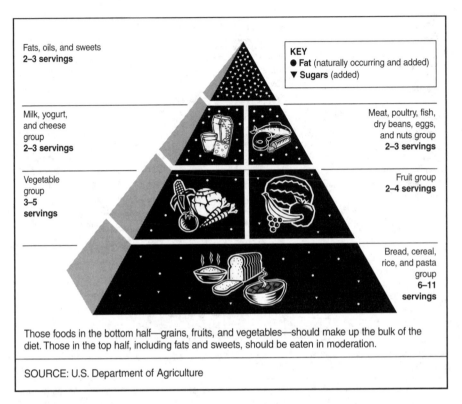

Fats, oils, and sweets
2–3 servings

KEY
● **Fat** (naturally occurring and added)
▼ **Sugars** (added)

Milk, yogurt,
and cheese
group
2–3 servings

Meat, poultry, fish,
dry beans, eggs,
and nuts group
2–3 servings

Vegetable
group
**3–5
servings**

Fruit group
2–4 servings

Bread, cereal,
rice, and pasta
group
**6–11
servings**

Those foods in the bottom half—grains, fruits, and vegetables—should make up the bulk of the diet. Those in the top half, including fats and sweets, should be eaten in moderation.

SOURCE: U.S. Department of Agriculture

FIGURE 1.1 The Food Guide Pyramid

tle else in the way of nutrients and should be eaten sparingly. This guide is intended for people who can eat "average" diets, but it must be modified for others.[10] We have illustrated some of the "daily servings" with the pyramid in Figure 1.1. If you did the Food Self-Inventory suggested in the Introduction, how did what you eat compare with these recommendations?

Typically, the establishment of government food guides were met with political opposition and surrounded by scientific controversy. The 1992 USDA/HHS pyramid stimulated enormous criticism, "ranging from the sublime to the ridiculous" according to the head of New York University's nutrition and food studies department.[11] Food industries like the dairy and beef producers were not happy when the pyramid recommended reducing the daily consumption of their products. Some nutrition scientists objected because the pyramid didn't distinguish between saturated and unsaturated fat. Others objected because it lumped meat with fish and beans—three high protein foods with very different health consequences. Recently some charged that the pyramid is unwittingly biased, ignoring the needs of minority Americans. It calls for 2–3 daily servings of dairy products even though some minorities, including most Asian Americans, are lactose intolerant.

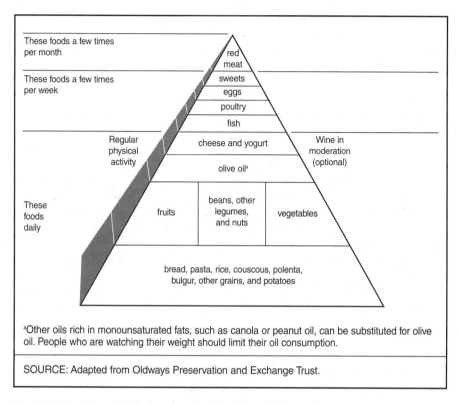

These foods a few times per month — red meat

These foods a few times per week — sweets, eggs, poultry, fish

Regular physical activity — cheese and yogurt, olive oil[a] — Wine in moderation (optional)

These foods daily — fruits, beans, other legumes, and nuts, vegetables

bread, pasta, rice, couscous, polenta, bulgur, other grains, and potatoes

[a]Other oils rich in monounsaturated fats, such as canola or peanut oil, can be substituted for olive oil. People who are watching their weight should limit their oil consumption.

SOURCE: Adapted from Oldways Preservation and Exchange Trust.

FIGURE 1.2   The Mediterranean Food Guide Pyramid

Since 1992, dozens of others food pyramids have appeared. There is a Mediterranean pyramid that downplays red meat and emphasizes fruits, vegetables, and olive oil. There are also vegetarian pyramids, a Latin American and an Asian pyramid reflecting their respective cuisines, one for children under six (created by the USDA), and one for adults over seventy. The problem, however, is not that Americans choose one pyramid or another, but rather that they ignore even those recommendations common to them all. For instance, the USDA/HHS pyramid calls for 5–9 servings of fruits and vegetables per day, and most Americans eat less than half of that. It suggests 11 servings of grain and most Americans average fewer than 7. Furthermore, few Americans have limited fats and oils as suggested.[12]

NUTRITIONAL SCIENCE: SOME CONCLUSIONS AND CONTROVERSIES

We have used material from *nutritional sciences*, including fields that scientifically study food and human well-being, such as food chemistry, clinical research about food and health, nutritional anthropology, and demographic concerns about food issues. The people most directly engaged in clinical practice, education, and writing about food and health, however, call themselves registered dietitions, not nutritionists. *Registered dietitians*—in whatever setting they work—have university graduate degrees specializing in nutrition, and they take rigorous state board exams. In contrast, any persons with some knowledge and interest in food can call themselves nutritionists, including those whose primary interest is in selling things. The profession of registered dietitians grew with nutrition science, and like other professions one of its purposes is to protect people from fraudulent claims that are ever present. Nutritional sciences are comparatively new, as well as complex and rapidly changing fields. Thus nutritional scientists agree about some things but have many areas where they do not agree. We summarize our discussion of nutritional science by focusing on some important areas where they agree, and note a few where they disagree. We do this by responding to some common questions about food and nutrition.

What about chemicals that are in the foods we eat, like pesticides and additives? Are they healthy? That *is* an important question, but also a huge and complicated one. Scientists distinguish between *toxicity* (a property of all substances) and *hazard* (or the likelihood of a substance causing harm). All substances are potentially toxic (including water), but they are actually toxic only if consumed in large enough quantities. A chemical that is present in minuscule amounts does not become a significant hazard until it is consumed in excessive or toxic amounts. Chemical contamination, however, can be subtle and insidious, especially for heavy metals like cadmium, lead, and mercury. Lead poisoning is a case in point. Lead does not kill a person all at once, but builds up in body tissues, because the body can't distinguish between lead and calcium. Pregnant women and children are especially at risk, and lead poisoning affects at least three million children under the age of six in the United States.[13] Aside from the gross accidental contamination of foods, however, most experts believe that chemicals in foods pose a small hazard.[14]

Agrochemicals include *pesticides* that are added to crops to kill or repel insects, spiders, rodents, and other living things, and *herbicides*, sprayed on

---

LEAD IN THE ENVIRONMENT

Historically, lead entered food and water supplies from leaded gasoline exhaust, which, through rainfall, entered water and soil. Gasoline is no longer leaded, and lead solder is no longer used on food cans (another historic source). But all the lead previously produced and in the environment is still with us! For example, the authors live in an urban area that had a lead refinery for the last 100 years, and government screening programs found that many young children in nearby zip codes exhibit blood lead levels that are many times the national average for children.

croplands to prevent weeds from growing. Some of the earliest pesticides were potent and dangerous, like DDT. It was banned in the 1960s when researchers observed toxic effects on birds, fish, and humans. Such dangers were popularized by Rachel Carson's book, *The Silent Spring* (1962). By the 1970s, the U.S. Environmental Protection Agency (EPA) was charged with determining whether a chemical may be used on crops. From the best available evidence, the EPA determines the amount of pesticide residues that a person might be exposed to in the course of a 70-year life and the risk that might pose; then the *tolerance limit* or the maximum allowable pesticide residue left on food is determined. Finally, the EPA establishes a *reference dose* with a large margin of safety (usually $\frac{1}{100}$ the tolerance limit) that could be consumed daily without posing a health risk. EPA inspectors monitor food shipments by testing samples for pesticide residues, and it can seize shipments and press criminal charges. You can imagine how complex and uncertain this has been, because there are many chemicals applied to many kind of foods. Concerns persist about the adequacy of monitoring for agrochemical residues and food imported from other nations using pesticides banned in the United States. Even so, a 1993 five-year study of pesticide residues by the National Academy of Sciences concluded that the U.S. food supply was safe for children.[15]

Since then researchers have discovered new concerns about pesticides as a part of a category of synthetic chemicals called *persistent organic pollutants* (POPs). They have four common properties: they are toxic, they accumulate in the food chain, they persist in the environment, and they can travel a long distance from their source. POPs are ubiquitous and accumulate slowly. Studies found that we now have about 500 of these man-made chemicals in our bodies which are potential poisons that did not exist before 1920, including the chemical breakdown residues of the notorious DDT.[16] Building on earlier concerns, toxicologists in the 1990s found POPs to be significant *endocrine disrupters*. As such, they can interfere with the body's network of hormones and receptors, known as the endocrine system, and they produce long-lasting and permanent damage. The greatest effects, found among farm workers and others exposed to higher levels of pesticides, included higher rates of immune system cancers (leukemia, non-Hodgkin's lymphoma), infertility, genital defects, heart disease, and high rates of infections. But consumers are affected as well. Though the findings are still controversial, a 1992 study found significant drops in sperm counts among men in industrial nations over the last 60 years. A 1999 study in the United States found that domestic fruits and vegetables (like peaches, apples, and frozen green beans) often exceeded the EPA exposure limit for young children and could cause neurological damage.[17] You can see that the long-term dangers of exposure to many agrochemicals in use are pervasive and ominous. But you need to keep contrasting risks in perspective. Major health organizations still claim that the health risks posed by agrochemical residues are less than the certain risks of *not* eating any fruits and vegetables.[18]

From a safety standpoint, food additives are among the least hazardous substances in food, though consumers typically rank them high on the list of hazards. *Additives* are substances added to foods to improve the flavor, texture, color, shelf life, or the nutritional value of foods. Iodine, for example, has long been added to salt to prevent deficiencies. Common additives include yeast, sodium bicarbonate, glycerin, pectin, vitamins A, C, and D, BHT ben-soates, monosodium glutamate, Red dye #40, caramel, tumeric, aspartame, calcium carbonate, and many others. In the United States, food additives were either banned as dangerous or declared "generally recognized as safe" (GRAS). The GRAS list came under renewed scrutiny in the 1960s, when con-cerns were raised about cyclamates (artificial sweeteners), which in massive doses had produced cancer in laboratory rats. After a sweeping review, the Food and Drug Administration removed 300 substances from the GRAS list. Over strong industry objections, the "Delaney Clause" was added to the Food Additive Act of 1958. It forbids the approval of any substance known to cause cancer in animals, no matter how small the dose.

Does this mean there are no concerns about food safety in the United States? No, indeed! There are many concerns about long-term exposure to pesticides and herbicides, and food additives have not collectively been "proven" risk free. But most dietitions and health experts agree that the most clear and present danger from food is ancient and ordinary—that is from microbial contami-nation of food during processing, handling, storage, and cooking. In 1999 a Nebraska packinghouse shipped a batch of contaminated ground beef to fast food restaurants in the Northwest that resulted in many cases of food poison-ing. Although such contamination can enter the food chain during process-ing, it is quite rare. A more common hazard occurs when food is mishandled in restaurants or households, by keeping perishables in refrigerators too long or not cleaning utensils or cutting boards. Food poisoning from salmonella, botulinium, listeria, E. Coli microbes are quite common, resulting in severe abdominal cramps, diarrhea, fever, nausea, vomiting. Many cases are mild and never reported, but some result in death.

Some people think organic food is healthier. Is this true? The phenomenal growth of the market for organic foods is partly fueled by fears about food additives and pesticide residues. These are real but exaggerated compared to the more present dangers of microbial contamination. Once only a niche market in health food stores, "organic" fruits, vegetables, and pasta can now be found in mainstream supermarkets, for a premium price. Although the USDA recently established standards for use of the label "organic," foods touted as organic may not mean what you think. It is difficult to grow food without agrochemical residues. An organic farm situated in the midst of con-ventional farms may get agrochemicals through using the same water table, or from the air as the wind blows, or from insect pollinators. If organic foods are grown with organic fertilizer, it may come from the manure of animals that are routinely treated with growth hormones and antibiotics that remain as residues.[19]

None of this is to say that organic foods are a complete waste of money. You may choose to buy organic foods because organic farmers do use fewer agrochemicals, and are more likely than conventional farmers to use environment-friendly farming techniques that protect soil and water tables. You may choose to do so because "free range" animals raised without growth boosting injections or antibiotics may be healthier, or are more likely to be raised under ecologically more manageable and surely more ethical conditions than ones raised in factory farms (confined animal feeding operations).

Is a vegetarian diet healthy? It can be. While it will not in the foreseeable future become the dominant American cuisine, vegetarianism is growing in popularity for a variety of reasons. "Vegetarian," however, includes a variety of cuisines:

- Semi-vegetarian: reduced amounts of animal-produced products are eaten, including meat, poultry, seafood, eggs, milk, and cheese.
- Ovolacto-vegetarian: milk, milk products, and eggs are included (possibly limiting the nutrient iron).
- Lacto-vegetarian: milk and milk products are included, but not meat, fish, poultry, or eggs (possibly limiting the nutrient iron).
- Ovo-vegetarian: eggs are included, but no milk or milk products (possibly limiting nutrients iron, vitamin D, calcium, riboflavin).
- Strict vegetarian, or Vegan: No animal-derived foods (possibly limiting nutrients iron, vitamin D, calcium, riboflavin, Vitamin B_{12}).

People can be vegetarians for a variety of reasons. Some are so for religious reasons, believing that it is inherently wrong to eat the flesh of animals. Hinduism and Buddhism teach this, although it is not strictly required or universally practiced. Some are vegetarians for health reasons, believing that consuming meat is unhealthy. To the extent that this means a diet low in saturated fat, they are probably right. Vegetarians have lower rates of cardiovascular disease and lower rates of incidence for certain kinds of cancer. Some become vegetarians for reasons of social justice. At least one-third of the world's grain is fed to animals, and if vegetarian diets became more widespread, they argue, there would be much more food to go around. Others become vegetarian for environmental reasons because, pound for pound, raising livestock makes far greater demands on the environment and creates more pollution than growing plant crops.

Why do people eat the foods they do, anyway? What factors shape food preferences and choices? Answering these questions illustrates just how complex the relationship is between people and food. What people eat—their food intake behavior—is responsive to both hunger, reflecting physiological needs of the body, and appetites, reflecting psychological needs and cultural preferences. Appetites rather than hunger are food advertisers' stock in trade! The rest of the answer starts with two kinds of societal systems that shape food intake behavior. They include the social, economical, and political structures of society, and, more specifically, the food production and distribution system. While these large, abstract, and complex systems may seem remote from concrete individual choices, they are, in fact, powerful and pervasive forces. You connect with the second system each time you buy food at a supermarket.

In between these large societal systems and food intake behavior are individual persons who are usually parts of household structures. Households vary in composition and characteristics, and individuals interact with households to create lifestyles that concretely determine food intake behavior. Factors that contribute to how they construct their lifestyles include income, occupation, education, family role, ethnic identity, cultural traditions, religious beliefs, emotional needs, physiological needs and health, age and place in the human life cycle, media exposure, and nutritional knowledge. These "lifestyle factors" may be a property of individuals, households, or both, and within their context a lifestyle that determines food intake behavior emerges.[20] Figure 1.3 summarizes these relationships.

Among the lifestyle factors that shape what we eat, nutritional scientists hope that nutritional knowledge will become more influential. Mass media exposure is a powerful force for most people and households, and the media can present scientific nutritional information reliably. But how can you tell if it does? An expert panel judged and "graded" some American magazines on the reliability of nutritional information. Out of a possible 100 points they rated a few excellent (more than 90 points), most either good (80–89 points) or fair (70–79), and several poor (less than 70 points).[21]

Few of us have access to such expert assessments. There are, however, some questions to ask about what you read or watch on TV that should make you leery of nutritional misinformation:

- Is something being sold?
- Are you being offered a remedy for problems that are not easily or simply solved (e.g., obesity, arthritis, poor immunity, low energy, weak muscles, wrinkles, aging)?
- Are such terms as "miraculous," "magical," "secret," or "studies prove" used?

HOW DOES YOUR MAGAZINE RATE?

An excellent one? *Cooking Light*. In order, among the good ones were *American Health, Consumer Reports, Good Housekeeping, Better Homes and Gardens, Reader's Digest, Prevention,* and *Redbook*. In order, among the fair ones were *Harpers' Bazaar, Runner's World, Self, Mademoiselle, Vogue,* and *Ladies' Home Journal*. A poor one? *Cosmopolitan*. Keep in mind that the content of a magazine often varies from year to year, as editors come and go.[22]

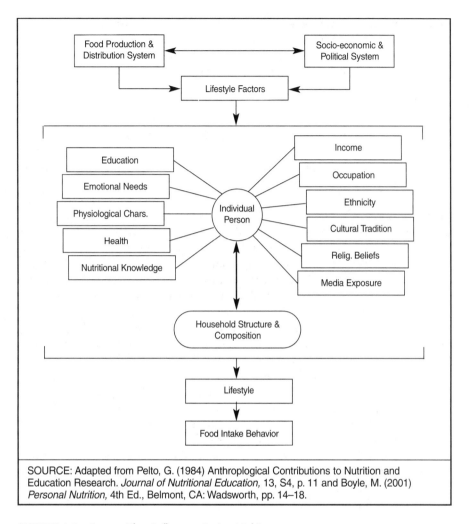

FIGURE 1.3   Factors That Influence Eating Habits

- Are testimonials, before-and-after photos, or nonexpert endorsements used?
- Does the information sound too good to be true?

The more of these questions you can answer "yes," the more likely you are to be dealing with misinformation. The last question is undoubtedly the most important one.[23]

You said that there is plenty of food to feed the world, but that malnutrition from having both too little and too much to eat is a serious problem in America as well as the rest of the world. How can this be? This is indeed a supreme irony. Today our food supply is nothing less than cornucopian, with more food varieties available to more people than ever before. Yet more people today are malnourished—hungry, deficient of minerals and vitamins, or overfed—than ever in human history.[24] This is an important part of the food story, and we discuss its deeper causes in later chapters. Here we discuss the seriousness and magnitude of the "three faces of malnutrition."

The best and most recent statistics about the incidence of global malnourishment are truly stunning. Those who are hungry from deficiencies of calories and protein constitute at least 1.2 billion people of the world's 6.2 billion. Those who are overnourished from an excess of calories constitute another 1.2 billion. Another 2.0 billion people, suffer from micronutrient deficiencies from lack of vitamins and minerals. These overlap those who are undernourished and overnourished, but include some who are otherwise healthy.[25] See Table 1.2. Neither overweight nor underweight are subjective categories. They are defined using the *body-mass index* (BMI), a scale calibrated to reflect the health effects of weight gain and loss. A healthy BMI ranges from 19 to 24. More that 25 signals overweight, and above 30 means obesity. The United Nations World Health Organization (WHO) estimates that nearly half of the world's population in all nations suffer from one of the forms of malnutrition.[26]

Hunger, the worst of the three forms, often cuts short lives that have just begun. It is most common in the world of developing countries, where one in five people is hungry—a proportion that has fallen by about 10 percent in the last two decades. That trend is good but does not capture inequality among the many people of the developing world. The United Nations Food and Agriculture organization, for example, recently estimated that in India 49 percent of adults and 53 percent of children are hungry, measured by being underweight. In terms of absolute numbers, more are hungry than ever before. Hunger is found in the industrial world as well, including the United States. The USDA estimated in 1999 that 27 million people representing about 10 percent of all American households were hungry, on the edge of hunger, or worried about being hungry. These households were home to 11 million chil-

TABLE 1.2   Types of Malnutrition and People Affected Globally, 2000

Type of malnutrition	Cause	Number and Proportion of People Affected	
Hunger[1]	lack of calories and protein	1.2 billion	20%
Micronutrient deficiency[2]	lack of vitamins and minerals	2.0 billion	
Overconsumption[1]	excess of calories	1.2 billion	20%

[1] Measured by the number of underweight and overweight persons.
[2] Partly overlaps hunger and overconsumption.
Adapted from Gardner, G., and Halweil, B. (2000), Nourishing the Underfed and Overfed, pp. 59–78. In L. Starke (Ed.), *State of the World 2000*. New York: W. W. Norton, pp. 59–78.

dren, nearly one in five American children. In Western Europe, Australia, and Japan, where social safety nets are more widespread, hunger is rarer.[27]

While the ranks of the hungry are shrinking modestly, overeating is more prevalent today than ever before. The WHO calls it "one of the greatest neglected public health problems of our time." In the United States, over half of adults are overweight (55 percent have a BMI of over 25), while the share of the measurably obese has climbed from 15 to 23 percent since 1980. Significantly, being overweight or obese is no longer found only in wealthy nations. Even in poor nations, wealthy classes are likely to be overweight, and in some poorer countries today the proportion of overweight people exceeds those who are underweight. Consumption of fat and sugar has surged far beyond earlier levels as people eat more livestock products and as oil and sugar are added to foods of all kinds. In Europe and America, fat and sugar account for more than half of the caloric intake, and they have squeezed complex carbohydrates, such as grains and vegetables, to only a third of total calories. This represents a near reversal of the diets of our hunter-gatherer ancestors.[28]

These two kinds of malnutrition overlap with micronutrient deprivation resulting from lack of variety—three bowls of rice a day and little else, or heavy dependence on hamburgers and French fries. Low intake of iodine, vitamin A, and iron are of particular concern because they are so widespread. Iron, found in green leafy vegetables and meat, is the most commonly missing micronutrient. A 1999 United Nations' report estimated that 5 billion people, more than 80 percent of the human family, suffer from varying degrees of iron deficiency! Among the most severely affected are women and children in poor countries, where lack of iron leads to cognitive disability and anemia.

In the historic "great nutritional transformation" leading to modern times, food shortages or bad weather were not the most general causes of malnutrition problems, as is commonly believed. Rather, as we noted earlier, they are caused by people's lack of access to food—by how societies are organized, by the decisions people and governments make, and particularly by the extent of poverty and inequality. Important causes of overeating are the changing agricultural technologies that make foods cheap, and urbanization that transforms lifestyles and, consequently, cuisines. Urbanization broke the close ties between food producers and consumers. Processed and packaged foods came to have a more powerful place in the human food system. To maximize profits, food sellers invested heavily in promoting less healthy foods. And urban consumers began to demand convenience foods, often high in fat, cholesterol, and sugars and low in fiber, vitamins, and minerals. In theory, food sellers and companies could have promoted healthy foods. But two factors encouraged them to produce "tasty" but unhealthy ones. Foods high in sugars, fats, and oils were tasty *and* profitable. That combination was irresistible to consumers and producers alike. In 1909 in the United States, for example, when many fewer foods were sold prepackaged, two-thirds of the sugar added was added in the household. Today three-fourths is added by producers, out of the consumers' sight.[29]

However, human choices and social factors did not cause all of the shift to chronic overeating. The desire for sugars and fats seems partly innate, evolving from our Homo sapien and hunter-gatherer roots before the agricultural revolution. Then, such energy-dense foods were scarce and had an adaptive value for weathering lean times. They were also easily overconsumed, with a low satiation level, unlike complex carbohydrates, such as starches and whole grain products that leave one feeling full. But these physiological traits were largely constrained until the twentieth century, when a host of social forces transformed the food system and allowed our desires to be largely unconstrained.[30] Fortunately, people are not doomed to live out a biological dietary imperative. Like many biological traits, these are quite malleable by the forces of society, culture, and learning.

For Americans, what is an important controversy among nutritional scientists? We have already mentioned one area where research findings are complex and often confusing: the relationship between fats and cardiovascular disease. Another is about vitamins. In the past ten years scientists have been exploring the possibility that vitamin supplements will stave off chronic diseases like cancer and heart disease, that rank as prominent causes of death. These were a class of vitamins called *antioxidant vitamins*. Antioxidant research is one of the hottest and most widely publicized areas in nutrition research today. Nobody had heard of antioxidant vitamins ten years ago, because it is a new way of describing the functions of some well-known vitamins. Antioxidants fight oxygen, in a manner of speaking. They include beta-carotene (that is converted to vitamin A), vitamin C, and vitamin E.

Earlier we noted that the oxidation of food is essential to provide energy. Oxidation, however, may lead to the formation of highly toxic compounds called *free radicals*. In addition to oxidizing food, environmental pollutants like tobacco smoke and ozone also cause the formation of free radicals in the body. Left unchecked, free radicals can injure cells and lead to serious chronic diseases like cancer and heart disease. Fortunately, the body's defense system uses antioxidant nutrients to combine with free radicals and prevent potential damage. Vitamin E seems to thwart free radicals that would otherwise damage the walls of blood vessels and contribute to hardening of the arteries. Vitamin C seems to help prevent heart disease and to be a particularly potent "scavenger" of environmental air pollutants (The National Academy of Sciences advises smokers to consume twice as much vitamin C as nonsmokers). Beta-carotene seems to work with the others to protect the respiratory tract, preventing lung cancer and other chronic conditions.[31]

The promise of antioxidants is now public knowledge but, as with much new research, findings of these early studies are not clear or consistent enough for public health information. How much of these antioxidants is required to fight diseases? By taking massive doses is your body better able to fight the millions of free radicals produced in your body? Or is the RDA enough? Large doses of antioxidants may be as harmful as not enough. Vitamins are biologically active compounds, and taking large doses might have dangerous side effects. Scientists discovered, for instance, that in a test tube-type environment when vitamin C is in the presence of iron or other metals, it could have a *pro-oxidant* effect and actually stimulate free radical damage. Whether this happens in the body, or whether having too much antioxidant will do more harm than good is uncertain. At present, data about antioxidants cannot be used for diet and public health recommendations, because there are too few studies using large human populations. Moreover, the findings of studies have not all pointed in the same direction.

While nutrition sciences cannot presently recommend taking massive amounts of vitamin supplements, antioxidant research does underline the importance of eating lots of fruits and vegetables, as recommended by the new food pyramids. In addition to being good sources of antioxidants, they are low in fats, which also reduces cardiovascular and cancer risk. Furthermore, unlike vitamin supplements, fruits and vegetables have other chemicals, called *phytochemicals*, found only in plants. They are not nutrients like vitamins or minerals, but they appear to play a role in fighting diseases like cancer. For instance, evidence suggests that those in soy-based foods like tofu help fight breast cancer by blocking the action of hormones that encourage the growth of cancerous tumors, and that those in garlic lower blood cholesterol levels and protect against some kinds of cancers.[32]

What do dietitians recommend for a healthy diet? Registered dietitians generally believe that there are no intrinsically good or bad foods. Whether they are good or bad for you depends on how much you consume. They also agree that eating a variety of foods is healthier than only a few, because food variety provides a variety of essential nutrients. A monotonous diet is likely to provide the same kind of nutrients and nutrient deficiencies. That having been said, most dietitians and nutrition researchers recommend that typical Americans eat less meat, particularly red meat, less saturated fats and oils, and less refined sugars and salt. They recommend that when we eat fats, they should be unsaturated, and that we eat more whole grain carbohydrates, fruits, and green and leafy vegetables. Alcoholic beverages, if any, should be consumed in moderation. "Moderation, " means for an average-sized man per day, not more than two mixed drinks (with 1.5 oz. of alcohol), or two 12 oz. beers, or two 6 oz. glasses of dry wine. For an average-sized woman, the recommendation is only one of each per day. These recommendations are purely about physiology and health; they do not consider the preferences or restrictions from culture, ethics, or religion.

Most foods in the typical American diet, and among affluent people around the world, are not intrinsically unhealthy. Most contribute to health, if eaten with moderation. Nor, as we shall see, were American diets historically healthier. But in typical modern American proportions, our food makes more than half of us overweight, subject to serious illnesses, and shortened lives. For all of its richness and bounty, eating in America often takes place in what a Yale University psychologist calls a "toxic food environment."[33]

CONCLUSION

We discussed the biological bases of food and human well-being in terms of food as related to human evolution, the basic categories of nutrients, and the development of nutrition science. Our discussion ended with some recommendations of nutritional science for improving the diet of typical modern North Americans. This chapter discussed how and why food is an important human value and presented a set of issues on many levels. From here we move to food history, ecology, political economy, and social justice issues.

SOME SUGGESTIONS FOR FURTHER READING AND INFORMATION

Boyle, G. (2001). *Personal Nutrition.* 4th Ed. Belmont, CA: Wadsworth.
Sonneberg, L. (1995). *The Health Nutrient Bible: The Complete Encyclopedia of Food and Medicine.* New York: Simon and Schuster.
Nutrition Information Line, American Dietetic Association. Call (800) 366–1655 to listen to nutrition messages by a Registered Dietition (RD) in English or Spanish, or to receive a referral to an RD in your area.
Food Research and Action Center, 1875 Connecticut Avenue N.W., Washington DC, 20009. (202) 986–2200 www.frac.org

United States Government Sources:

Food and Nutrition Information Center. Department of Agriculture, National Agricultural Library, Room 304, 10301 Baltimore Avenue, Beltsville, MD 20705–2351. (301) 504–5719. www.nal.usda.gov/fnic
Center for Food Safety and Applied Nutrition Outreach and Information Center. Food and Drug Administration, 200 C Street S.W., Washington DC, 20204. (888) 723–3366 http://vm.cfsan.fda.gov

CHAPTER TWO

Food and History

From Hunter-Gatherers
to the Preindustrial West

This chapter provides an overview of the history of food in the Western world prior to the modern period. It discusses the changing nature of food gathering, cultivating, and consumption, as well as the relationship between those changes and social, economic, political, and cultural life. We begin with a description of food gathering among the hunter-gatherers of prehistoric times and the dramatic changes brought about by the rise of agriculture and animal husbandry in the world's first civilizations. We look at the appearances of Western attitudes toward land ownership and tilling the land in the ancient civilizations of Greece and Rome, as well as advances in agriculture and changing social and religious practices related to food during the Middle Ages. Then we move to another of the truly revolutionary developments in world history that involved food—the Colombian Exchange—in which the continents of the world were brought together, and an exchange of peoples, ideas, disease, and food initiated that forever transformed how people lived. The chapter ends with a brief description of food in America prior to the Industrial Revolution. A pervasive theme is that the necessity for food, and changes in the way it is acquired and produced, have been powerful—and often unacknowledged—driving forces in the flow of human development and history.

FROM HUNTER-GATHERERS TO CULTIVATORS

Between 5 and 6 million years ago, the first humanlike beings, called hominids, evolved from earlier life forms in Africa. About 2 million years ago some hominids developed significantly larger brains and other recognizably human features, which earned them distinct genus names, such as Homo habilis (skilled man) and Homo erectus (man walking erect). Homo sapiens (wise men) evolved from these earlier Homo groups, while still in Africa it is now believed, appearing in Europe about 250,000 to 300,000 years ago. Their hands were equipped with a prehensile thumb, making them more dexterous than their primate ancestors, and thereby able to more easily grasp and work with tools and weapons. Males could chip rocks into hatchets to kill their prey, or wield two sticks to start a fire with which to cook their food. Females gathered fruits and grains found growing wild to share with their mates and children, whom they nourished and protected longer than mothers in the animal kingdom.[1]

Toward the end of the *Paleolithic*, or Old Stone, Age, about 100,000 to 120,000 years ago, the first Neanderthal people appeared in parts of Europe and Asia. Neanderthals lived in caves, hunted in groups, and appeased their gods—the spirits of nature—with comparatively elaborate rituals that involved sacrifices of what they had killed or gathered. They gathered around fires, wore clothing, and buried their dead with tools and ornaments to accompany them to the afterworld. But about 30,000 to 40,000 years ago, they were replaced by modern humans, as we would recognize them, known as Cro-Magnon people. They used more refined tools, and sewed clothes from animal skins, using needles of bone. They crafted statuettes of plump women with exaggerated breasts and bellies, who represented the source of life and new birth. They adorned their cave walls with paintings of beasts whom the hunters wished to kill, or had killed, and learned to apply their superior brainpower to explore and increasingly dominate the world around them.[2]

As humans evolved, so too did their adaptations to the biophysical environment. Between 1.6 million and 10,000 years ago, the Arctic ice cap repeatedly expanded over the landmasses of the Northern Hemisphere. Glaciers flowed into the valleys of the temperate zones of Asia, Europe, and North America, making life hard for humans and animals alike. They responded by migrating to warmer climes. Taking advantage of the lower sea levels and extended coastal areas that resulted from the spreading glaciers absorbing water, modern man migrated to every continent of the earth except Antarctica.

The final recession of the ice cap, around 10,000 years ago, was a turning point in the evolution of human culture. As the climate warmed, human beings in the *Neolithic*, or New Stone Age, laid the foundations for the development of what we would call civilization. Foremost among these developments were farming and animal husbandry. Securing sufficient food to satisfy

Prehistoric cave paintings of large animals from France probably had a magical significance about successful hunting.

the needs of its members has been essential to the existence of any society. In early communities men hunted for food and women and children gathered it, picking fruits from trees and bushes, gleaning grain from fields sown with seeds borne by animals or wind, and digging edible roots from the earth. Indeed, for most of human history, food was found in grasslands or forests, growing wild or running free. The cultivation of foodstuffs, whereby humans attempted to increase the reliability of their subsistence, is a very recent phenomenon.[3]

There were great variations in food gathering among our primitive ancestors. In its most rudimentary form, food foraging, they used little or no special technology. Hunting, fishing, and food collecting, on the other hand, required a more sophisticated level of activity and the employment of special, if still simple, tools. Foragers had a largely unprocessed, vegetarian diet, supplemented by insects, larva, and meat obtained by scavenging for dead animals. Only in the later stages of human development did humans become more reliant on meat and prepared foods.[4] However, according to recent research, meat constituted 90 percent of Neanderthal man's diet. Paul B. Pettit, Erik Trinkaus, and Fred H. Smith theorize that Neanderthals were able to organize complex and efficient hunts that brought down much bigger and more dangerous game. When modern people replaced the Neanderthals and turned to a mixture of foraging and horticulture, diets returned to a more omnivorous fare, 20 to 30 percent meat, but animal products continued to be an essential element.[5]

The discovery that planting crops or harvesting them repeatedly would bring forth grain created a revolution in the way early humans obtained food. It initiated what we today call agriculture, but its impact would be felt far beyond the fields. For the first time in the millions of years of their existence, human beings cultivated the land and produced their own food, but in order to do so most efficiently, they had to settle in one place, rather than wander from one place to another, and form stable communities. The first farmers were really *horticulturists* who grew yams, squash, corn, and other root crops in small patches they cleared from forests and jungles. This practice was initiated in widely scattered locations around the world, and people used digging sticks and hoes rather than plows. They typically combined this with hunting and gathering. Their "slash and burn" agriculture, as it was called, was fairly sustainable. After several years when the animals were depleted or the soil fertility diminished from erosion, they picked up and moved on, perhaps returning to the same location in ten or twenty years. As they led a semi-settled life, their numbers began to increase dramatically. Settled people weaned children much earlier than nomadic foragers, thus increasing fertile periods of females and reducing the length of time between births.[6]

More intensive agriculture emerged about 8000 B.C.E. in the highlands of the Middle East. They turned up fertile topsoil with plows powered either by humans or animals, and they grew wheat, millet, oats, and barley, which could be stored much longer than horticultural root crops. Food was prepared by boiling, soaking, pounding, grinding, and baking those grains. They stewed them in water to form porridge, molded them into a loaf or cake for baking, and brewed them to make a fermented sludge, the precursor of modern beer. They domesticated cows, goats, sheep, pigs, and fowl, which provided clothing and milk, as well as meat, and learned to use oxen, water buffalo, horses, and dogs to haul loads, provide transportation, and help them with their work. They began to cook their food on a regular basis (boiling of food may have begun at about 5000 B.C.E.) and to employ various means of preserving it, such as drying, freezing, the use of salt, curing, and smoking.[7]

Raising crops and animals entailed a new way of life for humans. They built shelters close to the fields. They grew into communities larger than the smaller groups necessary for—and that could be supported by—hunting and gathering. Whereas hunter-gatherer groups were limited to about thirty or so persons, organized into family groups or loose confederations of families, agricultural villages numbered in the hundreds or thousands, a development that proved both beneficial and detrimental.[8]

The conventional view of this change from hunting and food gathering to agriculture is that inhabitants of these new farming communities were better fed, housed, and protected than their hunter and gatherer forebears. But that view has been challenged by archeologists and other researchers, who have concluded that the invention of agriculture was "the worst thing that ever happened to the human stomach."[9] University of California physiologist Jared Diamond provided the substance of this position in "The Worst Mistake in History of the Human Race," first published in 1987. He argued that recent discoveries suggest that the adoption of agriculture was "in many ways a catastrophe from which we have never recovered." He pointed to a negative effect on man's diet, as well as the emergence of exploitive social hierarchies, patriarchy, the spread of nutritional and infectious diseases, despotism, slavery, and warfare.[10]

Diamond reported that skeletons discovered in Greece and Turkey show that the average height of hunter-gatherers toward the end of the ice ages was 5'9" for men, 5'5" for women. With the adoption of agriculture, by 3000 B.C.E. average heights declined to 5'3" for men and 5' for women. By classical times heights began to rise again, but modern Greeks and Turks have still not regained the average heights of their ancestors.[11] A study of Indian skeletons found in Dickson burial mounds in the Illinois and Ohio river valleys revealed that farmers had a nearly 50 percent increase in enamel defects indicative of malnutrition, a fourfold increase in iron-deficiency anemia, a threefold rise in bone lesions reflecting infectious disease in general, and an increase in degenerative conditions of the spine, probably reflecting a lot of hard physical labor. Life expectancy dropped from twenty-six years to nineteen.[12]

When the Indians at Dickson Mounds, and other primitive peoples, took up farming they adopted a less varied, and less nutritious, diet. Whereas prehistoric peoples found food in over 1,500 species of wild plants, and at least 500 major vegetables, "civilized" man came to obtain 75 percent of his calories from wheat, rice and maize. Further, the first farmers ran the risk of starvation if one crop failed. The crowding of people into smaller areas, which carried on trade with other population centers, led to the spread of parasites and infectious diseases like tuberculosis, measles, and bubonic plague. As

---

AGRICULTURE AS PROGRESS?

Diamond also offered the following "indirect test" of the progressivist view that the lives of people improved when they abandoned hunting and gathering for farming:

> Are twentieth-century hunters and gatherers really worse off than farmers are? Scattered throughout the world, several dozen groups of so-called primitive people, like the Kalahari Bushmen and the Yanomamo in the forests of Brazil and Venezuela, continue to support themselves that way. It turns out that these people have plenty of leisure time, sleep a good deal, and work less hard than their farming neighbors....One Busman, when asked why he hadn't emulated neighboring tribes by adopting agriculture, replied, "Why should we, when there are so many mongongo nuts in the world?"[14]

Tribal women from islands near the African nation of Guinea-Bissau pound the fruit of oil palms to extract cooking oil while caring for children.

these population centers grew, they produced class divisions. "Only in farming populations could a healthy, nonproducing elite set itself above the disease-ridden masses," Diamond wrote, the results of which can be seen in the skeletons of royalty and commoners.[13]

So, why did humans turn to agriculture, or as Diamond put it, get "trapped" by it despite its pitfalls? As growing populations of seminomadic people gradually decimated wild game and "gatherable" plants and roots, they had no other choice than to rely more and more on horticulture or pastoralism (herding sheep, goats, etc.), regardless of the social or environmental consequences. Agriculture was the only means of producing sufficient food supplies, and such settled populations even forced the remaining hunter-gatherers either to join them, or move to land the farmers did not want. As in many things, they found that "you can't go back."[15]

THE FIRST CIVILIZATIONS

Between 5,000 and 6,000 years ago, some complex Neolithic communities crossed the threshold between prehistory and history and formed the first civilizations. They were marked by greater concentrations of population, more complex social organization, and many technological innovations. They came together to sow and harvest, but they also walled their cities, became administered by sophisticated (if often despotic) forms of government, raised armies, and established more religions with more formal cosmologies administered by a "priestly" class. They developed systems of writing, metallurgy, began to keep records, and speculated about the world around them and beyond.

Such civilizations developed at different times at different points on the globe. The earliest arose about 3500 B.C.E. in the valley of the Tigris and Euphrates Rivers in the Middle East, in what is often referred to as the Fertile Crescent. The second developed in Egypt, along the Nile, about 3000 B.C.E. Another civilization appeared in the Indus River Valley around 2500 B.C.E.; the next in the valley of the Yellow River (Huang Ho) in modern China about 500 years later. From these first four Old World civilizations developed all of the subsequent modern cultures of Afro-Eurasia. That development (with some differences) was paralleled at a somewhat later time by the Mesoamerican civilizations of the Aztecs, Mayans, and Incas. Early Spanish explorers found incipient civilizations in the lower Mississippi basin of North America that featured large walled cities along the river and elaborate social hierarchies that kept slaves.

What the Old World civilizations had in common—indeed what served as the basis for their development as the first civilizations—was the presence of rivers and fertile soil, linked to the flooding of those rivers. In the valleys formed by the Tigris and Euphrates and Nile Rivers, for example, the soil was potentially very fertile. The use of water management, especially irrigation from those rivers, made it possible to grow crops in an otherwise hot, dry climate. In Egypt the Nile could be counted on to flood every summer and recede every fall, creating a green strip on both banks of alluvial soil that formed an ideal bed for the cultivation of grains. Plant and animal life soon flourished providing food not only for the Egyptian population but enough to store and trade—the first evidence of substantial trade in foodstuffs among peoples.[16]

Mesopotamia presented a more difficult challenge. Unlike the Nile, the Tigris and Euphrates Rivers flooded on an unpredictable schedule and therefore were as dangerous as they were life giving. Laborers constructed dams to hold back the floodwaters and canals to channel them, and in time managed a level of control that had a similar effect on the Fertile Crescent as it did on the Nile River Valley. By the early third millennium B.C.E., the Sumerians founded the first civilization in the region and a dozen walled cities soon appeared. Uruk had about 50,000 people by 2700 B.C.E.; Ur 25,000; and others 10,000 to 20,000.[17]

More pronounced hierarchies developed in these cities. At the top of the social hierarchy were those who ruled: kings, priests, and nobles. The members of this privileged elite lived in palaces, or administered temple buildings and land. They ruled over, and were supported by, a much larger population of rural villagers who grew food, but owned nothing. In between these two levels of the social hierarchy existed merchants and artisans.[18] Families, the basic unit of society, changed as well. Prehistoric people grouped themselves in clans, but when agricultural communities found that the control of property was the key to survival, nuclear family units became more important.

Women were increasingly excluded from public life, as marriage and motherhood became their whole life. Fathers arranged their daughters' marriages. Contracts specified exchanges of property given by the bride's family to a desirable groom, and by the groom's to a valuable bride. Marriage was an economic arrangement that answered the aspirations of families for status, offspring, or allies. It was not designed to suit the inclinations of the individuals whose lives it affected. Once married, a woman became subject to her husband's authority. In general, she could not act independently in society, and much as she had little choice in entering a marriage, she had little choice in its dissolution. Nevertheless, harsh as were the restrictions that encircled married women, their status was higher than that of unmarried women who were not under male protection. Similarly, these first "civilized" families preferred male to female children, who were occasionally cast out after birth. Girls caused great expense because of the dowries they were expected to provide. And they could not carry on the family line. Farmers could use their sons' labor, and sons stood to inherit the family lands.[19]

Human beings first learned to write so that they could keep lists of the measure of grain in storage, as well as the amount to be paid in taxes or tribute to the gods. They kept inventories of tools and recorded the laws that became more encompassing and complex, like the Babylonian law code of Hammurabi assembled around 1760 B.C.E. They noted planetary motions, the rise and fall of the rivers, and more. Priests, the guardians of the temple, were the first list makers and first scribes, and they formed schools to transmit the art of writing to others, thereby further advancing civilization—important because of the changing nature of food cultivation.[20]

Finally, given the centrality of food to the human experience, it is perhaps to be expected that it would be central to the religious experience of the first civilizations as well. Much like their prehistoric ancestors, the people of the first civilizations engaged in sacrifices to the gods, most commonly to ensure their food supply. The gods required sustenance and were fed on the altars with foodstuffs or domesticated animals offered up by worshippers, or more commonly by their priests. In time worshippers created myths, or stories, about the gods that helped explain the working of the cosmos, and in time they began to believe that what was required of them was not only the sacrifice of plants and beasts, but obedience or faith as well. They had storm gods and flood gods, as well as round and full-breasted earth mothers. The gods looked like animals or human beings, or—in the case of the Egyptians, for example—both. They resided in splendid temples, on mountaintops, or in trees, streams, or oceans. There were gods of the harvest and of the earth and to their altars people brought offerings. They scattered grain, spilled wine, and slew rams and goats.[21]

ANCIENT GREECE AND ROME

What we now call "Western Civilization" is rooted in ancient Greece. Although people first occupied the land in about 2000 B.C.E., the Greeks gave birth to the *polis* during what is called the Archaic Age (about 750 to about 500 B.C.E.) and became the first citizens of the Western world. A *polis* generally developed when one or several villages coalesced around a common religious center. The cult celebrated a local deity as patron, and built a temple to that deity on a hill, called the *acropolis*. At the foot of the hill was a flat, clear area, the *agora*. There people brought goods to market for exchange, wealthy landowners listened to civil disputes, and citizens gathered for debate. The Greek *polis* (which evolved into the word "political") was an association of people united by place, custom, and principle, from which the modern concept of citizenship derives.[22]

The emergence of hundreds of *poleis* and their increase in size and influence enriched the world around the Aegean Sea. Such poleis never grew terribly large. A population of 4,000 to 5,000 free men and women was common; only a few exceeded 40,000, to which should be added at least an equal number of foreigners and slaves. During the Golden Age of Greece, from 477 to 431 B.C.E., the Greeks made high attainments in philosophy, the arts, and in the development of a democratic government. Athens became the center of this rich cultural development, and its population peaked at about 310,000: 172,000 free men and women, 110,000 slaves, and 28,000 foreign people of commerce.[23]

The people ruled the *polis*—not all of them, of course, but approximately 15 percent, or between 40,000 and 50,000 adult males, in the case of Athens. Nevertheless, some consortium or committee drawn from the people organized city life. The primacy of the people resulted from the demotion of kings and the disappearance of the priesthood as a separate and privileged social class. Although the Greek world knew both priests and priestesses, they were either ordinary citizens performing special rites on ceremonial occasions or inspired oracles attached to particular deities, public places, and temples. They did not constitute a priesthood such as that which had dominated the first civilizations.[24]

Importantly, the Greek polis was a dramatic contrast to the hierarchical "top down" structures characterizing Egyptian and Mesopotamian civilizations. Scholars have argued that Western attitudes toward the land, as well as democracy, originated in Ancient Greece. Much as Thomas Jefferson would explain in his *Notes on Virginia* (1785), the Greeks believed in a beneficial relationship between the percentage of what would be known as yeomen farmers and a people's virtue, democratic form of government, and general welfare. For four centuries (700–300 B.C.E.), when Greece flourished, much of what we honor as the heart of the Western tradition was linked to, if not based on, what we would consider today traditional agrarianism or family farming.[25]

Family farming has not been a typical pattern of land tenure or agricultural practice in history. It did not exist in the ancient worlds prior to the Golden Age of Greek civilization. Indeed independent and private property holding free citizenry did not exist. Instead, once man turned to agriculture and entered the "cradles of civilization," central bureaucracies controlled land from the palace and prescribed all agricultural regimes, including harvests and the distribution of food. The palace owned the land, the food, and in some ways the people themselves.[26]

Thus, Western agrarianism and the polis arose simultaneously. In the polis, a citizen was defined by title to his own parcel of land. Land entitled him to vote in governing the polis, as well as obliged him to fight in its defense. Lack of land ownership relegated the person to various inferior positions, from limited citizenship and participation in government to chattel slavery. Further, Classical Greek farming was characterized by the ideas that each farm family would hold its ancestral plot—roughly 10 to 15 acres—in perpetuity, and that the network of such plots would provide stability for the community. Laws forbade farm sales outside the family, and, for the first time in history, people began to live on the land they farmed. The result was an autonomous and middling citizenry that would invest time and energy in improving their farms for their offspring.[27]

In sum, the Greeks believed that the family farm was the moral cement of the community and that farmers were the ideal citizens. Thus the Greeks turned to agriculture to serve society at large in ways that transcended the production of food. Its antithesis, at least during the Classical Period, was specialization and trade, which they—much like Jefferson at the founding of the American Republic—believed would lead to an increased dominance of non-farming, or commercial, interests.[28] Commerce flourished in ancient Greece, to be sure, as they engaged in trade throughout the Mediterranean world. But merchants occupied an uncomfortable place in Greek society. Their work brought wealth to Greece, which fueled its achievements. Nevertheless, they were perceived as outsiders. Those who engaged in manufacture and commerce were looked down upon by the landowners. The ideal state, wrote Aristotle, cannot allow its citizens to "live a mechanic or a mercantile life (for such a life is ignoble and inimical to virtue)." Thus most merchants were foreigners, immigrants who formed a separate class of resident noncitizens.[29]

The public life of the *polis* was based on distinctive patterns of private life, the fundamental unit of which was the household. The household was *patrilineal* in origin and purpose, and *patriarchal* in character. The patrilineal family traced its foundation to a male forebear on the father's side. Only

THE ANCIENT GREEKS AND AGRICULTURE

Ancient Greeks speak for themselves: Xenophon, in his *Oeconomicus,* a "Household Manager," wrote: "When farming goes well, all other arts go well, but when the earth is forced to be barren, the others almost cease to exist." Farming is "the best life" because it gives the body "the greatest degree of strength and beauty," and the farming community is the backbone of the state, because it makes "those who work the soil brave, the best citizens, most loyal to the polis." The word *oeconomicus* (household manager) is the root word for our word *economic,* which now has a somewhat different meaning.[30]

males were considered as descendants. The family was patriarchal in that a senior male exercised power within the family and over all its members. Any authority a woman might yield resulted from the labor she performed. In Greek peasant families that labor was tied to food production and preparation: she sowed and harvested, ground grain, carried water, milked and herded, gathered and stored surpluses, and prepared meals. In wealthier urban families that were farther removed from the land, the wife became a full-time manager of the household. She became a producer of textiles, spinner, weaver, embroiderer, and preparer of food. However, in both cases women spent their lives first in her father's household and then in her husband's, and were sequestered in the home, seldom venturing out even to shop, which was a male activity.[31]

Ancient Greece's food supply was the product of its environment, supplemented at its height by imported products. Agriculture in Greece lagged behind that of Mesopotamia and Egypt by as much as 1,000 years. Most of Greece was covered by rocky, light soil, but as long as the population remained small, it provided people with an adequate food supply. Greeks never made much use of animals as beasts of burden. The early Greek diet was simple. Porridge and bread were made from wheat and barley, which they supplemented with olives, olive oil, some fish, figs, honey, and an occasional pig. Goats were commonly kept for milk and cheese. Richer farmers had flocks of sheep, but meat was scarce due to the difficulty of grazing on the Greek terrain. Because of its scarcity and resulting value, the Greeks used meat mainly for feasts and religious sacrifices.[32]

As you might guess, Greeks were largely vegetarians, their diets commonly included beans, cabbage, leeks, lentils, onions, turnips, and various fruits. Although at first adequate, as the population increased there was increased competition for the limited amount of available land, which was farmed more intensively. The land suffered from overcropping and overgrazing by sheep, which left the ground almost bare. People were forced to clear the remaining trees from the land, which increased the erosion of the thin, dry soil. The dry, warm climate encouraged the buildup of salinity in the soil, further discouraging the growth of most crops. Olives and grapes, which could be grown under these conditions, replaced livestock, barley, and wheat, requiring the importation of other foods to ensure an adequate food supply.[33]

Such conditions brought about the demise of the "citizen-farmer society." Land holdings became enormous, ranging into the thousands of acres. The law was changed to allow such private accumulation of the land, and slaves were brought in increasingly to work the large estates. Thus, the very basis of citizenship was undermined. Land was bought and sold under imperial directive. Agriculture became an investment opportunity like mining or shipping, and it drew investment capital into the countryside in return for competitive profits from harvests. Greek investors exhibited no consideration for civic consequences, other than that which affected their investment.[34]

By the end of the fifth century B.C.E., a great disparity appeared between rich and poor cuisines that had not previously existed. Trade brought in a wide range of foods from throughout the Mediterranean, but only the wealthy could afford them. As a result, while the rich dined on exotic foods, and even produced fine cookbooks, the poor ate black pudding made from pork stock and blood, vinegar, and salt. The decline of Athens is commonly attributed to its defeat by Sparta in the Peloponnesian War in 431 B.C.E. and a severe plague that struck the next year, but it was also related to food shortages. In its defeat, Athens could no longer import the food it needed to sustain its population. The war devastated the countryside. Villages were razed and crops ruined. Greece soon fell to the Romans.[35]

Much like the Classical Greeks, Roman republican society—begun in 509 B.C.E.—was rooted in the ancient social organizations of tribe, clan, and family. Much like the Greeks, the Romans idealized the small farm and based citizenship on land ownership. Men dominated the household with much the same authority of their Greek counterparts. The mission of the family continued to be to preserve the male line and to transmit property down through the generations.[36]

In 27 B.C.E., however, the Roman Republic came to an end. After twenty years of civil war, Rome became an empire under the benevolent dictatorship of Octavian, titled Augustus. He returned domestic peace and prosperity, and at the same time Rome conquered others to form the largest empire in history. Trade routes were established throughout Eurasia and northern Africa, as far east as China and India. The city of Rome became colossal. Baths, aqueducts, and sewers, as well as magnificent public buildings, temples, and arenas graced the city. It attracted about 1 million residents, making it the largest city in the Mediterranean world. About 400,000 of that population, however, were slaves. The wealthy lived well, in private town houses built around a central courtyard. The urban poor lived in tenements several stories high, shoddily built, inadequately supplied with light, air, heat, or water, without kitchens, and vulnerable to fire. By the fourth century, Rome is said to have contained more than 46,000 of these tenements, in contrast to fewer than 2,000 homes of the rich.[37]

Through the Republican Period, most Romans ate well, if frugally, with little distinction between classes. They were largely vegetarians and bread was the staple. When Rome began to extend its boundaries beyond the Italian peninsula, however, things changed. Rome defeated Carthage in North Africa in the second century B.C.E., and gained control of North African and Sicilian wheat, which it imported. Further conquests added foods from Mesopotamia and the far reaches of Europe, most of which enlarged the diets of the upper classes. Increased amounts of meat and fish became available, as did wine—consumed largely by the wealthy.[38]

Roman Empire society was known for its eating orgies among the upper classes. Such behavior led to the passage of sumptuary laws—an attempt to control such excesses, which were really signs of conspicuous consumption.[39] In contrast, in both quantity and quality, the poor ate a polenta-like porridge made from millet, grain pastes, coarse bread, olive oil and water, in addition to which some ate turnips, olives, beans, figs, and cheese. Meat was scarce, although a little pork or fish was occasionally available. Cooking was kept to a minimum among those who lived in urban tenements, due to the primitive and dangerous conditions. In a fate similar to that of the Greeks, military defeats and the ravages of German tribal occupation meant Rome could no longer import a sufficient amount of food to feed its urban population. The capital of the Mediterranean world collapsed, and people moved to the countryside where they would remain for over a thousand years, or until near the modern period.[40]

THE MIDDLE AGES

In the fifth century, the accumulated energy of various German tribes that had been massing on the frontier overwhelmed the Roman Empire. Although its Eastern sector, Byzantium, with its capital at Constantinople, survived for several more centuries, the Roman Empire in the West came to an end in 476 C.E. While there was the "devolution" of a high civilization, historians no longer use the phrase "Dark Ages" to describe what followed. A debasement of literary culture paralleled a loss of population, a decline of urban life, the collapse of commerce, an increase in lawlessness, and a deep isolation. But at the same time, beginning as early as the sixth century, and certainly from the end of the eighth century, profound changes did emerge that laid the foundation for modern European and Western culture. It was a period of transition, as the focus of European life shifted from the Mediterranean to the forested interior of Western Europe. Central to the story of the development of this new and vigorous civilization were the developments in agriculture and food.

The Middle Ages (c. 476–1500) were marked by periodic crop failures, famines, and plagues, but it was also a period of remarkable achievements, those in farming being the earliest and most fundamental. They were accomplished by peasants, who made up 90 percent of all Europeans. These workers invented the techniques of medieval agriculture, felled forests for settlement, and built stable village communities. As in antiquity, peasants struggled to produce the minimum amount of food necessary for survival. The soil was stubborn and unpredictable. Nature imposed hardships of bad weather and disease, but human beings imposed others.[41]

The agricultural economy of medieval Europe was characterized largely by the phenomenon of *serfdom*. A serf was neither free nor slave. Many were the descendants of late Roman peasants and slaves. By the last centuries of the Roman era, many peasants had already fallen into a desperate condition, forced into dependency by the relentless demands of landholders and tax collectors. These oppressed smallholders surrendered their freedom in order to gain the right to stay on the land and farm it. Serfs came with the land. Unlike slaves, they could not be sold, or even removed from the land they had bargained sacrificially to win. But neither could they leave and seek a different occupation, or richer soil, elsewhere. Slaves escaped their servitude, but, ironically, they ascended into the condition of serfdom.[42]

During the early Middle Ages, the farmers of northern Europe faced the challenge of tilling soil that was more difficult than the land around the Mediterranean. The land was also more fertile, however, and a series of innovations in plowing and managing the soil made northern European agriculture more productive. North of the Alps, the soil demanded a different pattern of land cultivation from that common in the earlier Mediterranean civilizations. The Mediterranean climate was warm and the soil thin, but easily cultivated with a lightweight plow. To the north, the climate was cool and wet, the soil heavy, damp, and deep, and the land was a great forested plain from the Atlantic shore eastward into modern Russia. Once the forests were cleared, that rich and well-watered plain was suitable for growing grain, particularly rye and barley which had shorter maturation times than wheat.[43]

AGRICULTURAL INNOVATIONS AND EATING IN THE MIDDLES AGES

The peasants of northern Europe developed new techniques to meet the demands of climate and topography. By about 1000, they developed a heavy plow, called the moldboard plow, the key to Europe's future prosperity. Drawn by a pair of yoked oxen or a team of horses, this powerful implement pierced the tough skin of the northern soil, sheared the grass at the roots, turned the sliced soil, and mounded it alongside the deep furrow. The deep cultivation of the soil accomplished by the heavy plow permitted the intensive cultivation of grains. By the beginning of the fourteenth century, thanks to this invention, grain yields climbed to a peak that would not be surpassed until the eighteenth century.[44]

To mill grain, serfs used human or animal power. They also built water-wheels and windmills, which were used for brewing, for fulling of cloth, and for papermaking, as well. Horses are quicker and more dependable than oxen, but ancient people, who harnessed their horses the way they yoked their oxen, never utilized horsepower effectively. The harness strangled horses hauling a heavy load. By the ninth century, medieval peasants learned to employ a device imported from the Asian steppes—a rigid, padded collar. Equipped with such a collar, which rested on the shoulder blades rather than on the neck, the horse could pull heavy loads without choking. At about the same time, peasants began to equip their horses with another device, also Asian in origin—iron shoes. Now teams of horses with armored hoofs and hitched in teams could work faster than the oxen.[45]

Another important innovation was neither a machine nor a device, but a farming method called *fallowing*. Peasants learned that planting the same crops on the same fields year after year resulted in the impoverishment and mineral depletion of the soil. Leaving one-half of the soil idle, or fallow, for a season enriched it. This practice allowed nutrients to be reintroduced through the normal process of the decay of vegetable matter and the interaction of elements in the soil with those in the air. The late-medieval, early modern period peasants developed a "three-field system," where the cultivation of a staple but soil-depleting grain, was complemented by alternate crops of legumes, such as peas, beans, and alfalfa, whose roots released soil-enriching nitrogen back to the soil.[46]

Peasant families ate a supper of bread, which was the largest part of their diet, perhaps accompanied by a stew of vegetables flavored with garden herbs. Rye became the principal cereal grain in northern and Western Europe. Wheat was available in the south, which was often made into frumenty, made by soaking the husked grains in hot water. It was eaten with milk and honey (a sort of medieval equivalent of oatmeal). Peasants in the north drank ale, in the south, wine. Occasionally they ate cheese from the milk of sheep, goats, or cows. They ate meat rarely, and then most often pork, salt pork, or mutton from the superfluous or elderly beasts slaughtered before the onset of winter, when no fodder could be spared to feed them. Only the rich had spices. During the early Middle Ages, except for cabbage, leeks, and onions, vegetables were scarce, and fruit was rare, as well.[47]

Large and wealthy property owners dined on a variety of meats, roasts, wild boar, venison, veal, game, ducks, geese, and chicken. If they lived near the sea, a lake, or a river, they also had fish. Bread, cheese, and honey were common, but vegetables were largely absent from their diets until the eleventh century, when previously noted developments in crop rotation added legumes to their diets. At that point closer contact with the Arab world,

FEASTING AND MEDIEVAL ELITES

Norbert Elias provides this description of the food practices of the social elites of medieval society: "The dead animal or large parts of it were often brought whole to the table. Not only the whole fish and whole birds (sometimes with their feathers) but also whole rabbits, lambs, and quarters of veal appear at the table, not to mention the larger venison or the pigs and oxen on the spit....The diet of the Northern German court showed its resident members to consume two pounds of meat a day in addition to large quantities of venison, birds, and fish.[49]

especially the Middle East, led to the importation of a greater variety of foods, including sugar cane, rice, and additional spices.[48]

RELIGION, FASTING, AND MEDIEVAL EATING DISORDERS

As in today's world, there were those who chose to deny themselves food of any kind. Indeed, students of eating disorders often begin their histories among one particular group of women who lived in the Medieval Period. Women saints in the Middle Ages starved themselves in what has been labeled "holy anorexia." Men engaged in such practices as well, but women were represented in disproportionately high numbers. As Rudolph Bell found, self-starvation affected between 37 and 61 percent of women saints from the thirteenth to the seventeenth centuries.[50]

As alluded to earlier in passing, food has always played an important role in religion. Certain foods were sacrificed to the gods for their blessing or at least avoid their curses. But it is also the case that refraining from eating and drinking—fasting—played a role as well. In the Hebrew Bible, we read of people fasting in preparation for holy war (1 Sam. 14:34), in mourning for the dead (2 Sam. 3:35), and in reaction to calamity or distress (Joel 1:11). And there were "unclean foods" that were prohibited at all times (Lev. 11: 1–43). Similarly, in the Christian Bible, or New Testament, Jesus fasts in the desert after his baptism (Matthew 4:2). The Roman Catholic Church made fasting obligatory on special days like Ash Wednesday and Good Friday, for many years forbidding the consumption of meat on Fridays, in remembrance of Jesus' crucifixion. Not coincidentally, the practice of eating fish on Fridays did not develop until the heavily Roman Catholic Basques, Spanish, and Portuguese developed important fishing industries in the 1400s, and sought to created large markets for their dried and salted fish over much of Europe.

Refraining from certain foods may have arisen out of dietary or health considerations in a primordial past or the relative availability or plentiful nature of certain crops or animals. It may also have served to provide a sepa-

A SAMPLING OF RELIGION-BASED DIETARY PRACTICES

Buddhism

The central tenet of Buddhism is vegetarianism. In the eyes of Buddhists, to eat meat is to destroy the seeds of compassion. All plant foods are considered appropriate to eat except for the "five pungent goods": garlic, leeks, scallions, chives, and onion. These are considered unclean and believe to generate lust when eaten cooked and to induce rage when eaten raw.

Hinduism

Hindus believe that food was created by the Supreme Being for the benefit of humans. Beef is prohibited, and many Hindus are vegetarians.

Islam

Islamic food laws prohibit the consumption of "unclean food" such as swine, animals killed in a manner that prevents their blood from being fully drained from the bodies, carnivorous animals with fangs (such as lions and wolves), birds with sharp claws, and land animals without ears (frogs and snakes, for example).

Judaism

The traditional dietary laws of Judaism prohibit the consumption of swine, carrion eaters, and shellfish and specify other practices, such as the ritual slaughtering of animals. The term *kosher* indicates that the food was prepared according to certain methods. For example, that meat was salted to help remove the blood, or milk and meat were prepared using separate utensils.

Seventh-day Adventism

Vegetarianism is the foundation of dietary practices for the sect of Christianity. In addition, dietary standards call for abstaining from alcohol and avoiding caffeine. Followers typically eat a wholesome diet consisting of whole grains, fruits, nuts, vegetables, a little milk, and eggs.[52]

rate identity for groups of people, Jews and Christians, for example. Fasting was often penitential, that is, an attempt to have God forgive one's sins, but it was also intended to make the faithful more aware of God's presence.[51] For medieval saints, it was understood in these and other ways.

We will return to anorexia nervosa in its modern medical context in Chapter Five, but here we simply note that it was more common in societies where women are expected to be morally, spiritually, and bodily pure—which is often achieved by food restriction, virginity, and asceticism. Related ideas commonly include forbearance, passivity, self-denial, and dependence. Food refusal, Littlewood argued, functions as an attempt at self-determination that can be accomplished without breaking cultural norms, especially when other forms of personal resistance are not available. This helps explain the disproportionate presence of anorexia among women in Western culture, in general, and among medieval women saints in particular.[53]

Food was one of the few resources women controlled in the Medieval Period. Therefore, they found it easier to renounce eating than anything else. As a sign of their devotion to God, women gave up daily food for the Eucharist in their conviction that they were feeding on the body of God. As Caroline Walker Bynum has written: "Theologians and spiritual directors from the early church to the sixteenth century reminded penitents that sin had entered the world when Eve ate the forbidden fruit and that salvation comes when Christians eat their God in the ritual of communion." Further, fasting to these women was a form of suffering that they willingly endured in order to participate in the suffering of Christ, much as they and other saints endured self-inflicted injuries like whipping and burning. "Food was not only a fundamental material concern to medieval people; food practices—fasting and feasting—were at the very heart of the Christian tradition." So too, it would seem, was the suppression of excretory functions and even menstruation, which often resulted from starvation, among saintly women. Conversely, gluttony was often associated with heightened sexual appetite.[54]

FOOD, POPULATION, AND CHANGE IN THE MIDDLE AGES

Western Europe experienced dynamic growth, underwent economic crisis, suffered the devastations of the plague, and saw frequent outbreaks of peasant rebellion. The biggest change was the steady increase in population. The productivity of the land, tended by the plow and nursed by fallowing, and greater prosperity, meant that people could live longer; healthier mothers, their fertility enhanced by ample diets, gave birth to more children; and children, adequately nourished, more often survived. From about 700 to around 1300, the population of Europe grew from approximately 27 million to 73 million.[55]

Territorial expansion followed upon population growth. Prodded by their lords, the peasants of western Europe undertook the enormous task of clearing for cultivation the forests and swamps of the eastern region. At the beginning of the Middle Ages, most of Europe was wilderness. By 1000 Europeans completed the conquest of the soil within the western region and began pushing the boundary of the zone of settlement to the Elbe River and beyond. "Claiming the wilderness for the plow was the epic tale of medieval agriculture, and the peasant was its hero."[56] Thus begins the long tale of the accumulating impacts of agriculture on the earth's ecosystems, a tale that continues today.

The explosive population growth of Western Europe halted around 1300. The years that followed brought cycles of famine and disease. The most serious famine occurred in 1315–1317, in part the result of an epochal climatic cooling later called the "little ice age." In those years, cold, wet winters were followed by cool, sterile summers. Famine paved the way for disease, culminating in the terrible onslaught of the Black Death, probably bubonic plague, which ravaged Europe from 1347 to 1351 and recurred in every generation thereafter until the eighteenth century. The Black Death took so many lives—estimated as high as one-third of the total population—that a labor shortage developed in some regions, benefiting, ironically, the peasants who survived. They could now negotiate a good price for their labor. Many bargained for their freedom. But frustrated hopes on the parts of many others provoked numerous peasant revolts—in 1358 in France, in 1381 in England, and so on.[57]

For three centuries, beginning in the eleventh century, Europeans engaged in a series of wars intended to liberate the Holy Land from the

WET RYE AND THE FIRE OF ST. ANTHONY

From the ninth to the fourteenth century a strange madness accompanied by a devastating illness reached epidemic proportions in Western Europe. Now known as ergotism, then people commonly believed it was the wrath of God. Whole villages would suffer convulsions, hallucinations, gangrenous rotting of the extremities, and often death. Pregnant women would abort, and in its acute form, the disease brought great abdominal pain, violent convulsions, and a speedy death. Monasteries were founded to care for those who did not immediately die, and in 1096 the order of Hospital Brothers of St. Anthony was founded for the same purpose. The climate was cold and wet. Growing seasons were short, and summers were often not dry enough to work the land or properly dry the harvest. It is now known that much of the rye consumed was infected with the fungus blight, *ClACeps purpurea*. Blighted kernels were blackened and swollen, and only a few incorporated into a sack of grain were enough to make those sick who ate bread therefrom. Why? Blighted grain, if stored damp, ferments and produces a second chemical—a form of the hallucinogenic drug now known as lysergic acid diethylamide (LSD). The religious and medical madness of the Middle Ages had a pharmacological basis. As the European climate warmed and dried by the 1590s, the incidence of the disease was dramatically reduced.[58]

infidels, the Seljuk Turks. The Crusaders fought in the name of the cross. In the end thousands of lives were lost on both sides, and barbarities committed by both forces, but the Holy Land remained in the hands of the Turks. The impact of these wars and Europe's continuous contact with the Near East, however, had implications far beyond the battlefield. In the process of supplying the troops fighting in the east, merchants returned to Europe with Asian goods that proved irresistible to their clients. Italian merchants and soon their counterparts throughout Europe mastered the techniques of international commerce and opened up Europe to the outer world—and that included food.[59]

Finally, at the same time that Europe was advancing its techniques at producing abundant and nourishing food, the medieval elite began to "civilize" their appetites—to voluntarily curb their food consumption and shun their earlier gluttony. To this point, the wealthy indulged in gluttonous banquets, even in times of widespread dearth. It was a sign of relatively low level of identification with the sufferings of the less fortunate, marking in Norbert Elias's terms, a low point on the curve of the civilizing process.[60]

Stephen Mennell further argued that gluttony, as well as fasting, in the Medieval world was not simply connected with the insecurity and unpredictability of the food supply but also with the more general insecurity of conditions of life—mortality, disease, war, and more, all of which affected the well-born the same as the lowly, if to a lesser degree. Mennell associated wealthy Europeans' shunning gluttony with the previously noted Christian valuing of abstinence, sumptuary laws that demonstrated the interest of the state in suppressing gluttony, and medical opinion that counseled moderation. He also argued that it was a statement of class. Much as earlier the elite distinguished themselves by epic banquets and feasts, by the early modern period they increasingly did so by showing that they exercised greater control over their appetites than those beneath them on the social scale. As Mennell put it: "Courtly fashion moved towards the proliferation of small, delicate and costly dishes, and…knowledgeability and a sense of delicacy in matters of food became something of a mark of the courtier."[61]

THE EARLY MODERN PERIOD

The early Middle Ages saw a near-eclipse of trade. Bandits and pirates roamed at will. Roads and bridges fell into disrepair. Water routes became more dangerous after 700, when Arab ships controlled the Mediterranean, and in the ninth and tenth centuries when Vikings prowled the northern seas and rivers. Political disarray made it difficult for merchants to employ an acceptable currency or enforce contracts. After 900, however, beginning in northern Italy, cities began to flourish once again and to reengage in trade beyond Europe's borders. The Crusades, which began in the eleventh century and lasted some 300 years, may not have achieved their goal of "liberating" the Holy Land from the infidels. They certainly led to much death and destruction on both sides, but they also reopened trade between Europe and the Middle East and Asia.[62]

Historians disagree as to what motivated Europeans to take this step, which ultimately resulted in the development of a world food system. Some suggest that food shortages resulting from wars and epidemics pushed Europeans to search for staples in the Far East and Africa.[63] Others argue that they sought spices for both practical and symbolic reasons. They used sugar, salt, and other spices to season their foods, to preserve them, and as medicine. Spices were expensive, however, so they were luxuries, as well, and, signs of wealth.[64]

Italian trading cities began by supplying European Crusaders, but they soon engaged in bringing Asian luxury goods back to Europe. Venice, Genoa, and Pisa led the way, which in turn paved the way for the cultural resurgence in Europe known as the Renaissance. The Renaissance began in those same Italian cities in the fourteenth century—the great wealth of their commercial success providing the means by which cultural opportunities could be pursued. The development of this world food system also coincided, perhaps abetted, the development of capitalism in the West, the demise of feudalism, and the rise of the yeoman farmer.[65]

NUTMEG AND THE SPICE TRADE

Nutmeg, the seed of the tree, was the most coveted luxury in seventeenth-century Europe, a spice held to have such powerful medicinal properties that men would risk their lives to acquire it. Always costly, it rocketed in price when the physicians of Elizabethan London began claiming that their nutmeg pomanders were the only certain cure for the plague, which started with a sneeze and ended in almost certain death. Overnight, the withered little nut—previously used to cure flatulence and the common cold—became as sought after as gold. There was one drawback: No one was sure exactly where it came from. London's merchants bought it from Venice, where in turn it was purchased from the Turks in Constantinople. But nutmeg came from much further east, from the fabled "spice islands." On the vague and nebulous maps of the times, and as far as the merchants were concerned, it may have well have been on the moon. Even the merchants of Constantinople had only vague notions about where it came from, and there were lurid rumors of sea monsters that preyed on ships, hidden reefs, and bloodthirsty savages along the way.

But none of this deterred Europe's profit-hungry merchants who would chance everything in their desperation to find nutmeg's source. Soon the shipyards of Portugal, Spain, England, and Holland were alive to the clatter of shipbuilding, and a flurry of activities that would later become known as the spice race, a desperate and protracted struggle for control of one of the world's smallest island archipelagoes.[66]

The expansion of European commerce was so dramatic as to be called a "commercial revolution." Italian merchants dominated the Mediterranean, but when Spanish, Dutch, English, and French merchants joined in, they took to the Atlantic. The tiny Iberian country of Portugal took the lead, reaching India in 1498 by a route around the southern tip of Africa. The Spanish, Dutch, French, and English soon followed suit. In 1492, Christopher Columbus, an Italian sailing for Spain, in an attempt to reach the East Indies, sailed west across the Atlantic in search of gold, spice, and converts to Christianity. He stumbled on the shores of the Western Hemisphere, joining all of the major continents of the world for the first time in history. This led to an incredibly influential biological and cultural development dubbed the "Columbian Exchange." Some have referred to it as the beginning of the globalization of the world's eating habits.[67]

In 1492 the entire population of the Western Hemisphere probably equaled that of Europe (60–70 million), with the highest concentrations of settlement in what is today Mexico, Central America, and Peru among the Aztecs, Maya, and Incas.[69] Rather than a New World, Columbus actually discovered another Old World, populated by numerous and diverse people with distinct cultures, whose ancestors migrated from Asia via the Bering Straits 20,000 or more years earlier.[70] European explorers encountered a mixture of hunter-gatherers and horticulturists in North America, and complex civilizations in Mesoamerica and South America. But even the latter were lacking in military technology that would help them resist European invasion and colonization. As a result, they were swept aside by tiny bands of conquistadors. Indian bows, arrows and slings could not match Spanish steel, horses, and cannon. Even more important, according to some scholars, was the transmission of European diseases, such as small pox, measles, typhus, diphtheria, and mumps, as well as malaria and yellow fever from Africa, to which Indians had no immunity. Their numbers were rapidly decimated and the remainder became peons on the plantations of the Europeans, or herded into "reservations" on what was taken as useless land.[71]

A BASQUE TALE

"A Medieval fisherman is said to have hauled up a three-foot-long cod, which was common enough at the time. And the fact that the cod could talk was not especially surprising. But what was astonishing was that it spoke an unknown language. It spoke Basque." This Basque folktale, as summarized by Mark Kurlansky, shows the close ties between the Atlantic cod and the Basque. They were among the great fishermen of the Middle Ages. They supplied Europe with whale meat and cod, for which they had to travel long distances. They fished for cod off the coast of North America decades before Columbus happened on the "New World," but they didn't tell anyone![68]

North American Indians, those within the bounds of what would become the United States, were a mixture of foragers and horticulturists. According to one estimate the pre-Columbian Indian's diet consisted of about 35 percent meat and 65 percent plant food. When agriculture expanded into North America—in to the American Southwest, and to a lesser extent elsewhere—in the period from 1500 B.C.E. to 300 C.E., their diets developed a greater reliance on plant foods. They cultivated staple crops like corn, beans, pumpkins, and squash, and lent variety to their diets with wild fruits, roots, and berries.[72]

The native inhabitants of the Americas, then, had their own foods. Many of those foods were taken back to Europe, where they were joined by imports from Africa and Asia. And, of course, Europeans brought the foods of the world to the Americas. On his second voyage in 1493, Columbus brought with him the first contingent of horses, dogs, pigs, cattle, chickens, sheep, and goats, plus new seeds and cuttings, thereby initiating an unprecedented exchange of flora and fauna between the Eastern and Western hemispheres. The listed domesticated animals not only supplied inhabitants with meat and poultry, but milk and cheese as well. Europeans established plantations to produce foods and fibers not known in the Western Hemisphere, like sugar and cotton, which in turn led to the institution of slavery and the importation of Africans as slaves.[73]

In 1951, the Russian botanist, Nikolai Vavilov, compiled a list of the 640 most important plants cultivated by man. Roughly 500 originated in the Old World, 100 in the New.[74] Today over three-fifths of the world's wealth comes from plants unknown to the Eastern Hemisphere before Columbus. This includes such nonfood items as tobacco, rubber, and certain cottons indigenous to the New World. The Europeans encountered maize (corn) for the first time, made it a staple in their own diets and exported it to Africa and Asia, as they did other New World crops.[75]

Vavilov listed the fifteen most valuable New World crops, including maize, various beans, peanut, potato, sweet potato, manioc (cassava), squash, pumpkin, papaya, guava, avocado, pineapple, tomato, chile pepper, and cocoa.[76] "Collectively," Crosby observed, they "made the most valuable single addition to the food-producing plants of the Old World since the beginning of agriculture." Maize and manioc became especially important to Africans; potatoes, followed by beans and maize, made a significant contribution to the European diet.[77]

Among the most valuable food contributions of the Old (Europe, Asia, and Africa) to the New World were wheat, rice, barley, oats, rye, sorghum, millet, bananas, cane sugar, coffee, and eggplant. Although Native Americans benefited little from them—after being nearly decimated by military conquest and disease—the colonization of the Western Hemisphere would not have progressed so rapidly without the importation of foods with which Europeans were familiar, and that could be supplemented by native crops. By 1600 all of

THE GLOBAL DIFFUSION OF FOOD

Historian William H. McNeill commented on the impact of New World foods on the Old: "Columbus and the innumerable discoveries that followed his venture across the Atlantic changed many things for the inhabitants of the Old World, but for most people what mattered most was not the new information about the lands, peoples, plants, and animals...nor was it the gold and silver....Instead it was a change that historians have overlooked: the spread of American food crops to Europe, Asia, and Africa....If you cannot imagine the Italians without tomatoes, the Chinese without sweet potatoes, the Africans without maize, and the Irish, Germans, and Russians without potatoes to eat, then the importance of American food crops becomes self-evident....their share...of the world's food supplies constitutes by far the greatest discovery that the Old World acquired from the New."[78]

the most important food plants of the Old World were being grown in the Americas.[79]

One major result of the "Columbian Exchange" of foods was the world's population explosion of the next 300 years and the Industrial Revolution. During the next three centuries, the number of people on earth quadrupled. Between 1650 and 1850 the number doubled. It was not until after the year 1800 that the world's population hit 1 billion and by 2001 it exceeded 6 billion. Prior to 1900 Europe grew the most rapidly, but after 1900 the Americas, Asia, and Africa grew even more quickly. Factors like advances in medical science and hygiene undoubtedly played a major role in this development, but it is no coincidence that such rapid worldwide human population growth has occurred only twice in history: first when humans invented agriculture and again following the Columbian Exchange. Thomas Malthus's famous theory that population numbers are tied to the size of the food supply may have been erroneous in many ways, but he was basically right about food and population cycles in the preindustrial world.[80]

The Age of Exploration transformed trade between Europe and the rest of the world in many ways. That transformation included, but was certainly not limited to, foodstuffs. Before about 1500, European wealthy elites craved the spices and gems, exquisite porcelains and finished silks found in the East. But, having little of value to offer in exchange, they paid mostly in gold or silver. That changed after the opening of the New World. The Americas provided new sources of gold and silver; from 1492 to 1800, the New World supplied 85 percent of the world's silver and 70 percent of its gold. But the New World also provided new commodities and raw materials for Europe's manufacturing enterprises. By the 1700s the products of those enterprises found markets in Asia. Eastern luxuries still satisfied the appetites of the rich, but other imports fed the European economy in more productive ways. By

1750, instead of draining Europe of coin, trade with other regions of the globe contributed to Europe's wealth.[81]

Among the most important crops in this global transformation that made its way from the Americas into the European diet was the lowly potato. Initially, Europeans looked upon the potato with fear and contempt. Many thought it caused leprosy or was poisonous, others that it was an aphrodisiac. Even more labeled it food for the pigs or the poor and a cause of flatulence.[82] As anthropologist Sidney Mintz observed, the acceptance of new foods by a group usually requires major disruptions, like war, or crop failure, or migration, in their ordinary diets. Both migration from one country to another and migration within a single country are important (particularly rural to urban migration), as are agricultural reforms, especially if they result in the displacement of a segment of the population from the land. Industrial change, which disrupts the distribution of people and land, is also an important factor. Even then the diffusion of new foods requires adapting that food to local tastes and dietary habits, mixing it with other indigenous foods. In the case of the potato, Europeans gradually learned to enjoy the potato by making it their own.[83]

It was the Irish who first accepted the potato, with which they were to become famously identified. Desperate to find a crop that would feed the population on so little, poor land, they discovered that 1.5 acres planted with potatoes would provide enough food, when supplemented with milk, to feed a family for a year. The Irish soon grew dependent on the potato, which proved to be both a blessing and a curse. Until the mid-nineteenth century, it proved a boon to the population. In 1845, the potato crop occupied some 2 million acres and was planted as a virtual monoculture in many areas. A 13.6 million-ton harvest was anticipated for a population whose adults consumed six to fourteen pounds of potatoes per day. With the coming of the potato blight and famine—the Great Hunger of 1845–1847—dependence on the potato proved catastrophic. As Alfred Crosby put it: "The Irishman who had lived by the potato died by the potato." While masses of poor Irish people were starving, however, Ireland continued to grow wheat commandeered by their colonial masters and shipped across the channel to make bread for the English![84]

From Ireland acceptance of the potato spread eastward. German farmers resisted it until the end of the eighteenth century. Then, after famine and war years, they were ordered to grow it. By the mid-nineteenth century potatoes spread across Central and Eastern Europe into Russia. As late as 1840 "Old Believers" continued to reject potatoes as "Devil's apples" or "forbidden fruits of Eden." In that year when the government ordered peasants to grow them, they responded with "potato riots" that lasted for three years, when the order was lifted. Left to their own devices, the peasants adopted the potato in their own time, but adopt it they did. By the early years of the twentieth century, potatoes became Russia's "second bread."[85]

Rich in vitamins, easily grown, capable of being prepared in innumerable ways, the potato became a staple of the European diet. Capable of producing more calories and protein per unit area with less labor than any other major grain or root crop, its consumption in some places came to rival that of bread. And as population expanded in Europe and people moved in increasing numbers to the cities, setting the stage for the Industrial Revolution, first in England and then elsewhere on the Continent, the potato assumed even greater importance in the diets of both peasant and laborer. Indeed, many historians credit potatoes with allowing the rapid rise of population associated with the Industrial Revolution in Europe.[86]

In time New World foods like corn, manioc, peanuts, various squashes, pumpkins, sweet potatoes, beans, tomatoes, and cacao became staples in the African diet. By some estimates, Africa so appropriated these foods that today the continent produces 5 to 6 percent of the world's corn, 25 percent of its peanuts, and perhaps as much as 50 percent of the maniac, sweet potatoes, and yams. This transplanting was linked to the slave trade, wherein, for example, corn was bartered for slaves, who were used to work the rice, sugar, and cotton plantations in the Western Hemisphere.[87]

And finally, as indigenous Asian foodstuffs were imported into Europe and eventually to the Americas, so too American foods found their way to Asia. India welcomed American fruits, corn, sweet potatoes, and peanuts.[88] The Japanese adopted American potatoes, sweet and white, while the Chinese not only took a liking to sweet potatoes, they became the world's largest producer. China now grows and consumes peanuts and corn in large amounts as well.[89] In fact, it is curious that the Chinese became stereotyped as rice eaters. Many, particularly from South China, were rice eaters, but the Northern Chinese produce their staple diets with wheat and corn (to experience this diversity, order "lo mein" made with noodles, at an American Chinese restaurant). By discussing this transformation, we underline the point that the ultimate consequence of the Columbian Exchange was that the same food staples became shared by most of the world's people.

THE EARLY AMERICAN DIET

The United States evolved from the thirteen British colonies of North America. Most of those colonists were English, but Dutch, French, German, Scotch-Irish, Spanish, Africans, and Swedes were also included. They came for various reasons, and some, like the Africans, had no choice. But all had to adapt or modify their cuisines.

Native Americans helped many of the first colonists obtain adequate food and taught them their methods of agriculture. As we noted, some of their foods, like maize, became a staple in the colonial American diet. The colonists not only adopted ways of growing it, but also they accepted many

Indian dishes and their Indian names, like pone, hominy, and succotash. Curiously, they refused the Indian word maize and persisted in calling it corn, a generic term for cereal grains in England.[90]

Colonists adopted these and other Indian foods and then changed them to suit their European tastes in dishes like corn pone, hoe cakes, hominy (including grits), corn sticks, Johnnycake, and hush puppies. They combined native beans with corn to make succotash. They also adopted wild rice, baked beans, Indian pudding, maple sugar, pinto beans, and chili peppers. "Hogs 'n' hominy," a combination of salt pork and preserved corn, kept pioneers alive during westward migration, and was to become the dietary staple of many Americans. And colonists adopted seasonings from the Indians, like filé, a powder made of dried, pounded sassafras leaves, to thicken soups and stews, and later gumbo.[91]

But as the colonists drove Indians inland, they also began to import the foods to which they were accustomed, and they created hybrid and blended cuisines. Diets varied, especially at first, according to the origins of the colonists and their location in the colonies. The first settlers at Jamestown, Virginia—the first permanent English colony in the New World—brought with them cheese, cured fish and meat, oatmeal, bread and biscuits, beans and onions, dried fruits, seasonings, butter, beer, cider, water, and seeds for future planting. Indians provided the 650 immigrants with corn and taught them where fish could be caught and what game was edible. Nevertheless, food was still scarce and during the winter of 1609–1610, so many settlers died that it became know as the "starving times." In the years that followed, corn became the staple grain, supplemented by imported hogs and wild game, and, to a lesser extent, beef.[92]

The Dutch established the fur trading post of New Amsterdam on Manhattan Island in 1613 and transported settlers to the area. Again, the native inhabitants helped them survive the first few years in much the same manner. As early as the second year, however, the Dutch East India Company supplied the colonists with substantial numbers of livestock, horses, hogs, and sheep. The fertile soil of the lower Hudson River Valley lent itself to the raising of grain, fruit, and a wide variety of vegetables, including native beans, pumpkin, and squash.[93]

The Pilgrim's story closely approximates that of Jamestown, Virginia and is already well known. Expecting to settle in Virginia, they landed on the coast of Massachusetts during the winter of 1620–1621, their supplies nearly exhausted. Instead of having their needs met by the already thirteen-year-old Virginia settlement, they were on their own and unprepared for where they had landed. Unable to leave, they lost about half their numbers during that first winter due to disease and famine. The losses would have been even greater if the Indians had not intervened, much as they had in Virginia. One year later, in the fall of 1621, the Plymouth colony and their Native American guests celebrated a day of thanksgiving with cornbread, cranberries, wild turkey, pumpkin baked in maple syrup, venison, and fish of various kinds.[94]

THE FIRST AMERICAN THANKSGIVING

Only two short accounts of the "First Thanksgiving" have survived the centuries. Pilgrim Governor William Bradford recorded this one in his journal, *Of Plymouth Plantation*: "They began now to gather in the small harvest they had, and to fit up their houses and dwellings against winter, being all well recovered in health and strength and had all thing in good plenty....All summer there was no want; and now began to come in store of fowl, as winter approached, of which this place did abound....And besides waterfowl there was a great store of wild turkeys, of which they took many, besides venison, etc. Besides they had about a peck of meal a week to a person, or now since harvest, Indian corn to that proportion. Which made many afterwards write so largely of their plenty here to their friends in England, which were not feigned but true reports."[95]

Edward Winslow wrote one of the letters to which Bradford referred in his journal. Whereas Bradford's entry is undated, Winslow's letter was dated December 11, 1621. Winslow added: "Our harvest being gotten in, our Governor sent four men on fowling, that so we might after a more special manner rejoice together, after we had gathered the fruits of our labours. He wrote that upon the Governor's invitation, Indian Chief Massasoit and ninety of his braves joined the gathering, adding five deer to the feast, which lasted three days."[96] The actual date of the "First Thanksgiving" is unknown.

Our point is that the first colonists owed much to the Native Americans they encountered in the New World. Some of the first ventures, like Jamestown and Plymouth, may not have survived if the Indians had not shared with them their food, food gathering skills, and knowledge of hunting and fishing. Nevertheless, after several difficult years, especially by the eighteenth century, adjustment to this new land and the merging of the two food cultures provided a plentiful food supply—a food supply more bountiful than that of any other people in the world.[97]

Although it varied from section to section, from one ethnic group to another, an American diet began to take shape. The basic corn diet was supplemented with produce from the kitchen garden found behind most farmhouses. Colonists grew vegetables to which they had become accustomed at home—parsnips, turnips, onions, peas, cabbage, and carrots—all served in traditional ways. They rejected the native sweet potato and did not adopt the white potato until it was returned to British North America by the Scotch-Irish as the "Irish potato" in the eighteenth century. Orchards were common as well, providing fruit, especially apples and peaches, as well as cider, applejack, and brandy.[98]

The colonists raised chickens and goats, but hogs became the staple meat in most diets, mainly as salt pork. Hogs were excellent foragers, able to live on what they found in the woods. Sheep were welcome mainly for their wool, but cattle provided cash income, and may be called "the first major industry" for

American farmers. Settlers caught and ate just about every kind of fresh and salt water fish, except salmon, which for unknown reasons they did not like, and shad which they "profoundly despised." And they laced their meats in season with huckleberries, blackberries, blueberries, and strawberries.[99]

In spite of the variety of potentially tasty foods available to them, the diet of most settlers through the end of the eighteenth century was dull and tasteless to modern palates, especially in households that stuck closely to English ways of preparing food. To put it mildly, most were not adventuresome cooks. The colonists of British North America prepared their food by boiling, roasting, steaming, or baking. They cooked vegetables into a tasteless pulp and used few condiments. Except for salt and pepper, most condiments came from their gardens and were limited to parsley, hyssop, thyme, and marjoram, all of which they had known in England. Breakfast usually consisted of some kind of mush diluted with milk or molasses. Something similar was served for supper in the evening. The main meal, dinner, came at midday and consisted of a stew or pottage whose contents varied with the season. In the eighteenth century portions of vegetables and meat began to appear on plates.[100]

Early Americans preserved their food by drying, salting, pickling, and cooling. Nevertheless, their diet varied by season, as well as climate, storing food being a particular problem. Some meat, especially pork, could be salted or smoked, while certain vegetables were dried or pickled. Root vegetables and some fruits (e.g., apples) were kept in cool dry cellars, but bread and meat often were the standbys during the winter.[101]

Colonists drank large amounts of beer, cider, rum, or wine, rather than water, which, like most Europeans, they believed to be unsafe. Milk, first from goats and later from cows, was a principal beverage in the North, where cattle were fenced in and the weather was cool enough to delay spoiling. They also enjoyed apple cider, while Southerners enjoyed their peach brandy. Madeira wine, imported from the Portuguese island of the same name, was popular, but by 1800 tea, coffee, and hot chocolate were popular beverages as well.[102] As in Europe, social status determined dietary variations. The well-to-do enjoyed imported wines and French brandies; beer was favored among the rest, as was rum—the alcoholic staple of commoners—which was referred to disdainfully as the "diabolical liquor." In colonial New England, type and color of bread, quality and source of animal protein, and frequency of consuming butter were class related. The well-to-do ate more fresh meat (particularly beef, which was expensive because it could not be successfully preserved like pork or fish), white bread, and butter, while their poorer neighbors consumed more salted meat, fish, baked beans, Indian-meal bread, and rye (dark) bread.[103] Most Americans developed a fondness for sweets. Sugar was a luxury in America, so it was consumed mostly by the wealthy. But there were substitutes—like molasses, honey, and maple sugar. They were used in desserts and other dishes to counter their blandness. By 1750, Americans were second only to Englishmen in per capita sugar consumption.[104]

By the end of the Colonial Period, new food production systems had emerged from the merging of the two agricultural traditions, Indian and European, and the natural food supplies of the New and Old Worlds. The result was the basis of an American diet that still persists and that continues to focus on animal meat as the central entrée, augmented by fruits, vegetables, grain products, dairy products, legumes, sweet meats, sugar, and alcohol. The American diet was, and would remain, high in fat, salt, and sugar. It lacked certain key nutrients, and colonists' health suffered as a result. Low life expectancies, high death rates, and high infant mortality rates were the rule. But European diets and health statistics at the time were worse.[105]

The American diet changed little in the first half of the nineteenth century. Rural staples remained corn and potatoes, pork, bread, and butter. Hogs and hominy were mainstays, while consumption of perishable foods like milk, fresh fruits, and vegetables, as well as fresh meats, was inadequate. Inadequate consumption of vitamins and minerals necessary for good health continued— including vitamin A, C, and D, riboflavin, and calcium. In fact, the diet of many Americans resulted in widespread micronutrient deficiency diseases, particularly Pellegra in the rural South and Midwest. Compared to rural dwellers, urbanites—who could not raise their own food and had more limited resources—were even less well fed.[106]

Importantly, dietary deficiencies were matched by dietary excesses. Fat and salt intake remained high, particularly on farms, where people had access to large amounts of butter, cheese, lard, and salted pork products like ham and sausages. This was supplemented by continued high intakes of sugar and molasses. Even so, people worked hard in early America, especially on the farms, so obesity appears not to have been a problem. They burned off excess calories, but harm was being done in other ways.[107]

Finally, Americans slowly began to drink less alcohol. In 1825, annual per capita consumption of alcoholic beverages in terms of absolute alcohol was 3.7 gallons. Thereafter old-stock Protestants began to mobilize to discourage such consumption, in what became powerful Temperance and Prohibition movements. Despite the substantial consumption of alcohol by newly arrived immigrants, by 1840 annual per capita consumption of alcohol plummeted to 1.8 gallons (in absolute alcohol). The decline continued for the rest of the century. While there was a popular groundswell for abstinence, a major contributing factor for the decline in alcohol consumption came from middle-class Americans, who replaced whiskey and other distilled liquors with beer as their preferred drink.[108]

SOME SUGGESTIONS FOR FURTHER READING

Diamond, J. (1987). *Guns, Germs, and Steel: The Fates of Human Societies.* New York: W. W. Norton.
Bynum, C. (1987). *Holy Feast and Holy Fast: The Religious Significance of Food to Medieval Women.* Berkeley: The University of California Press.

Crosby, A. (1972). *The Columbian Exchange: Biological and Cultural Consequences of 1492.* Westport, CT. Greenwood Press.

Elias, N. (1978). *The Civilizing Process* (1939). Volume 1 of *The History of Manners* (1978). Oxford: Basil Blackwell.

Grover, K. (1987). *Dining in America, 1850–1900.* Amherst: The University of Massachusetts Press.

Kiple, F., and K. Ornelas (2000). *The Cambridge World History of Food* (two volumes). Cambridge, U.K.: Cambridge University Press.

Kurlansky, M. (1997). *Cod: A Biography of the Fish that Changed the World.* New York: Walker and Company.

Mennell, S. (1985). *All Manners of Food: Eating and Taste in England and France from the Middle Ages to Present.* Oxford: Basil Blackwell.

Milton, S. (1999). *Nathaniel's Nutmeg, or, The True and Incredible Adventures of the Spice Trader who Changed the Course of History.* New York: Farrar, Straus and Giroux.

Mintz, S. (1985). *Sweetness and Power: The Place of Sugar in Modern History.* New York: Viking Press.

Montmarquet, J. (1980). *The Idea of Agrarianism: From Hunter-Gatherer to Agrarian Radical in Western Culture.* Moscow: University of Idaho Press.

Salaman, R. (1985). *The History and Social Influences of the Potato.* Cambridge: Cambridge University Press.

Tannahill, Reay (1988). *Food in History.* New York: Crown Paperbacks.

Viola, H., and C. Margolis (1991). *Seeds of Change.* Washington: Smithsonian Institution Press.

CHAPTER THREE

Food and America
Early Industrial Era Transformations

We continue to focus on how changing foodways and food systems interact with social change, but now we move to the early industrial era in America, roughly from 1850 to 1945. This chapter focuses in particular on increasing American population diversity, urbanization, and technological innovations, and how they transformed the ways in which food was produced, transported, processed, and consumed. As we noted in Chapter 2, Americans were comparatively better fed than in the rest of the world, even though many suffered from dietary deficiencies during the first half of the nineteenth century. The consumption of perishable foods, like milk, fruit, vegetables, and meat, was inadequate, and urban workers were less well fed than the rural population. They could not raise their own food and had limited resources with which to buy what foods were available in the cities. In any case, nutritious food was limited or unavailable because appropriate means of preserving and transporting it from the country to the nation's cities did not exist. That began to change after mid-century.

So too did the agrarian ideal expressed by Thomas Jefferson in his *Notes on Virginia*:

> Those who labor in the earth are the chosen people of God, if ever he had a chosen people, whose breasts he has made his peculiar deposit for substantial and genuine virtue. It is the focus in which he keeps alive that sacred fire, which otherwise might escape from the face of the earth. Corruption of morals in the mass of cultivators is a phenomenon of which no age nor nation has furnished an example.[1]

If the success of the new republic depended on the virtue of its citizens, as Jefferson and others maintained at the end of the eighteenth century, and the virtue of a nation depended on the existence of a "mass of cultivators," then by the end of the century addressed in this chapter, the United States was in trouble. It was no longer an agrarian nation.[2]

THE INDUSTRIAL REVOLUTION AND THE COMMODIFICATION OF FOOD AND FARMING

Major developments in the American economy began to take place in the first half of the nineteenth century, and they accelerated in the next fifty years. In 1800, approximately 95 percent of the population lived on small farms. After 1830, the *Industrial Revolution* rapidly changed that. The second half of the nineteenth century witnessed a dramatic increase in industrialization, modernization, urbanization, and immigration. In 1850 about 85 percent of the American population engaged in farming or farm-related occupations. By 1900 that figure dropped to 60 percent.[3] Those that left the farm moved to the cities, where they became workers for America's burgeoning industrial economy.

Paralleling industrialization, eating patterns and agriculture were undergoing their own remarkable transformation. Both producing food and eating were becoming *commodified*, meaning that fewer people produced food for their own consumption. Like many other things, it was increasingly produced and sold for money as a commercial commodity. The structure of the modern food system and foodways was emerging. Dietary patterns and nutrition became major concerns, and—speaking more broadly—a revolutionary *age of consumerism* began. By the 1870s middle-class and working-class Americans had more money and time to purchase goods, which were increasingly mass-produced, cheaper, and advertised more widely—including food. At least in urban areas, earnings rose while the number of hours spent working declined (from sixty-six hours in 1850 to fifty-five in 1914).[4] Agriculture, food, nutrition, and commerce became increasingly interdependent, and government became involved with food issues in unprecedented ways.

Important agricultural inventions preceded 1850. The steel plow was invented in 1837. Cyrus McCormick invented the reaper in 1832, and soon thereafter the binder and threshing machine made their appearance.[5] After 1850, the pace of mechanization accelerated. Increased demand and high prices for farm products during the Civil War and immediate postwar period encouraged the development of better tools. Farm mechanization and specialization combined to bring about a dramatic increase in the supply of food. Seeders, combines, binders, mowers, and rotary plows moved onto the plains during the 1870s and 1880s. Since the beginning of farming, the acreage a farmer could plant was limited to the amount that could be harvested by hand, or at best with simple tools pulled by draft animals. Machinery dramatically increased productivity. Before mechanization, a farmer working alone could harvest about 7.5 acres of wheat. Using an automatic binder that cut and bundled grain, the same farmer could harvest 135 acres. The time and cost of planting and harvesting dropped dramatically, thereby allowing the cultivation of much larger plots of land available in the middle and western regions of the United States. By 1900 one farmer could harvest as much grain as twenty could in his great-grandfather's day.[6]

As farmers spread west, the nation's food suppliers and railroads followed them to transport farm produce to cities—where population was beginning to swell due to rural-urban migration and the influx of immigrants from abroad. During the first half of the nineteenth century, few immigrants came to the United States, but the first great wave of immigrants started coming in the 1830s. During the next three decades, the number of immigrants rose from 600,000 to 1.7 million and 2.6 million, respectively. Most of these immigrants were from Great Britain, Germany, and especially Ireland. As we mentioned earlier, the Irish suffered severe famines in this period due to the failure of their potato crop in the potato blight. Following widespread failures in 1845 and 1846, nearly one-fifth of the Irish population died. Many of the survivors fled to the United States, as well as to other English colonies like Canada and Australia, where they tended to settle in urban areas.[7]

A second wave of immigration occurred between 1860 and 1890, triggered by the Homestead Act of 1862, which promised nearly free land for people willing to live on and develop their property, usually 160 acres to start. The largest proportion of these people were from northern and western Europe—from Germany, Great Britain, Ireland, and the Scandinavian countries.[8] The Morrill Act of 1862 gave states federal land to sell, the proceeds from which were to be used for the endowment of Land Grant colleges. These colleges were directed to offer instruction in agriculture and the mechanical arts, which included home economics. A second Morrill Act in 1890 aided more schools, including a number of black colleges. The Hatch Act of 1887 provided for agricultural experiment stations in every state, all of which led to the development of many "extension programs" aimed at the diffusion of scientific agronomy to farmers and other rural groups. These programs resulted in more efficient methods of farming the comparatively arid plains, as well as the spread of hardier hybrid seeds for wheat, corn, soybeans, and so on.[9]

Railroads similarly supported farm development in the West, and the first transcontinental railroad, the Union Pacific, was completed in 1869. These railroads connected farmers to markets back east, enabling them to ship their produce to be sold in the nation's cities. Food preservation improvements—like the refrigerated railroad car in 1870—allowed these same railroads to ship fresh eggs, meat, milk, and produce to urban dwellers for the first time.[10] Railroads had been paid in large part in land for their efforts to span the continent. Now land-rich, they lured farmers westward, from the East and Europe, by advertising cheap land, low credit terms, and reduced shipping rates.[11]

These developments greatly facilitated not only the transformation of agriculture into big business, but also the expansion of farming into the nation's plains and prairies. During the 1870s and 1880s hundreds of thousands of people settled in the Trans-Mississippi West, putting more acres under cultivation during these two decades than had been in the previous 250 years. The number of farms tripled from 2 million to over 6 million between 1860 and 1910. Between 1875 and 1915 the acreage under cultivation doubled, and production of most staple crops more than doubled. Wheat production tripled, as the United States became the world's breadbasket. Whereas in the 1850s the United States exported about 19 million bushels of wheat and 33 million pounds of beef products, by the late 1870s the annual levels of both increased sevenfold. In 1900 the United States exported 34 percent of its wheat, 10 percent of its corn, and 66 percent of its cotton.[12]

As commercial farming spread, so too did cattle ranching. Early in the nineteenth century, cattle introduced by the Spanish centuries earlier were introduced by Mexican ranchers in the Southwest. There they bred with cattle brought by Anglo settlers, resulting in the longhorn breed for which there was increased demand by mid-century. By 1870 drovers herded cattle northward to railheads in Kansas, Missouri, Wyoming, and elsewhere, where they would be shipped to Chicago and St. Louis for slaughter and distribution.[14]

Ranchers discovered that crossing Texas longhorns with heavier Hereford and Angus breeds produced cattle able to survive winters on the central and northern plains. This curtailed the need for cattle drives, which were being hindered by increased settlement, farming, and fencing of the West. Between 1860 and 1880 the cattle population of Kansas, Nebraska, Colorado, Wyoming, Montana, and the Dakotas increased from 130,000 to 4.5 million.[15]

Paralleling nineteenth-century agricultural developments were those in

---

AMBER WAVES OF GRAIN

"You are in a sea of wheat," rhapsodized the author of an 1880 magazine article about Oliver Dalrymple's farm in Dakota territory's Red River valley. "The railroad train rolls through an ocean of grain....We encounter a squadron of war chariots...doing the work of human hands....There are 25 of them in this one brigade of the grand army of 115, under the marksmanship of this Dakota farmer." Dalrymple's farm exemplified two important achievements of the late nineteenth century: the taming of windswept prairies and the transformation of agriculture into big business by means of mechanization, long distance transportation, and scientific cultivation.[13]

Cowboys and cattle herds, like these on a Montana ranch, were a rich part of American history and folklore. Today cattle are more likely to be raised in huge feedlots with commercially produced food.

food preservation. Louis Pasteur's development of the process of pasteurization helped protect consumers from disease-causing organisms in liquids, especially milk. The invention of a simple canning process by Nicholas Appert, a French chef, in 1809, led to the development of the canning industry.[16]

In the 1850s an American man named Gail Borden developed a means of condensing and preserving milk. In 1859, the Mason jar was perfected, and the American Civil War provided a powerful impetus for the canning industry, so as to feed the soldiers. Large pressure cookers were marketed beginning in 1874, and combined with Mason jars, canning emerged as a form of food preservation in the home as well as in factories. By 1880 a process for mass producing cans from tin plate was developed. The Underwood family of Boston produced canned seafoods and meats, including a highly seasoned, "deviled," canned meat for sandwich spreads, and by 1875 advances in preventing spoilage in canned foods allowed Gustavus Swift and P. D. Armour to establish meatpacking plants in Chicago.[17]

The ice-cooled refrigerator, invented in 1803, became common, followed at mid-century by a process to make artificial ice.[18] The invention of mechanical refrigerators is quite a saga, and because it was such a strategic innovation that allowed the whole modern food system to come into being, we elaborate.

PROGRESS AND PROBLEMS: A CAUTIONARY TALE

Until almost the end of the nineteenth century, refrigerating food and drink depended on ice from natural sources. It was chopped from local lakes and ponds and stored in warehouses or pits for use in the summer. Households used this ice, but breweries and restaurants were the heaviest users, and stored winter ice was sometimes shipped hundreds of miles to provide refrigeration (Boston ice merchants shipped ice as far south as South Carolina and the Caribbean). But this was difficult and expensive, and most food was preserved with ordinary salt (sodium chloride). Ice-refrigerated railway cars were first used in the 1870s by meatpackers who raised their profits by shipping cars of dressed beef, slaughtered and chilled in Chicago to customers hundreds of miles away. Soon this technology was used to ship fruits and vegetable from urban hinterlands to remote customers. As you can easily imagine, refrigeration eventually changed the whole nature of the American diet.

But there were problems. Natural ice was unreliable, and in two warm winters, 1889 and 1890, the "crop" failed completely. Packers and others sought more reliable refrigeration. The principle of mechanical refrigeration—by which compressed gas was allowed to expand rapidly and lower temperature—had been known since the mid-1700s. Urban brewers were first to use commercial adaptations of this principle in the late nineteenth century, but these early refrigerant systems had serious drawbacks. They used ammonia, sulfur dioxide, or methyl chloride as refrigerant gases, and to be efficient they required huge and powerful compressors, which created a risk of dangerous explosions. The toxicity of these gases, as well as their ponderous size and expense kept mechanical refrigeration from making headway among retail customers, who represented a huge potential market. In 1931 the barrier was broken by Thomas Midgely, who, working for General Motors Frigidaire Division, developed a small refrigerator using a chlorinated fluorocarbon compound (CFC) patented as "Freon 12." It was perfect: safe, nonexplosive, and required only a small compressor to get the desired cooling effects. American households could soon own their own "refrigerators," making it possible to sell frozen foods in retail-sized packages. Such frozen foods massively entered the American food system by the 1950s, as did fresh fruits and dairy products that rapidly became accepted as ordinary parts of the American diet. It was a truly revolutionary transformation, but much more than food was revolutionized.

The same freon-based refrigeration technology was applied to space cooling in buildings, thus creating another huge market—for the development of air conditioning. For many of us, it would be difficult now to endure the summer months or warm climates without air conditioning in our homes, autos, stores, and offices. It changed the pattern of American urban growth, particularly in the cities of the Sunbelt. In fact, without air conditioning, it is unlikely that much of the recent development and population shift to the

Sunbelt cities—Phoenix, Los Angeles, Miami, among others—would have even taken place. It also shifted the nation's peak use of electricity from winter (when it is used for lighting and space heating) to summer, when air conditioning systems use power at prodigious and unprecedented rates.

Refrigeration had an enormous and largely positive impact on improving peoples' nutrition, comfort, and the physical quality of life. But the freon-based refrigeration story is not only one of progress: It had a long-term catch. The very advantage of the compound (its nonreactive, nontoxic, and nonexplosive nature) meant that it stayed around when it leaked from refrigeration compressors. It gradually floated up to the stratosphere, where it "collected" ozone molecules that in turn were destroyed by incoming ultraviolet radiation from the sun. Over the decades, enough CFCs have escaped and accumulated there, and enough ozone has been destroyed, to create huge seasonal "holes" in the high "ozone layer." That destroyed one of the earth's protective layers that ensures we don't get too much ultraviolet radiation, thereby increasing the incidence of eye and skin cancers in humans and animals. As a result, over the last few decades, the world's nations have banned the manufacture and sale of CFCs and sought substitutes for refrigeration. Like many innovations of the early industrial era, long-term problems and complexities often accompanied short-term progress.

To recap: The invention of the railroad, grain and refrigerator cars, and grain silos, along with the growth of meat packing plants and marketing boards, contributed to the distribution of food stuffs well beyond their point of origin and to more distant markets and consumers. Americans were treated to a greater variety of foods at lower prices. These developments also increasingly separated food from its source of production, however, and increased the possibility of adulteration and contamination by the unscrupulous. As the distance from the original site of production and the number of hands through which the product passed increased, problems with food safety and customer suspicion grew.[19]

As a result the United States experienced the first attempts on the part of government to ensure food quality. It began at the state level. In 1850 Massachusetts law prohibited the adulteration of milk. Locales like Brooklyn, New York, established milk commissions, which set standards and began certifying bottled milk, in an attempt to insure safe milk. But soon after the turn of the century, the federal government began to take action. We will return later in the chapter to this subject.

CHANGES IN FOOD MARKETING AND CONSUMPTION

One of the major changes in American society accompanying industrialization and urbanization in the second half of the nineteenth century was the expansion of a comparatively prosperous urban middle class. As both their numbers and wages increased, by the end of the nineteenth century their influence was felt in a major way. Earlier in the century milk and fresh fruits and vegetables were scarce and expensive in urban areas. Fresh meat was rare; rancid and stale foods were common. For reasons noted above, in the second half-century both the amount and quality of food improved in urban areas, especially for comparatively prosperous middle- and upper-class people who could afford the fresh foods that became available. But, the diets and nutrition of the working poor remained poor. Their wages increased as well, but not as rapidly as the cost of living in the nation's cities and, as a result, their health suffered while that of the middle and upper urban classes and rural people improved.[20]

After 1840 food costs in relation to wages began to fall. By the 1850s and 1860s, middle-class workers were able to buy lean meat, milk, leafy vegetables, and fruit. And that pattern continued for the rest of the century, despite the short-term setbacks of the Civil War and the Depressions of the 1870s and 1890s. By the end of the century, the middle class entered an era of food abundance. As soon as their status permitted it, they typically began to buy beef. Although more pork continued to be consumed nationwide, beef became popular, especially among more prosperous Americans. Once again, after 1880, largely as the result of improved diet, most measures of improved health showed marked improvement for nearly all classes of Americans, rural and urban, except for the urban working poor.[21]

The manners and mores of the growing urban middle classes also shaped foodways. The Victorian middle class of the late nineteenth century was described as "proper and prosperous." To demonstrate their newly won place in society, they meticulously observed the rules of etiquette. Thus, dining rituals—how they ate; the dining room furniture, decorations, and table settings; how they dressed for dinner; and the menus they chose—became very important. To middle-class Victorians, dining habits provided visible evidence of their place in society.[22]

Really wealthy Americans, in what Mark Twain called the "Gilded Age," entertained friends at elaborate, multicourse dinner parties at well-appointed tables, attended by servants. Those who were extremely class-conscious patterned their meals after overly mannered and pretentious European models. But people also developed pride in things American. According to Susan Williams: "While Americans continued to look to their European past for refinement, they selectively scrutinized their own colonial past for evidence of moral supremacy, national mettle, and personal ingenuity. Thus 'civilization' for them became an amalgam of anything from the past, be it European or distinctively American, that proved useful in ordering their increasingly complex world."[23]

The marketing of food changed as well in the Victorian era. Prior to the end of the century, most Americans bought their groceries in markets on a credit system. Customers presented their orders to clerks who filled them and

Attending huge banquets like these were signs of elite status in the "Gilded Age." This one was hosted by President Grant.

periodically billed the purchasers. Cash-and-carry transactions were atypical; so too were fixed prices, thereby necessitating bargaining for many items. What changed was the rise of national-brand advertising in the growing number of national publications and prepackaging. Food producers and store-owners learned that attractive advertisements, especially in women's magazines—women having become the principal consumers of domestic goods—and attractive boxes or bottles, with recognizable trademarks, enhanced sales. The trend away from displaying general goods in barrels, jars, bins, and bags to preparing individual consumer units of wrappers, packets, cartons, and containers began. Quaker Oats, to cite just one example, switched from a plain eight-pound sack to an attractive sixteen-ounce cylinder.[24]

The concept of prepackaged foods further transformed marketing strategies by demonstrating that raw goods could be turned into standardized products with national brand names. This led to three developments. First, it led to the introduction of hitherto unknown foods to a wider market (including ethnic food, to which we will return). Second, it provided easier access to diverse foods in formerly isolated regions. And third, it began the emphasis on "convenience" that allowed middle- and working-class women to escape some of the labor-intensive work in food preparation.[25]

Advertisers touted processed foods as sophisticated and up-to-date. Condensed, evaporated, and concentrated foods and drinks promised more for less. Campbell's told consumers that one of its cans of soup could be a meal in itself for lunch. So too could prepared spaghetti, meat stews, and casseroles. Moreover, all one had to do to prepare any of these was to heat it.[26]

CONTINUING TRANSFORMATIONS IN THE NEW CENTURY

It should be obvious that urbanization, industrialization, an increasingly industrialized and commercialized agriculture, as well as innovations in food processing and transportation and distribution had profound impacts on the American food system and foodways, as well as the whole American social pattern.[27] The elements of this emerging system formed a tightly bound positive feedback system.

For example, by the early 1900s, more efficient farming methods encouraged the increased migration of people to the city, because fewer farm workers were needed. Coupled with a sharply increased influx of immigrants to the nation's cities, by 1920—for the first time—a majority of the American population were urban dwellers (51.4 percent) living in cities of 2,500 people or more. This fact was as symbolically important as the official closing of the frontier in 1890. The era of Jefferson's yeoman farmer was over in reality if not in myth.[28]

Between 1870 and 1920, the number of Americans living in cities increased almost 550 percent, from 10 million to 54 million. The number of cities with more than 100,000 people grew from fifteen to sixty-eight, and the number of cities with more than 500,000 swelled from two to twelve. These and other factors worked together to stimulate the food industry. The increase in both size and heterogeneity of the population, along with increased urbanization, changed the social environment, creating greater demand for more food, both in quantity and diversity, and the food system responded accordingly.[29]

Food processing became commonplace, both in factories and in the home, so that people no longer were restricted to eating seasonal foods. By 1900 the American food-processing industry accounted for 20 percent of the nation's manufacturing, and the main food sectors already were dominated by a few giant corporations. Improvements in canning technology greatly increased the productivity of canners, as well. By 1910, more than 68,000 people turned out over 3 billion cans of food, and the real heyday of American canning was yet to come![30]

As we noted earlier, there had been growing concern on the part of consumers regarding the safety and healthfulness of their food. The conditions under which food was processed and marketed were often unsanitary. Spoilage was common, and unsafe ingredients were occasionally added. A drive for meat inspection, which had begun in the 1880s, led to the passage of a federal meat inspection law in 1891. It was followed by the new, tougher federal Meat Inspection Act of 1906.[31]

Harvey Wiley, chief chemist of the U.S. Department of Agriculture, was a leading crusader in the movement to obtain federal regulation of food additives and compulsory labeling of ingredients. The efforts of this movement culminated in the enactment in 1906 of the *Pure Food and Drug Act*. This law was undoubtedly one of the most significant pieces of legislation in American history. In 1908 concern over the purity of milk led to the enactment of the first compulsory pasteurization law, in Chicago. By 1920, many similar laws were passed at other state and local levels. All of these regulations led to the consolidation of the milk, meat, and food-processing industries. Giant corporations replaced many smaller companies, who could not afford the investments necessary for the equipment and monitoring required to comply with the new "pure food laws." The names Nabisco (National Biscuit Company), Heinz, Van Camp's, and Campbell were well known, as well as the names of the Big Five in meatpacking: Armour, Swift, Wilson, Morris, and Cudahy.[32]

One of the results of these advances in food production and marketing, wherein food became more plentiful, was that an increasing number of people ate more than was necessary. Obesity and digestive problems related to overeating became common. Both upper and lower classes tended to overeat, albeit for difference reasons. The upper class tended to overeat because their affluence afforded them a wide selection of food and drink, while the lower classes overate in part because they were likely to be doing hard physical labor.[33]

Generally, American diets contained much more meat than was necessary for adequate protein intake, and certainly more meat than immigrants had been accustomed to eating in their native lands. Pork, which initially had been America's prime animal meat source, remained the country's most common meat. In the 1900s, frowned on by the nutritionists of the day due to its fat content, pork began to lose popularity among affluent Americans, but it continued to occupy an important place in the diets of factory workers, midwesterners, and southerners.[34]

IMMIGRATION AND ETHNIC CUISINES

Between 1901 and 1910, 1 million new immigrants arrived, helping to increase the total number of newcomers between 1870 to 1920 to 26 million. Earlier immigrants came from northern and western Europe. After 1900 most came from central and southern Europe, including large numbers of Italians, Jews, and Poles. A bi-level working class began to form by the 1880s, consisting of the relatively well-off skilled and semiskilled workers and struggling unskilled workers. After 1900, this socioeconomic class division was amplified by ethnic differences, since most of the new immigrants were unskilled workers. These groups observed different foodways, reflecting their different cultural and geographical origins, as well as their economic status.[35]

Bread, potatoes, cabbage, and onions were essential items to workers' diets. Fortunately, both potatoes and onions (often called the poor man's sources of vitamin C) provided much-needed ascorbic acid. More skilled workers, mainly with origins in the British Isles, tended to follow modifications of the typical "New England cuisine" that had developed during the colonial days. Their diets were more varied, clearly reflecting their prosperity and the greater diversity of foods becoming available. Their meals included fresh meat of all kinds, eggs, potatoes, white sauce, fruits, and vegetables (particularly the canned variety), as well as desserts (including apple pie).[36]

New immigrants were fond of multifood dishes such as stews, goulashes, and Italian pasta, tomatoes, and sausage. But these were frowned upon by the native-born Americans, as well as by dietitions and home economists. Curiously, food professionals of the day believed that foods mixed together were not assimilated as well as those served separately—not taking into account that all foods, when taken in the same meal, become mixtures in the stomach anyway. Most immigrants came from cultures in which bread had been a much-depended-on staple, and it remained an essential component of their diets in the United States. And, they bought their bread from bakeries where breads like those eaten in the old countries were available.[37]

By the late 1920s, ethnic eating habits began to become Americanized. The Immigration Act of 1924 curtailed immigration from southern and eastern Europe, reducing a driving force for the maintenance of ethnic cuisines that fed earlier arrivals. Furthermore, as first generation immigrants gave way to a second generation, their children brought home American ideas gained from their outside contacts in school and in the community at large—even about food. Second generation immigrants were more likely to abandon old country food habits. Increasingly, they began to use dry breakfast cereals, canned goods, and other typically American prepared foods.[38]

At the same time, ethnic foods became big business as the entrepreneurs in enclave communities (ethnic ghettoes) developed monopolies over food products there and began to market modified forms of those ethnic foods to the wider population. As early as the 1880s Chinese importers in California began to dominate that market, followed by German businessmen and then Italians, East European Jews, and others. The marketing of ethnic foods came under the control of fewer and fewer companies that not only distributed their products more efficiently but also standardized it to appeal to a "general taste." Among the earliest such entrepreneurs was the Ghiradelli family of San Francisco and the La Rosas of New York. The La Rosa Company, founded in 1914 by a Sicilian who imported olive oil from his native land, employed 300 workers by 1930, with sales worth $3–5 million per year.[39]

Before World War II most of these ethnic food entrepreneurs, as large as they were, were restricted to their ethnic niches, determined by nationality and geography—New York Italian, for example. However, increasingly they offered more "American" foods for sale, especially to second generation immigrants, and built bridges to the larger population and foodways. They

EATING KOSHER IN AMERICA

Kosher eaters could not depend on imports, so the arrival of Eastern European Jews led to the rapid growth of a variety of food industries in America. Kosher butchering attracted particular attention. During the first decades of the twentieth century there were more than 10,000 Kosher butcher shops in the United States, as many as 9,000 in New York alone. By 1917 a million Jews ate 156 million pounds of Kosher meat each year. Because the rules of Kashrut required meat to be soaked and salted (to remove blood) within seventy-two hours of an animal's slaughter, Kosher meat generally sold for four or five cents more per pound than other beef. When shops increased prices beyond that, Jewish women in New York were known to take to the streets, boycotting and even destroying shops that sold meat at inflated prices.[40]

also began to lure those outside their ethnic enclave to buy their product, but in this effort they ran into considerable resistance.

Novelty, entertainment, and a sense of participating in the excitement of big city life provided bridges for some immigrant entrepreneurs. Inexpensive snack food could be marketed by street vendors, from frankfurters to knishes, bagels, and other products with "foreign" origins, to people outside those ethnic enclaves. When individual, small-time enterprises achieved some success in their efforts, much larger "cross-over" businesses arose to supply them and push further into nonethnic groceries. To many Americans, however, that marketing development posed a threat to Americanism. Nativism and xenophobia, both prominent features of United States politics in the early twentieth century, reared their heads. As Donna Gabaccia put it: "Between 1880 and 1980, a veritable 'food fight' erupted over what it meant not only to be, but to eat, American."[41]

Americans' preference for variety and novelty eventually won out, but over strong resistance from nativists. This was helped by the fact that in the early twentieth century, it was impossible to identify an American cuisine. This problem plagued the depression era Federal Writers' Project which attempted to define and detail a guide to American cuisine in 1938. Some attempt was made to promote early New England meals as American, but that was not welcomed by proponents of other regional cuisines. Furthermore, New England cuisine, based on English food patterns, was not particularly tasty to Americans, by then tempted by a variety of national cuisines.[42]

Patriotic middle-class Americans associated ethnic foods with the eating habits of poor immigrants and the "threats" they represented. They not only violated "100 Percent Americanism," but were also believed to be lower class and unhealthy. It was therefore necessary, during World War I, to rename sauerkraut "victory cabbage" and the frankfurter the "hotdog!" Even many less patriotic Americans believed that Americanizing the immigrant diet was in the immigrant's best health interest. Home economists of the times employed "domestic science" to teach the foreign-born how to prepare healthier, American meals. Ellen Richards, in *The Cost of Living as Modified by Sanitary Science* (1900), promoted such foods as New England's codfish, brown bread, and baked beans as healthier alternatives to ethnic dishes. She further urged new Americans to emulate American "virtues of self-control, self-denial, regard for ethics, good temper, good manners, [and] pleasant speech." Progressive Era reformers even turned to government regulation of suspect eating establishments and food processors, which was particularly burdensome for smaller and poorer neighborhood ethnic businesses.[43]

By World War II the "food fight" waned, and Americans became more accustomed to ethnic diversity and acceptance of ethnic foods. During the Great Depression some dietitions began to acknowledge the value of these foods, reasoning that by the very fact that they were poor, ethnic groups "learned to know a lot about food substitutes and economy in buying." Spaghetti, in particular, entered the "advised" list for inexpensive nutritious foods recommended by New York social workers.[44] Perhaps more influential in this change of heart was the success of some food companies in marketing "ethnic" foods to broader American markets.

One of the earliest successful labels to accomplish this was Chef Boyardee. The business originated with Hector Boiardi, a chef from Piacenza, Italy, who began an Italian restaurant in Cleveland, Ohio. He decided to can and distribute his sauce, packaging it with dry spaghetti and a packet of grated cheese, through his own company, Chef Boiardi Food Products Company. In the 1930s he changed the name to Boyardee because it was easier for non-Italians to pronounce, and by the late 1930s he was selling canned spaghetti to the earliest national supermarkets. During World War II he supplied the U.S. army and cultivated a taste for the product which lasted when they returned home. In 1946 Boiardi sold his company to American Home Foods, a large conglomerate, who built the line into the household product it became. Interestingly, American Home Foods was still prospering in 2001, when it was bought by a much larger food conglomerate, ConAgra. Other entrepreneurs followed Boiardi's lead in the post war years, forming conglomerates that joined the mass marketing of "ethnic" foods that appealed to many Americans—whether of that nationality or not.[45]

As a result of all of these developments, what we term "typical" American food changed over the course of the first half-century. Many of the foods central to our diet today came into being. In 1901 the frankfurter was served in a bun at New York's Polo Grounds; some argue that the "hot dog," as it became known in 1906, dates to the 1880s. People who attended the St. Louis World's Fair of 1904 were introduced to hamburgers on buns, ice cream cones, and peanut butter. The nation's first pizzeria opened in 1905 in New York City. Oreo cookies were marketed in 1912, Kraft processed cheese in

1915. Model T cars rolled out of factories, providing Americans the means by which to patronize new "cash-and-carry" grocery stores, which, due to their larger volume of sales, could sell at lower prices. The Great Atlantic and Pacific Tea Company (later A & P) opened in 1912. Piggly Wiggly, the first modern grocery store opened in 1916 in Memphis, Tennessee. It had aisles that led customers in a set pattern through all the merchandise and then through the checkout counter. Piggly Wiggly sold only prepackaged and individually priced items, eliminating the need for store clerks to wrap and weigh the goods.[46]

The pace of growing commodification of the American food system accelerated after World War I. In the 1920s the following foods became household names: Kool-Aid, White Castle hamburgers (the first hamburger chain), Eskimo Pie, Popsicles, Caesar salad, Velveeta, and a myriad of candy bars including Baby Ruth, Mounds Bar, Milky Way, Reese's Peanut Butter Cup, and more. The Jazz Age also witnessed a wave of mass-produced items like Campbell's condensed soups. Smaller kitchens and kitchenettes became popular, and gas ranges and refrigerators became more common.[47]

Scarce dollars encouraged homemakers to favor casseroles composed of scalloped potatoes with ham, macaroni, and cheese, baked beans with frankfurters, and rice with chicken gizzards and livers. Frozen foods made their appearance during the 1930s, long before home freezers became common. So too did Toll House cookies, Wonder Bread, Twinkies, Bisquick, Ritz Crackers, Spam, and Lay's Potato Chips. The Philadelphia Girl Scouts baked and sold cookies, and they were so successful the organization had them commercially produced and sold nationally. The blender was marketed, as were *The Better Homes and Gardens Cookbook* (1930) and *The Joy of Cooking* (1931). Such cookbooks helped to standardize American cooking with common recipes and standardized measurements. Not all food innovations were for the masses, however—*Haute Cuisine* representing elite European cuisines was introduced in the 1939 New York World's Fair.[48]

EARLY FOOD REFORM MOVEMENTS

After 1900 nutritionists focused much of their energies on changing the diet of the middle class, but they were not the first to do so, even in the United States. Reformers sought to reshape the American diet decades earlier. The most famous of the early health/diet reformers was Sylvester Graham. He began his campaign in the 1830s as a lecturer for the Pennsylvania Society for Discouraging the Use of Ardent Spirits, but he soon expanded his agenda. He began to lecture on diet, criticizing those physicians who urged Americans to eat hearty, stimulating food to build up their systems to withstand the ravages of disease. Graham dissented. He saw irritation of the stomach as the primary cause of illness and recommended a more bland diet of fruits, vegetables, and coarsely ground grain—no meat, spices, coffee, tea, or alcohol. He also preached the importance of diet in a virtuous life. Rich and spicy food, be believed, excited passions that led to sexual excess. His *Treatise on Bread and Bread-Making* (1837) was influential and led to the "invention" of the Graham Cracker.[49]

In the 1850s Seventh Day Adventists began experimenting with cereals to meet the need of their vegetarian diets in Battle Creek, Michigan. In the 1870s, John H. Kellogg, a nutritionist and manager of the Western Health Reform Institute in Battle Creek, began serving patients new health-providing foods, including peanut butter and wheat flakes. He produced granola, the first ready-cooked cereal food, made from a mixture of oatmeal, wheat, and corn baked in an oven until thoroughly mixed. Several years later his brother, William K. Kellogg, invented corn flakes, and Charles W. Post, an ex-patient of John Kellogg, introduced Grape-Nuts and Post Toasties. Illustrating both his ingenuity and the abstemiousness of Seventh Day Adventists, we still have Postum, a grain-based coffee substitute. Ironically, although from today's perspective many recommendations of the early reformers were based on suspect and oddball nutritional theories, their consequences were not always bad. They were, for instance, the first to promote whole grain products at a time when the popular flour was bleached of nutrients, and they revolutionized breakfast by replacing eggs, potatoes, meat, and bread with much healthier ready-to-eat cereal.[50]

In the 1880s nutritionist Wilbur Atwater and his followers taught Americans that they could obtain proteins, fats, and carbohydrates from diverse but not necessarily expensive food sources. They recommended getting protein from beans rather than meat, carbohydrates from cornmeal, oats, and grains other than wheat, and their fats from lard and vegetable oils. Home economists devised recipes and menus that would employ substitutes for wheat, beef, butter, and sugar, recommendations that would accelerate the coming food-strained war and depression years.[51]

Efforts of the "nutrition reformers" of the 1890s to reach the poor and urban factory workers failed. But many middle-class people, who were better educated and more impressed by science, showed interest. Advocates of the "new nutrition" set their goal to convince Americans to jettison their greasy meat-and-potatoes diet and their penchant for cakes, pies, and fried foods in favor of a more balanced program of fruits, vegetables, carbohydrates, and proteins. They emphasized the health advantages of their recommended dietary change, and their promotional strategy was effective. Just before World War I scientists discovered the dietetic value of vitamins A and B (C and D were discovered after the war). A growing number of publishers offered cookbooks, which, in conjunction with the opening of cooking schools, heightened American's interest in healthy and enjoyable food.[52]

The demands of feeding the troops during World War I helped change the American diet, as well. Americans were urged to consume less, especially

AMERICA'S WAR FOOD POLICY

The central strategy of the U.S. Food Administration during World War I was voluntary restriction of white wheat flour, meat, sugar, and butter. In addition to calling for general reductions in food consumption, it promoted wheatless and meatless days. It prescribed substitutes, established by the nation's premiere nutritionist Wilbur Atwater. It encouraged Americans to get their protein from beans instead of meat, their carbohydrates from cornmeal, oats, and grains other than wheat, and their fats from lard and vegetable oils. The U.S. Food Administration also recognized the value of pasta and tomato sauce in limiting the consumption of meat, thereby making Italian food the first turn-of-the-century immigrant food to gain widespread acceptance.[54]

of the much needed meats, butter, sugar, and wheat flour, and to eat more fresh fruits and vegetables. Army cooking manuals stressed the new nutrition idea of balanced meals that included proteins, fruits, vegetables, and carbohydrates. New eating habits resulted. By 1928 Americans consumed 5 percent fewer calories than they had in 1890. They ate more fruits, vegetables, greens, milk, and cheese, and less cornmeal, wheat flour, potatoes, and sweet potatoes. They cut their annual per capita beef consumption from 72.4 pounds in 1899 to 55.3 pounds in 1930.[53]

By the early 1900s the middle class wanted to imitate the dining styles of the upper class. Middle-class Americans had experienced a rise in economic status, and the ready availability of foods made a shift in diet possible, as well. Moreover, women's interests were expanding beyond the home, and, whether for work or some form of community involvement, they needed more time from their domestic responsibilities. Either because they could not afford it or had difficulty in obtaining satisfactory domestic service, women sought to limit or decrease the number of hours they spent in household labor, including cooking. Thus, the warnings of nutritionists against overeating, combined with the pervasive desires of middle-class women to reduce the hours spent in the kitchen, changed what American society expected of middle-class cuisines—in both quantity and quality. The shift was toward smaller, lighter, and less elaborate meals. Women saved labor by simpler menus, fewer ingredients in dishes, fewer steps in their preparation, and fewer courses. One-dish dinners, once despised as reflective of European immigrant peasant dishes, became increasingly popular.[55]

It is important to note here a deep irony of the first half of the twentieth century. The accumulating innovations in food processing and preparation, along with the growing knowledge of nutritional science, interacted with the mandatory belt-tightening and deprivations of two world wars punctuated by the great depression. People learned to "get along with less," and responded to official recommendations and rationing. In retrospect, they adapted and they did so remarkably well. Many Americans made better food choices with less food than they had—or could have done—before these twentieth-century traumas. As in many things, deprivation is an important source of innovation and adaptation.[56] Though not uniformly, Americans were better nourished in 1950 than in 1900.

CORPORATIONS, FARMERS, AND POLITICS

To deepen this irony, as people were eating better, America's farmers and ranchers seemed to experience ever-accelerating difficulties and hardships. To begin to unravel this puzzle, we argue that even considering the impact of traumatic events, scientific progress, and government regulation, without a doubt the major driving force of the transformation and development of the American food system was big business. The growth of huge food corporations not only dramatically impacted the lives of urban dwellers but also framed the direction of an increasingly commodified American agriculture. Corporations proved to be the best instrument to raise capital for industrial expansion, and by 1900 they were responsible for two-thirds of all goods manufactured in the United States. Massive corporate conglomerates dominated the economy at the turn of the century—including the food sector.[57]

Corporate control of nearly every stage of food production and distribution from the purchase of farmland to marketing farm goods led to hard times "down on the farm." They produced a powerful revolt of the farmers, more formally known as *agrarian populism*. It began in the closing decades of the nineteenth century and lasted to World War I. This agrarian revolt began in the 1870s with state level organizations known collectively as the "Grange," which peaked in a decade but gave way to a more broad-based coalition known as the Farmers' Alliance in the 1880s. The immediate targets of this protest were the big banks, railroads, merchants, and all the middlemen who stood between farmers and urban consumers. Farmers perceived these as the culprits, as indeed they were in part. But the deeper causes of their plight were a tangled web of broader and more abstract forces that they could barely understand, much less control.

The first among these was the very mechanization that they willingly embraced to boost productivity. When increased efficiency and foreign competition produced surpluses that exceeded national and worldwide demand, prices dropped. In 1897–1901, for example, the United Kingdom purchased 72 million bushels of wheat and 74 million bushels of corn each year from the United States, but in 1910–1914 it was able to import only 27 million and 10 million bushels respectively. Germany's annual imports of American corn fell more than 80 percent. A bushel of wheat that sold for $1.45 in 1866 brought only 80 cents in the mid-1880s and 49 cents a decade later.[58]

In addition, many farmers carried debt from their investments in land and machinery. The Homestead Act's offer of free land notwithstanding, commercial farming required a significant investment of money, just to get started. Beyond the $500 or $600 the land itself might cost when purchased from a land company, it cost an additional $1500 to $2500 to establish a farm in Kansas, Nebraska, or Minnesota—to build a house and barn, to purchase the minimum necessary equipment, and to properly stock the farm. Nearly every new farmer had to borrow that money, and although state law limited interest charges to between 7 and 10 percent, various "technicalities," or fees, pushed rates to as high as 20 percent.[59]

The Census of 1850 reported that $6.8 million was invested in farm implements and machinery. In 1880 the figure had risen ten times; by 1900 it was $101.2 million—and the price of farm implements fell during this period. Transportation, storage, and sales fees remained high relative to other prices, as did prices for seed, fertilizer, manufactured goods, and taxes. Western farmers were dependent on railroads to get their produce to distant markets, and although there were four transcontinentals by the end of the century, practically speaking they were forced to use the closest track regardless of the cost. Farmers were forced to produce more, which only served to drive prices down further. Western farmers and cattlemen became enmeshed in national and international business, and they gained no exemption from the risks of either big business or farming, whether those were downturns in business cycles or drought. The ideal of the independent, hard-working, simple but honest farmer, if it had ever existed, was dead.[60]

Populist organizations took economic and political action. Granger political parties organized in eleven states and in the 1870s controlled state legislatures in Illinois, Wisconsin, Iowa, and Minnesota. Local branches formed cooperatives to buy equipment and supplies and to market crops and livestock. Farmers' Alliances took political action, not only organizing the farm vote behind supportive candidates, but also pushing for reforms such as a subtreasury plan to relieve shortages of cash and credit. They called on the federal government to build warehouses where farmers could store their crops while waiting for higher prices. The government would then loan farmers Treasury notes amounting to 80 percent of the market price that the crops could bring. Once the stored crops were sold, farmers would repay the loan, interest, and storage fees. Farmers also demanded low-interest loans from the federal government to buy land. Granger legislation tried to reduce "middleman" prices by regulating the price of rail transportation and the price of grain-elevator storage of crops, but the Supreme Court shortly ruled that unconstitutional.[61]

The Farmers' Alliances sprouted in the Southeast, Texas, and the Northwest. In 1889 they tried to form alliances with the burgeoning labor movement organizations of urban workers. In 1890 Farmers' Alliance and labor groups joined to form the Populist party. In 1892 it called a People's Party convention in Omaha, Nebraska, where the delegates drafted a platform and nominated James B. Weaver of Iowa for the presidency. The platform announced that "the fruits of the tens of millions are boldly stolen to build up colossal fortunes for a few." In one of the most colorful and raucous political gatherings in the nation's history, delegates adopted a platform that summarized the outlook of agrarian dissent. They advocated free and unlimited coinage of silver, a graduated income tax, government ownership (not just control) of the railroads and the telephone-telegraph system, the secret ballot, direct election of U.S. Senators, and restraints on immigration. The "silver plank" was intended to gain support from Western mining states, while resolutions supporting reduced working hours for urban workers were intended to attract them to the "cause," as well. Remember that at the time 12-hour days were common in industrial "sweatshops."[62]

While the populists made the strongest "third party" showing in American history, the 1892 election was still disappointing for them. They won 1 million of 17 million votes cast, carrying majorities only in Idaho, Nevada, and Colorado (then the center of the silver mining industry) and made strong showings only in the wheat and beef states of the great plains. Populist attempts to win black voters damaged their efforts in the South. Urban workers had little interest in policies that could raise the price of food, and the "specialty farmers" of the Northeast and Upper Midwest found little to gain in addressing the plight of the Plains states and Western silver interest. The Depression of 1893 made matters worse, by creating many bank failures. Attempts by President Grover Cleveland and financier J. P. Morgan to protect the gold reserve brought cries of corruption. The Populists rallied behind William Jennings Bryan, a former congressman and ardent supporter for coinage of silver, which he articulated in his fiery "cross of gold" speech at the Chicago convention. The Democratic party, hoping to attract the farm vote, nominated Bryan as well, and he won 39 percent of the popular vote and 176 electors.[63]

Bryan's "cross of gold" speech personified the split and tension between the old and new farmer. On the one hand he called the farmer "as much a business man as the man who goes upon the Board of Trade." On the other hand, he continued to articulate the Jeffersonian agrarian creed and to warn that if the farms are destroyed, "The grass will grow in the streets of every city in the country." The Populist-Democratic fusion proved uneasy, but by World War I many of their goals were eventually realized, including the elimination of the "gold standard" for currency, a graduated income tax, regulation of railroads, banks, and utilities, the direct election of senators, the secret ballot, and federal agricultural subsidies. The immediate plight of the farmer, however, did not improve, and it continued to spawn bankruptcies, land consolidation and migration to the cities.[64]

MID-TWENTIETH-CENTURY CRISES

The 1920s, 1930s, and 1940s were shaped by three major crises: the Great Depression, the Dust Bowl, and World War II. Most of the decade of the 1920s were prosperous for business. After a brief period of prosperity during World War I and the early 1920s, however, farmers were once again beset by economic problems. Between 1919 and 1929 the gross national product of the United States swelled by 40 percent. Wages and salaries grew, while the cost of living remained relatively stable. People had more purchasing power, and they spent more on luxury as well as basic goods and services. During the same period prices for farm products fell by about 40 percent in 1921 and then by 60 percent from 1929 to 1933. Drought, foreclosure, swarms of destructive grasshoppers, and, after 1929, bank failures plagued American farmers. Many abandoned farming altogether.[65]

The stock market crash of 1929 heralded the Great Depression, a worldwide business slump that continued through the 1930s. It was the worst and longest period of high unemployment and low business activity in modern times. Adding to the gravity of the situation were the severe droughts, dust storms, and erosion that hit parts of the Midwest and Southwest during the 1930s. The most severe droughts occurred in 1934 and 1936. Thousands of farmers were wiped out. Some organized protests, tried to block foreclosures, dumped milk and vegetables in ditches rather than sell them at depressed prices, and even engaged in sporadic violence against police, judges, and bankers. But many just quit and migrated to the fertile agricultural areas of California. Most of those who found jobs had to work as fruit pickers for low wages. Migrant families crowded into shacks near fields or camped outdoors, as described by John Steinbeck in *The Grapes of Wrath* (1939). The most immediate result was the rise of malnutrition, once again, affecting both urban and rural Americans. Urban ghetto dwellers and the rural poor, migrant workers, and even the jobless middle class were particularly affected.[66]

Under President Franklin Roosevelt, the Great Depression witnessed the beginning of twentieth-century federalism in the United States. Upon assuming office, Roosevelt immediately called Congress into session to pass laws to alleviate the depression, naming his program the New Deal. Government became intimately involved with America's food system, as well. It launched numerous efforts to safeguard the nation's agricultural base, including the Agricultural Adjustment Act of 1933. Food supports were authorized, and the federal government began to purchase farm products directly. The government paid farmers to reduce their acreage, thereby stopping the fall of prices and increasing farmers' purchasing power. A month later Congress passed the Farm Credit Act, providing loans that enabled farmers to refinance their mortgages and keep their homes and lands. It created the Commodity Credit Corporation in 1933, which bolstered crop prices by lending farmers money secured by their underpriced crops, thereby allowing them to withhold their

---

THE GRAPES OF WRATH

In his famous novel, John Steinbeck offered this description of rural Oklahoma families who had borne the brunt of yet another Depression Era dust storm:

> The people came out of their houses and smelled the hot stinking air and covered their noses from it. And the children came out of the houses, but they did not run or shout as they would have done after a rain. Men stood by their fences and looked at the ruined corn, drying fast now, only a little green showing through the film of dust. The men were silent and they did not move often. And the women came out of their houses to stand beside their men—to feel whether this time the men would break. The women studied the men's faces secretly, for the corn could go, as long as something else remained. The children stood nearby, drawing figures in the dust with bare toes, and the children sent exploring senses out to see whether men and women could break.

Neither the men nor the women broke, but many, including the Joad family, picked up stakes and headed for California.[67]

---

crops from the market until prices rose. The United States Supreme Court ruled the Agricultural Adjustment Act unconstitutional in 1936, but in 1938 FDR pushed through legislation that provided that the government could purchase and store excess farm goods, thereby supporting price levels.[68]

Some argue that the various New Deal programs were artificial, and that they helped farmers only for the moment, and then only marginally, without addressing the serious problems plaguing the economy. Others disagree, and argue that something had to be done to save the nation's farms. Nearly all agree that World War II returned prosperity to the American economy—including the farm economy. New Deal legislation, much of which had impact beyond the 1930s, ended the agricultural free-market economy. But as Carl Degler put it, the free-market economy in agriculture of the 1920s "succeeded only in making farmers the economic stepchildren of an otherwise prosperous decade."[69]

Several of the New Deal food-related programs had long term effects. For example, the Roosevelt administration authorized two food-subsidy programs under its commodity-food legislation in 1935. These programs distributed surplus agricultural products to families and to schools. The commodity products included canned meat and poultry, dried beans, canned fruits and vegetables, cooking and eating fats, cornmeal, flour, nonfat dried milk, peanut butter, rice, rolled wheat, and other cereals. These foods provided essential supplemental nutrition to the diets of many families and children. The commodity-food programs proved to be forerunners of stronger, expanded programs which still continue today, including School Lunch, begun in 1946, and the Commodity Distribution Program, initiated in 1949.

By the 1930s, the original Food and Drug Act had become inadequate because of the increased complexity and breadth of the food system. In response to increased needs and consumer pressure, the federal Food, Drug, and Cosmetic Act was enacted in 1938.[70]

For those farmers who survived the agricultural depression and Dust Bowl, agriculture became a very different enterprise by 1945 than it had been a half-century earlier—setting the stage for even more dramatic changes in the postwar period. For one thing, agribusiness had begun in America. Owners of giant commercial farms, heavily capitalized, banded together for promotional purposes and to work more closely with national food corporations. As one California wheat grower put it in the early 1940s: "We no longer raise wheat here, we manufacture it....We are not husbandmen, we are not farmers. We are producing a product to sell."[71]

Science and technology began to revolutionize the crops grown. Hybridization had been a laboratory success in agricultural schools and seed company research and development departments for decades, but the first commercial raising of hybrid corn (more for fodder than as food for people) began in the 1920s. The new varieties were available in quantity by the early 1930s, and between 1935 and 1939 there was a five-fold increase in the number of acres of the newer varieties under cultivation. Twenty-five percent of all corn grown in 1939 was hybrid; 77 percent of the corn acreage in Iowa was hybrid in 1940.[72]

Livestock production was altered as well and in some cases enhanced by the increased use of artificial insemination for large animals and incubation and scientifically mixed feeds for chickens. Fishmeal feeds, a by-product of the California fishing industry, were 20 percent cheaper than meat scrap and grain feeds, and fowl grew faster on the protein-rich product. California chicken production reached 21 million annually by 1930, twice what it had been in 1920. In 1918, 20 percent of baby chicks produced annually were hatched in incubators; by 1944, 85 percent came into the world under heat lamps. Ten thousand chick factories produced 1.6 billion chicks that, beginning in 1918, could be sent to farmers through the mail.[73]

THE FOOD BUSINESS

Food became big business. Between 1914 and 1929 capital investment in the food industry more than tripled, making it America's largest manufacturing industry. It also became the second-largest purchaser of newspaper advertising by the 1920s. "New" foods were introduced and mass-produced foods were common. By 1939 the value of mass-produced bread was estimated to be $514 million, while the value of privately baked bread was $20 million. Four times as much white pan bread was produced (7.2 billion pounds) as rye or whole wheat or hearth breads (1.7 billion pounds). By 1934 Americans bought 39 million pounds of frozen foods. Ten years later they purchased 600 million pounds.[74]

During the first half of the twentieth century the portion of Americans' wages spent on food, as well as what food they purchased with their money, changed. In 1901, for example, workers budgeted about 43.1 percent of their income for food. By 1924, a Bureau of Labor Statistics' study showed that figure had dropped to 38.2 percent. Moreover, the cost of key items in that budget, such as flour, potatoes, and some meats decreased substantially. As a result, most people were able to buy more and varied foods, such as more milk, cheese, fruits, and vegetables. They ate less flour and cereals, and more meat and grains. Their diets, by 1930s' standards, were judged to be much healthier than in 1914.[75]

Although the economic status and consumption patterns of the urban workers improved in this period, the first signs of an *urban underclass* appeared; beginning in the 1920s, at least one in ten workers was constantly unemployed. This underclass included especially blacks, who were migrating from the rural South to the urban North and Midwest in search of industrial jobs. Their diet tended to retain the salt pork and corn of their tradition diets, adding white flour, sweets, and highly processed foods newly available to them, but little milk, fresh fruits, and vegetables. The result was a nutritionally inadequate diet.[76]

Otherwise, the "core" eating pattern of modern America was set by the mid-twentieth century. This general pattern consisted of breakfasts of citrus fruit or juice and dried cereal or eggs and toast, a light lunch of a sandwich, soup, or salad, and a dinner consisting of meat as a central entrée with potato and vegetable side dishes, and a simple dessert, often ice cream. Sliced baker's bread became a welcome, convenient consumer product. The use of canned goods, especially by the middle class, became dominant.[77]

Beans, peas, and cheaper cuts of meat were substituted for more expensive meats. Thrifty homemakers used cooked cereals, rather than the more expensive commercial dry cereals. From 1830 to 1930 pork consumption decreased by 25 percent, but it still exceeded beef consumption at twice the rate of consumption per capita. Moreover, big food companies began to make heavy inroads into homemakers' food preparation. Some food companies began to employ home economists and made that fact known in order to promote their foods. Perhaps the best known of these "home economists" was Betty Crocker of General Mills. Although a fictional character, she provided consumers with helpful information regarding her company's food products, as she does still today.[78]

RESTAURANTS AND "EATING OUT"

Restaurants began to appear in the 1920s. Before the Civil War, food outside the home could be found in a variety of places. Travelers could obtain drink and "victuals" in inns and taverns. Hotels maintained dining rooms that catered not only to travelers but also to long-term residents renting rooms by the week, month, or year. Some, like the Waldorf in New York City, were well know for their elegance. As cities developed, boarding houses catered to bachelors; they could find lunch at saloons, as well.[79]

Members of the Delmonico family popularized the restaurant idea, applying the name to several eating establishments in Manhattan during the 1830s. They introduced a French "Parisian" cuisine, which appealed to the affluent. Rival high-style establishments soon followed, but the restaurant name and idea was soon expropriated by other entrepreneurs for more common fare and use. By the end of the century restaurants fed working men, industrial workers, clerks, and others from factories and offices.[80] But they remained male preserves.

John Wanamaker opened the first department store in Philadelphia in 1876, and soon department stores populated every city in the nation. Luncheonettes, featuring soda fountains and offering light food such as sandwiches to complement their soda drinks and ice cream desserts, appeared in the 1880s in larger stores, catering to women, as well as men, shoppers. Out of the luncheonette, in the 1920s, evolved the lunchroom, most retaining the lunch counter as a principal feature. Chains dominated the larger urban markets, locating their outlets near major pedestrian areas, streetcar lines, and subway entrances. Schrafft's, begun in Boston in 1898, had twenty-two stores by 1923, forty-two by 1934.[81]

Other new kinds of restaurants appealed to the growing new middle-class male and female office workers and shop employees who needed quick lunches at midday. Self-service cafeterias, which had been introduced before 1920, became big businesses when steam tables were added to provide the hot food still considered essential for a proper meal. Borrowing an idea developed in Sweden, Horn and Hardart developed "automats," which dispensed food through banks of small windows. Configured along the walls of these cafeterias were hundreds of small glass compartments, six by eight inches in

---

EATING OUT IN NEW YORK CITY

In some respects eating out in turn-of-the-century New York City foreshadowed that favorite pastime of today. In other respects it was different. New Yorkers ate out because they were wealthy enough not to have to cook, or because they were too poor to afford an apartment with a kitchen. They also did it "for the heck of it," or, as a recent museum exhibit suggested, to indulge in the outrageous. At a banquet at Sherry's, guests dined on horseback and drank champagne through straws from their saddlebags. New Yorkers ate out to soak up the noise of a crowd, to cure the chronic affliction of loneliness. And they ate out to sate homesickness on the foods of their native lands.[82]

size, each with a coin slot and knob. The customer could see the sandwich, salad, or dessert, insert the appropriate coins, lift the glass door, and remove the dish. Begun in 1902, Horn and Hardart operated 85 automats in 1950, their peak year, followed by rapid decline.[83]

By the mid-1920s, and especially during the 1930s, cafeterias began to give way to luncheon restaurants and an increasing number of luncheonettes featuring lighter foods. Old main street cafés were modernized, whole façades were replaced with "open fronts" with wide expanses of glass. Brightly lit interiors were opened to street views, featuring fixtures of streamlined light-reflecting materials attractive to motorists as well as pedestrians. Tables and booths offered seating arrangements that were more conducive to social interaction than automats. Perhaps the most highly personalized restaurants of all were the *diners*. Organized around the lunch counter, most diners placed employees and customers in almost intimate proximity. Although common at the turn of the century, beginning in the 1930s, diner manufacturers "streamlined" their buildings, adopting simplified modern designs suggestive of speed, to appear on the nation's highways. An estimated 4,000 "modular lunchrooms," or diners, operated in 1932; in twenty years the number grew to 5,000.[84]

Not surprisingly, these innovations in quick eating, or fast foods, built around coffee, soft drinks, and novelty sandwiches like hamburgers, brought condemnation. In 1924 an anonymous medical doctor wrote for an industry trade journal: "The good, old fashioned American meal...is being rapidly supplemented by sugary concoctions of the soda jerker's ingenuity. This indiscreet eating, with almost a total lack of exercise, now features the life of the average businessman. Up at 8 in the morning, a hasty breakfast, ride downtown in an automobile; a ten minute lunch of miscellaneous sugary drinks in the quick lunch or drug store, back to the office, home in an automobile—they call that a day....The consequences are indigestion, bad nerves, decaying teeth, restless nights, and cutting down the span of life."[85]

John Jakle and Keith Sculle offered the following important observations to keep in mind as we turn to post-World War II America and the flourishing of fast food. Although we tend to equate quick-service eating with the coming of the automobile, many important attributes of the fast-food restaurant appeared before automobile use became widespread, catering to a mushrooming of the urban lunch-time working class. By the 1920s the format hardly varied, except for formal hotel dining rooms and automats, and it was easily adapted to life along the nation's new highways. As Robert and Helen Lynd found in their study of "Middletown," it is also the case that such developments in eating outside the home initiated the decline in shared mealtimes in the home. Rather than being a recent development as most people assume, the Lynds wrote in 1929: "Mealtime as family reunion time was taken for granted a generation ago." The threat to that tradition by that date had spawned a conscious effort to preserve it.[86]

THE IMPACT OF WORLD WAR II

Finally, World War II had far-reaching effects on the American food system and food science in particular. The need to provide an adequate, safe, nutritious food supply for the armed forces resulted in food rationing and stimulated much government-sponsored research into new and improved food technologies, as well as the setting of dietary standards. The public benefited from these efforts as well. In 1940, the Food and Nutrition Board (FNB) of the National Research Council (NRC) was established to advise the federal government on nutrition as it related to national defense. Charged by President Franklin Roosevelt with the task of developing a set of dietary standards to serve as a goal for good nutrition, the FNB developed the first set of Recommended Dietary Allowances (RDAs) in 1943; they were revised periodically thereafter. These standards represent recommended levels of intake for most healthy males and females of various ages with respect to energy (at differing activity levels) and those nutrients for which sufficient information is available to warrant making a judgment.[87]

Sugar, fats, meats, and canned fruits and vegetables were rationed during the war. That encouraged the increased consumption of eggs, milk products, and fresh fruits. Growing out of concern that certain vitamins and minerals were being lost during the removal of cereal hulls during the milling and refining steps of processing, in 1943 the government ordered the enrichment of baker's bread with thiamine, riboflavin, niacin, iron, and calcium. After the war, federal law ceased to make such requirements, but most states stepped in to require enrichment of flours and breads, and because most companies wished to engage in interstate commerce, they complied even if they were not located in a state that required it. During the war the federal government required that oleomargarine be fortified with vitamin A, and that milk be fortified with vitamin D, again establishing a process continued thereafter.[88]

Dehydration techniques advanced during World War II as well, since dehydrated foods do not require refrigeration. They are also lighter (since up to 99 percent of the water is removed) and easier to transport. Such research led in the post-war period to the marketing of powdered instant milk, orange and grapefruit powders, dried eggs, dried mashed potatoes, as well as dried instant coffee, tea, meat, fish, fruits, and vegetables. But the development of frozen foods had an even more long-lasting impact. After the war, frozen foods became a major source of preserved foods available to consumers. Clarence Birdseye was the first major name in this area of food production, but the scientific ground work was done by researchers like C. R. Fellers at the Massachusetts State College (now the University of Massachusetts) and Donald K. Tressler at Cornell University.[89]

Finally, the war led to dramatic improvement in food packaging that became widely available and marketable after the war. The discovery of polyethylene and applications of polyvinyl chloride in the late 1930s, experimented with during World War II, led to the use of wax papers and aluminum foil, which housewives used after the war to cover and protect freshly prepared foods, as well as leftovers, before placing them in the refrigerator.[90] In sum, World War II was an important historical watershed, a technological one for agricultural productivity and food preparation, as well as for the growing impacts of nutritional science and government subsidy and regulation.

SOME SUGGESTIONS FOR FURTHER READING

Desrosier, H. (1963). *Food Preservation.* 2nd Ed. Westport, CT: Avi Publishing Company.

Jackle, J., and K. Sculle (1999). *Fast Food: Roadside Restaurants in the Automobile Age.* Baltimore, MD: Johns Hopkins University Press.

Levenstein, H. (1988). *Revolution at the Table.* New York: Oxford University Press.

Marx. L. (1964). *The Machine in the Garden: Technology and the Pastoral Idea in America.* New York: Oxford University Press.

Paul, R. (1988). *The Far West and the Great Plains in Transition, 1859–1900.* New York: Harper and Row.

Root, W., and R. deRouchmont (1976). *Eating in America.* New York: Ecco Press.

Schlereth, T. (1991). *Victorian America; Transformations in Everyday Life, 1876–1915.* New York: Harper Collins.

Worster, D. (1985). *Rivers of Empire: Water, Aridity, and the Growth of the American West.* New York: Pantheon Books.

CHAPTER FOUR

Food in America and the World 1945–2002

Continuing Transformations

In the last chapter we discussed changes in the American food system from the mid-nineteenth to the mid-twentieth century. We continue here with the ongoing dramatic transformations of that system from the end of World War II to the present, concentrating especially on three major trends so interrelated in reality that we separate them rather artificially for convenience. First, we discuss the ongoing changes in the technologies of farming and food preparation. Second, we note the continuing dramatic transformation of the political economy of the food system in terms of the growth in size, scale, and concentration in ownership of farms, agribusiness, and food corporations. Third, the chapter will address the growth of world trade in food and the emergence of a world market system and globalization regarding food. While still focusing mainly on America, in this chapter we begin to "widen the hourglass" by considering some global food issues and end with a discussion of some of the social and cultural implications of those transformations, which continues in Chapter 5.

TECHNIFYING FOODS

As we noted in the last chapter, Americans had an adequate diet during World War II, despite food rationing. By the mid-1950s, however, there was an abundance of food. As the postwar American economy boomed, new technologies continued to transform the food system. Improved transportation, preservation, processing, and packaging produced a sharp increase in the numbers and types of food products available, and an unprecedented percentage of the population could afford to avail themselves of this abundance. By 1960, the food industry was growing at a faster rate than the overall economy.[1]

Development of the interstate highway system, as well as the continued improvement of rail transportation, helped farmers get their produce to market more quickly and efficiently. Although begun in the prewar period, the use of frozen, precooked foods expanded dramatically, especially with the introduction of the home food freezer in the 1950s. A complete meal, commonly known as the TV dinner—to be consumed in front of the television on TV tables—became a popular item.[2]

As noted earlier, research on dried foods—begun during the war— yielded many new convenience products. Powdered, instant, skim milk came on the market in 1954, where it was soon joined by orange and grapefruit powders, dried eggs, instant mashed potatoes, and freeze-dried, air-dried, sun-dried, and mechanically dried coffee, tea, meat, fish, fruits, and vegetables.[3] And the introduction of new packaging materials, based on discoveries of polyethylene and applications of polyvinyl chloride during World War II, insured these products would be efficiently, safely, and attractively displayed on supermarket shelves. Plastic tubs, polyethylene jugs, all-aluminum cans, polyethylene-coated cartons, laminated plastic tubs, and plastic-foam cartons allowed a much greater number of perishable foods to be sold, retaining their nutrients for longer periods of time. Products like Saran Wrap were added to wax paper and aluminum foil to preserve prepared foods and leftovers, when placed in the refrigerator, and the appearance of the microwave in the 1970s made preparing meals and warming things up even easier and faster.[4]

While grocery stores in 1916 offered only about 600 items, by 1988 supermarkets carried 24,000 items, and the number continued to increase.[5] Changes in the variety of actual foods consumed, however, lagged behind this dramatic increase in numbers and types of food available to Americans. Indeed for a few decades American eating patterns were the same as in previous periods. Animal meat continued to be the central part of a meal, augmented by items chosen from a wide selection of fruits, potatoes and other vegetables, grain products, dairy products, pastries, and other desserts. What did change was the amount of these foods Americans consumed. As one scholar put it: "The public's implicit attitude seemed to be that, if a certain level of nutrient consumption (e.g., protein) was good, more would certainly be better."[6] This did not take into consideration their more sedentary lives, which resulted from Americans' more mechanized, and therefore less physically taxing, jobs, and lives made easier by the greater availability of the automobile, household appliances, etc. In sum, calorie intake increased, while energy expenditures decreased—with predictable consequences to which we will return.

All of this was made possible by the continuing "industrialization" of

TECHNOLOGICAL ADVANCES IN FOOD PROCESSING

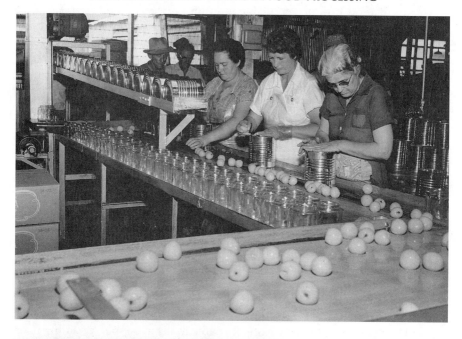

top: Assembly line workers can peaches after processing at a Meansville, Georgia, plant.

left: Female workers package meals of frozen foods into boxes on a conveyor belt.

American agriculture in the postwar period. Farmers began to use commercial fertilizers in dramatically increasing amounts, as well as insecticides and herbicides. Improvements in farm equipment and in livestock and poultry breeding, along with better nutrition and veterinary health care of farm animals, all led to higher farm productivity. Increasingly, crops were produced in more specialized monocultures. The use of specially bred, commercially produced hybrid seeds increased as well, so that by the early 1960s, more than 95 percent of all U.S. corn acreage was planted with hybrid seed.[7]

During the 1960s scientists introduced varieties of wheat, rice, and corn that produced much higher per-acre yields than traditional varieties. These new varieties were dramatically increased production in America, but they rapidly diffused to Third World nations, which needed higher crop yields to feed their growing populations. This effort, part of an international effort involving the United Nations, the World Bank, and many governmental and philanthropic organizations, has been called the Green Revolution.[8]

The Green Revolution was an intensive plant breeding program that relied on brilliant applied science, and some luck. It was dubbed the Green Revolution to distinguish it from "red" revolutionary politics that appeared to threaten the West as the cold war emerged. It began in the war years (1943) when the Rockefeller Foundation collaborated with the Mexican government to fund a research station in Northern Mexico to develop a high yielding variety (HYV) of wheat. Its director, American agronomist Norman Borlaug, later won a Nobel Peace Prize for his work. The center, known by its Spanish acronym CIMMYT, began releasing seeds to the world in the 1960s. By the 1960s a similar institute to produce HYV rice was founded in the Philippines, with financial backing from the Ford and Rockefeller foundations. After more than 18,000 experiments, it produced a HYV of rice that was more productive because it had shorter stems and would not fall into paddies, was of consistent height so plants did not shade each other from the sun, and was more rapidly maturing.

In 1971, a consortium of the World Bank, various regional banks, charitable foundations, UN agencies, and some national governments created the Consultive Group on International Agricultural Research (CGIAR). It gradually built over sixteen centers that collectively provided a wealth of knowledge about how to improve agricultural productivity. Importantly, CGIAR centers were funded by public and charitable sources, and the sums of money deployed were relatively small, in stark contrast to the 1990s, when private corporations became key forces in biotechnology crop and livestock improvements. In retrospect, the Green Revolution was a stunning technological achievement that dramatically increased per-acre crop yields in America, and also provided a model for how to develop institutions to rapidly diffuse such agricultural innovations around the world.

But, after initial euphoria about the Green Revolution, critics noted the HYVs were sometimes adopted where they were not as ecologically fit as traditional varieties, and as they spread they reduced the genetic diversity of crops that provided some manner of protection against drought and pests. HYV rice, for instance, was susceptible to 150 identified diseases and pests, to which many traditional varieties, developed over centuries, were immune. Hence HYVs required the adoption of a "package" that included not only seeds, but more irrigation, herbicides, and pesticides to compensate for their ecological vulnerabilities. And that "package" often meant that the HYVs could only be adopted by the most successful and largest landowners—who had the money or could obtain loans to capitalize such production. Green Revolution crops disadvantaged smaller and marginal farmers everywhere, who were less able to take risks, had less cash or credit to invest, or had poorer access to water. Thus, the Green Revolution increased social and economic polarization in that it benefited large-scale farmers, rather than poor ones. In fact, Green Revolution crops were likely to increase the disparities of wealth between people and regions in developing nations.[9]

The Green Revolution did increase food production in America and around the world. By the end of the twentieth century, each American farmer was producing enough food for more than seventy people. Less than 3 percent of Americans were living on farms, and only 1.9 million considered themselves farmers, as compared with 23 million fifty years earlier. Over the same period, however, the average size of farms more than doubled, and, coupled with increased production, American farmers were producing enough food to feed the nation and to export to other nations.[10] In fact, American agriculture became increasingly dependent upon food exports to avoid the accumulation of economically ruinous surpluses.

FEEDING THE HUNGRY

In a world literally awash with food, however, not everyone benefited from this remarkable second agricultural revolution—either around the world or in America. In America in the 1950s it was widely assumed that perceived poverty and hunger of the Depression era had been eradicated by a combination of New Deal programs and the postwar economic boom. In the early 1960s, however, serious poverty was "rediscovered" in the midst of that boom. It was estimated that between 22 and 25 percent of the U.S. population was living in poverty.[11] Michael Harrington brought it to the public's attention in *The Other America* (1962). John F. Kennedy made it a campaign issue and a concern and, after his untimely assassination, his successor, Lyndon Johnson, attempted to carry it out with his War on Poverty program.

Lyndon Johnson launched the War on Poverty in 1964, as part of his Economic Opportunity Act. It included the initiation or expansion of a wide variety of programs designed to provide the poor with a safety net of basic income, medical care, food, and shelter, as well as job training and education programs designed to offer an escape from poverty. Other important related pieces of legislation included the Food Stamp Act of 1964 and the Headstart program of 1965, which, by expanding on the School Lunch Act of 1946, emphasized the need for proper nutrition for children. A U.S. Senate Sub-committee on Employment, Manpower, and Poverty investigation, begun in 1967, encouraged the continuation of such programs into the 1970s. In 1969 it provided a graphic televised (CBS) report on the extent of poverty in America called "Hunger in America."[12]

In 1972, Congress passed legislation authorizing the Special Supplemental Food Program for Women, Infants, and Children, or the WIC program, funded and administered by the USDA through state health departments, Native American tribes, and other groups. In 1974, the Food Stamp Program became a nationwide program operating throughout the United States and its territories, based on a uniform set of federal rules. Two major nutrition programs designed especially for the elderly, the Congregate Meals Program and the Home Delivered Meals Program ("meals on wheels") were authorized by legislation in 1972 as an amendment to the Older Americans Act of 1965. All persons over age sixty were eligible for meals from one of these programs, regardless of income.[13]

As a result of these efforts to combat hunger, and with a generally strong economy, both poverty and hunger decreased significantly by the end of the 1970s. The official poverty rate fell from 25 percent of the population in 1959 to under 12 percent in 1979. Thereafter, however, it hovered at about the same level, only to begin to creep up as President Reagan's conservative policies dismantled most of the remnants of the War on Poverty. Poverty and resulting malnutrition continues to disproportionately affect blacks, Hispanics, Native Americans, members of households headed by women, and children.[14] Some of this may be due to historical problems of immigration and Native Americans, and new problems posed by a soaring divorce rate, as well as continuing cut backs in government "safety net" programs, including the food assistance programs noted earlier. It may also be due in part, however, to cultural attitudes about the poor in America.

Hunger in the United States was never the result of insufficient food-stuffs for the total population. In fact, national food production is now at unprecedented high levels, and food surpluses continue to plague the farm economy. It is, instead, a matter of some part of the population regularly having inadequate access to sufficient food. Recent increases in hunger are not solely a result of the policies and priorities of federal administrations, but are also the product of dominant American cultural ideas about poverty, work, and morality. American social Darwinists have long held that "the American cultural system rests on a belief that in this land of opportunity, the individual can and should shape his or her own destiny." Put another way, the poor are casualties not of society but of their own shortcomings. Poverty is a condition of individuals; the poor are poor because they are lazy and won't work. It is up to them to pull themselves up by their bootstraps.[15] This belief has under-scored recent—and popular—attempts to "end welfare as we know it" that was enacted by the Clinton Administration in 1996 (the Personal Responsibility and Work Reconciliation Act, known as PWORA).

As Janet Fitchen has argued, these beliefs about poverty and poor peo-ple shape societal beliefs about what and how poor people should eat. Because the poor have little money, the reasoning goes: "They should eat rationally on a cost/benefit basis, where costs are measured only in dollars, and benefits solely in terms of nutrition. If poor people would eat this way, then surely there would not be malnutrition and hunger in America."[16]

Anthropologist Mary Douglas observed that, unlike other animals, humans choose what to eat, when and how to eat, in what order, and with whom, rather than merely responding to physiological needs alone. As in any society, in America the definitions of acceptable and preferred foods are largely cultural. Contemporary food preferences that lean toward finger foods, fun foods, snack foods, and fast and convenient foods express basic American cultural values. Low-income people express their membership in the society and their adherence to its dominant values through many of the same food choices that characterize the rest of the population. And so they, too, desire and purchase foods with these characteristics. Unlike the well-to-do, who can afford both junk food and nutritious food, the poor can seldom afford both. Thus the effect of heavily promoted but nutritionally deficient junk foods carries a particularly adverse impact on the diet-related health problems of the poor.[17]

THE BIOTECHNOLOGY REVOLUTION

The period beginning in the 1980s and continuing to the present has been marked by biotechnological developments that are often termed revolution-ary. If biotechnology includes selective breeding to develop varieties of crops and livestock, then it actually dates back to at least the 1600s. However, dra-matic changes occurred when, in 1973, scientists cut a gene (a small piece of DNA) out of a cell and spliced it into a tiny bacterial chromosome (plasmid). The ability to specifically cut and recombine genes led to the development of recombinant DNA technology, the so-called "genetic engineering."[18]

The first impact of biotechnology on the food system has been in agri-cultural production from innovations that seek to improve the yield of plant products at the farm level. These improvements are being effected through the development of disease-resistant, herbicide-tolerant, and insect- or virus-resistant plant varieties by selection in tissue culture or by genetic engineering techniques. Hypothetically, these same technologies have been used to develop salt-tolerant, temperature-tolerant, or drought-resistant crop varieties.[19]

Large-scale investments by corporations for commercial applications of genetically engineered plants began in the 1980s, when the U.S. Supreme Court extended patent protections to genetically engineered plants, seeds, and tissue cultures. The Monsanto Company, for instance, developed soybeans with a built-in immunity to a plant virus, that was previously fatal to soybeans. Several companies developed genetically engineered varieties of corn and cotton containing a naturally occurring toxin that minimizes insect damage to plants while dramatically reducing the need for chemical sprays.

By 1999 roughly half of the U.S. soybean crop and about one-third of the corn crop came from genetically engineered seeds. The enthusiasm for genetically engineered crops among American farmers is not hard to understand: because the decreased need for spraying dramatically reduced production costs (for soybeans, from 10 to 40 percent). In fact, while seed companies made money, the biggest winners were farmers, capturing roughly half of the economic benefits. Seed companies got about one-third, and consumers somewhat less.[20]

European farmers stayed away from genetically engineered crops largely because European consumers became frightened of eating them, dubbing them "Frankenfoods." They boycotted genetically manipulated foods, and countries in other parts of the world followed suit. This, in turn, led export-minded companies—Archer Daniels Midland, Gerber, and H.J. Heinz, for example—to either require separate deliveries of the new and older crops or to ban genetically engineered food altogether. At home, such concerns led to a movement to provide food labels with information pertinent to genetic engineering.[21]

Genetic engineering also raises new concerns. For all of its benefits, real and potential, it poses health risks. All foods are potential *allergens* that can

---

THE GREAT FOOD FIGHT OF THE 1990s

The costs of the U.S.-European food fight and genetically engineered foods were not merely hypothetical, nor were corporate reactions merely paranoid. For health and environmental reasons, genetically engineered foods, and particularly beef injected with growth hormones, were banned by the European Union (EU). U.S. and Canadian beef imports were banned. A panel appointed by the World Trade Organization (WTO) found that there was little hard evidence for such fears and ruled in favor of the North Americans. When the Europeans defied the WTO and refused to revoke the ban, the United States imposed 100 percent tariffs on about $117 million worth of EU food imports, including fruit juices, and French mustard and cheeses. Europeans, particularly the French, reacted angrily and symbolically, picketing McDonald's Restaurants and doubling the price of Coca-Cola in places. The food fight became a significant trade war.[22]

cause severe reactions and even death. With such diverse sources of DNA in gene splicing, it is difficult to know exactly what allergens might be in our diet. Without the expensive regulation, separate production from traditional foods, and detailed, yet understandable labeling, it would be difficult—if not impossible—to protect consumers from painful, even fatal, allergic reactions.

There are also ecological reasons for proceeding with great caution about genetically engineered foods. If such crops increase productivity by accelerating photosynthesis, they may also amplify the impact on soil, including the loss of soil nutrients, and thus require more fertilizer and water. That could magnify the current assault on water and soil resources by agriculture around the world. New species would be inserted into natural food chains, predator systems, and mineral cycles with unpredictable results. Moreover, like earlier hybrid crops and new pesticides and herbicides, there is no reason to believe genetically engineered crops would not generate their own productivity-limiting pests and weeds. Critics believe that genetically engineered crops have a built-in "productivity plateau" and by killing nontarget insects and birds, they could further reduce the earth's biodiversity—a consequence of modern agriculture and indiscriminant pesticide use first noted by biologist Rachel Carson's popular work, *The Silent Spring*, in 1962.

Defenders of genetically engineered crops believe these ecological and health fears are greatly overblown. They argue, that the threatened ecological

Genetically engineered food is a promising but intensely controversial issue. Here biotechnology researchers examine experimental plant specimens in a high-technology greenhouse.

disruption posed by such crops pale by comparison with the invasion or introduction of exotic non-native species by humans in the last forty years—having
damage and control costs estimated to be $138 billion a year in the United
States alone. They point out that the health of Americans has benefited in the
past from technological developments in agriculture and that similar results
will result from newer biotechnological products. And, they insist, there is no
scientific evidence that organically grown products are any more nutritious or
safer. Any switch to totally organic production, they assert, would mean as
much as a 50 percent decrease in the world's food production. This would
result in the farming of marginal land, further destruction of rain forests and
other sensitive areas, and increased likelihood of widespread famine.[23]

In one compelling example of how genetically engineered food has a
real potential of improving the nutritional status of the chronically hungry in
developing nations, Swiss scientists announced in 1999 the perfection of
"golden rice." It is genetically engineered rice that contains beta-carotene
(Vitamin A), which could go a long way to address one of the world's major
nutrient deficiency diseases. Three billion people around the world depend
on rice as their major staple, and 10 percent of them risk some degree of

OTHER VOICES: GENETICALLY ENGINEERED FOOD HAS KEY ROLE

Even though too little research has been done to assure the safety of bioengineered foods, the eleventh annual *Human Development Report* of the United
Nations said that the world's richest nations must get over their fears of them if
they want to help eradicate poverty in the world's poorest nations. Crops altered
to produce higher yields could revolutionize farming in Africa, Latin America,
and across the underdeveloped world, the report said. Issued in July 2001, the
report added that the long debate in the United States and Europe over biotechnology "ignores the concerns of the developing world." John Doyle, director of
communications for more than 30,000 restaurant and tavern owners, argued that
we must pursue biotechnology without being hamstrung by the cautions commonly noted. He cites former Senator George McGovern's recent book about
hunger (*The Third Freedom*) that, "as the world moves from over 6 billion today
to 9 billion by 2050, if we fail to make genetically modified foods available to
the world's poor, untold millions will die as a consequence." Genetically modified foods could—without chemicals—resist pests and weeds, save soil and bring
better nutrition. Doyle notes that much of the American food system now contains genetically modified food (corn, soybeans) without a single recorded
instance of damaged health. According to former Senator McGovern, "I have for
years admired the principles and policies of...environmental groups. But I
believe their opposition to biotechnology as the newly emerging handmaiden of
agriculture is both ill-founded and threatening to human survival in the poor
countries of our planet."[24]

THE MAKING OF GOLDEN RICE

In the late 1930s, Ingo Potrykus, professor of plant science at the Swiss Federal Institute of Technology, was thinking about using genetic engineering to improve nutrition among the world's poor. He knew more than most scientists about hunger, because he grew up in war-ravaged Germany, and he and his brothers were often so desperately hungry that they ate what they could steal. About 1990 he met the director of food security for the Rockefeller Foundation, who had identified the lack of beta-carotene in rice as a good project for research, and Peter Beyer, a German biochemist and expert on the beta-carotene in daffodils. With a $100,000 grant from the Rockefeller Foundation, they launched what eventually became a $2.6 million, seven-year project backed by the Swiss government and the European Union. They began by inserting beta-carotene-producing genes from daffodils into "promoters," or small loops of DNA of other bacteria that activate genes. Then they added Agrobacteria to a Petri dish containing rice embryos which they "infected," transferring the genes that encode instructions for making beta-carotene. These genetically engineered plants must be crossbred with strains of rice that are suitable to local growing conditions around the world. By early 2000, they negotiated a deal with AstraZeneca, a London-based firm that holds an exclusive patent on one of the genes they used, to create golden rice. In exchange for commercial marketing rights in the United States and other affluent countries, AstraZeneca agreed to use its financial muscle and legal expertise to help get the seeds to poor farmers in developing nations at no charge.[25]

Vitamin-A deficiency disease. It kills a million children each year, and blinds another 350,000. Proponents view this as the harbinger of a new Green Revolution in which ancient crops would acquire all manner of useful properties: bananas that will not rot on the way to market, corn that could supply its own fertilizer, and wheat that could thrive in drought-ridden soil. As important and hopeful as "golden rice" is, it is the *only* case that we know of in which bioengineered seeds are being made available without the high prices that accompany corporate patents—which in fact makes them unaffordable to poor farmers in developing nations.

THE PRICE OF INDUSTRIAL AGRICULTURE

As in the case of other agricultural innovations, including the advent of agriculture itself, there is a price to be paid for "progress." To begin with, this latest agricultural revolution has contributed to the decline of the family farm.

Wendell Berry wrote eloquently in defense of the family farm. He linked the decline of the family farm to a decline in family values. He argued that "land that is in human use must be lovingly used," and only family farms can be trusted to provide that loving care.[26] But there are other issues as well.

As Jack Kloppenburg observed, "The development of hybrid corn has long been regarded as the supreme achievement of public agricultural science." By 1965 over 95 percent of U.S. corn acreage was planted with this seed. But, whereas, before hybridization farmers reused their seed, thereafter they bought their hybrid seed from seed companies. Hybrid seeds were more productive, but in almost all cases they also required a management system that required greater mechanization and the application of agrichemicals— fertilizers , herbicides, and fungicides.[27]

Farming not only became more scientific, but it also became more dependent on agribusiness, more specialized (monocropping) and potentially more threatening to the land and water table as a cause of erosion and pollution, and more expensive. Those farmers who could afford it did well; those who could not failed, resulting in the declining number of farms and growing size of surviving farms noted earlier. By 1978 the largest 5 percent of landowners owned 75 percent of the land. There were 25,000 superfarms, representing 1 percent of all farms and receiving 66.3 percent of total net farm income. Moreover, fifteen companies accounted for 60 percent of all farm inputs, forty-nine companies processed 68 percent of all the food, and forty-four companies received 77 percent of all wholesale and retail revenues. Clearly, American food production has undergone a fundamental concentration of land and productive assets, which will be discussed further. To quote a U.S. Office of Technology Assessment: the United States is "at the brink of a new scientific revolution that could change the lives and futures of its citizens as dramatically as did the Industrial Revolution and the computer revolution."[28]

Some who did not welcome this agricultural revolution, or who feared its negative aspects, sought alternatives in organic and regeneration farming. Plant geneticist Wes Jackson, at his Land Institute in central Kansas, for example, began conducting experiments in crops and methods that would minimize the high-technology, high-chemical agriculture that is now dominant. His objective is to imitate nature's own solution to food production, as one source succinctly put it. Similar research is being done at the Rodale Research Center in Maxatawny, Pennsylvania, and other institutes, as well as in the nation's leading land-grant universities that have retained agricultural research programs. To date, however, the impact of such research into alternative forms of agriculture has been minimal. The use of diversity and other ecologically based cures for agricultural ills have tended to be popularly viewed as more politically correct than economically viable.[29] We will discuss these initiatives for an alternative agricultural system in more depth later.

SAFEGUARDING THE FOOD SUPPLY AND THE ENVIRONMENT

The dramatic postwar transformation of American agriculture by means of an increased reliance on commercial fertilizers, insecticides, and herbicides, crop breeding, and biotechnology spurred the federal government to pass legislation further safeguarding the food supply. The Poultry Inspection Act of 1957 regulated all poultry products involved in interstate commerce. The Food Additives Amendment to the Federal Food Drug and Cosmetic Act of 1938, passed in 1958, established the *Delaney Clause*, still in use today. The Delaney Clause mandates that "no addition shall be deemed safe if it is found to induce cancer when ingested by man or animal, or if it is found after tests which are appropriate for the evaluation of the safety of food additives, to induce cancer in man or animals." The Food Additives Amendment also prohibited the marketing of any additive until the Food and Drug Administration (FDA), after a careful review of test data, pronounced it safe at the intended levels of use. Data pertaining to safety must include toxicity tests on two or more species of animals.[30]

In 1966 Congress authorized the FDA to set up requirements for complete information on contents in labeling and packaging. The Fair Packaging and Labeling Act went into effect July 1, 1975. It required labeling for any food to which a nutrient was added or for which a claim is made regarding nutritional value. That was enacted over howls of protest from food processing corporations, who claimed that it would bankrupt them.[31]

FAST FOODS, DIET FOODS, AND CONTEMPORARY AMERICAN CUISINE

Three other major developments in the second half of the twentieth century include the proliferation of fast food, growing concerns over diet and health, and a dramatic diversification of American cuisine. The origins of fast food in the prewar period have already been noted. The fast food phenomenon took off in earnest, however, in the 1950s. As the automobile became ubiquitous, especially among teenagers, so too did eating in one's car. Local carhop restaurants appeared to cater to this market, typically serving hamburgers, hot dogs, French fries, and soft drinks. A & W Root Beer was among the earliest of these new eateries, actually establishing the first "drive-in" in Sacramento, California, in 1923. In 1924 it offered the first food service franchises, and by the mid-1930s A & W had about 200 outlets.[32]

The best known fast food chain, however, was the fabulously successful drive-in restaurant begun by Richard and Maurice McDonald. The McDonald brothers opened their first restaurant in Pasadena, California, in 1937. They based the restaurant on the principles of high speed, large volume, and low price. They offered customers a limited menu, and, instead of personalized service and traditional cooking techniques, an assembly line procedure for cooking and serving food.[33]

In the early fifties, Richard and Maurice (Mac) introduced the Golden Arches and decided to sell McDonald franchises. In 1954, when they employed Ray Kroc as their franchise agent, the McDonalds had only one drive-in hamburger stand—in San Bernardino, California. Kroc turned that single restaurant into an empire of franchises. In 1961 Kroc bought out the McDonalds for $2.7 million. Some economic historians argue that Kroc invented little that was new. He took the McDonald brothers' products and combined them with the principles of other franchises, scientific management, and the assembly line. Kroc's genius was in bringing all these well-known ideas and techniques to bear on the fast food business and adding his ambition to turn it into an international business. As George Ritzer put it: "McDonald's and McDonaldization….do not represent something new, but rather the culmination of a series of rationalization processes, that had been occurring throughout the twentieth century."[34] McDonald's was soon joined by the equally successful Burger King and Kentucky Fried Chicken, which employed the same marketing model.

The pace quickened in the 1960s, added to by the success of home food delivery and even greater convenience in the fast food industry. Home-delivered pizza actually began in the 1950s, but it flourished during the 1960s, while deliveries of other foods—Chinese, for example—were soon added. During the 1970s, Wendy's popularized drive-through windows. By the 1990s fast food accounted for 40 percent of the money spent on meals away from home.[35]

Much as in the prewar period, the popularity of fast food has stemmed from the need for reduced time for food preparation, with more women in the work force; a greater number of people who live alone and lack the incentive to cook for themselves; less formal lifestyles; convenience of fast food restaurants; increased amounts of disposable income; and greater opportunities for recreation and travel—to say nothing of reasonable prices and mass marketing to the mass "baby boom" generation of young and healthy appetites.[36]

The dramatic growth in the consumption of fast foods, as well as "ad hoc" meals and snacks, caused concern among health professionals about nutritional quality. Meals from fast food establishments tended to provide adequate amounts of carbohydrate and B-complex vitamins, but they were also generally high in calories, sodium, fat, and cholesterol, and low in calcium, dietary fiber, and vitamin C. Moreover, Americans generally began to question the "implicit, if not overtly articulated ideology of the 1950s that 'more is better' as far as food and nutrition was concerned." Americans rediscovered the nutritional adages presented by Wilbur Atwater and others at the turn of the century. Health professionals, as well as a growing number of consumers, became increasingly concerned over the high prevalence of diet-related chronic diseases and conditions.[37]

The fast food industry has responded to these criticisms by offering such foods as grilled chicken sandwiches, baked potatoes, and fresh salads, among other foods more acceptable to food critics, as well as a decreased reliance on saturated fat. For example, for decades McDonald's cooked its French fries in a mixture of about 7 percent cottonseed oil and 93 percent tallow. The mixture gave the fries their unique flavor—and more saturated beef fat per ounce than a McDonald's hamburger. In 1990, amid a barrage of criticism over the amount of cholesterol in its fries, McDonald's switched to pure vegetable oil.[38]

Diet foods became available during the 1960s, health and organic foods during the 1970s. By the 1980s all three became major staples in the food industry. The food industry developed several low-sugar and sugar-free foods, fat replacements and fat substitutes, with Nutrasweet, Aspartame, and Olestra, for example. In 1977, the Senate Select Committee on Nutrition and Human Needs established dietary goals and guidelines, revised periodically since, to prevent such chronic diet-related conditions as obesity, hypertension, coronary heart disease, cancer, and Type II diabetes. As J.W. Erdman concluded, with publication of these recommendations, the *preventative nutrition era* began in earnest.[39]

Based on the Dietary Goals of 1977, the USDA and USDHHS jointly issued the first edition of the Dietary Guidelines (1980, subsequently revised). In 1982, the National Cancer Institute published an initial report containing related guidelines for reducing cancer risks, and subsequent reports having been consistent with those recommendations. All of this information has been well distributed to the public both by the media and improved package labeling. The Nutrition Labeling and Education Act of 1990, which went into effect in March 1994, represents a response to nutritional concerns. A major premise of the act is that it should assist consumers in maintaining healthy dietary practices. By using the information provided by new and better labels,

---

THE HISTORY OF THE FORTUNE COOKIE

The fortune cookie is not ancient, nor is it authentically Chinese. The Chinese fortune cookie was invented in the United States sometime in the early part of the twentieth century, probably by either a Japanese-American gardener in San Francisco or a Chinese-American in Los Angeles. It may have antecedents among Chinese moon cakes, which carried hidden messages in the fourteenth century, but little else exists to establish authenticity. Whoever invented fortune cookies, they remained regional California oddities until 1948, when a San Francisco truck driver, Edward Louie, devised a machine that automated the formerly labor-intensive process of making the confection. Louie then partnered with a local restaurant that began the tradition of serving the cookies as complimentary desserts and after-dinner entertainment.[42]

consumers should be able to reduce consumption of total and saturated fat, increase fiber intake, and reduce caloric intake.[40]

Finally, significant changes made inroads on the "traditional " American diet, as we described it earlier, that had dominated American foodways for most of the century. Influenced by the large numbers of immigrants from Asia and Latin America, whose meals traditionally emphasized multiple vegetable dishes, plant foods began to play an increasingly important role in the American diet. Meat continued to occupy a central place in the meal, but beginning in the 1970s, the emphasis on red meat, particularly beef, began to decrease. The varieties of vegetarianism gained legitimacy. Traditional southern African American cuisine made a revival, while many more or less assimilated ethnic groups sought to rediscover their native cuisines.[41]

FOOD CONSUMPTION TRENDS: A SUMMARY

Let us summarize these trends in food consumption since the 1940s. To begin with, per capita consumption of animal products in the United States increased in relation to crop products, but not dramatically. Total per capita food consumption has declined since 1945, but the largest share has been taken out of crop products. After a downward trend in the consumption of meat, poultry, and fish between 1910 and 1935, there was a spectacular rise during the remainder of the century. This has been especially true in the consumption of poultry, which, by some measure, now exceeds beef. Consumption of beef grew dramatically from 1950 to 1970, but has since declined as a percentage of all meat, poultry, and fish consumed in the United States. Pork and fish consumption has remained stable.[43]

The decline in beef consumption relative to chicken is perceived health benefits. In fact there appears to be a significant relationship between health concerns about fat and cholesterol and decreases in the past few decades in consumption of milk, beef, pork, and eggs. Although overall consumption of fat increased in the twentieth century, consumption of animal fat declined after 1940 and was surpassed by vegetable oils in 1950.[44]

There was a substantial drop in the consumption of flour and cereal products from the turn of the century to the 1970s, followed by a significant increase in both. Americans are eating more pizza, pasta, pitas, and fajitas, as well as breakfast cereals, particularly those made from oat bran. Once again, this has been attributed to the public's health concerns and their seeking more fiber in their diet. Fiber intake has increased markedly since the late 1970s, but it is still well below the recommendations of the National Cancer Institute.[45]

Per capita consumption of fresh fruit declined from 1900 to 1970. It has increased since then but only to 1950 levels. This has been attributed to the demise of homegrown and home-processed fruit, but there has been a steady increase in vegetable consumption, especially after 1970. Potato consumption has declined markedly, largely replaced by pasta. Even so, potatoes, along with iceberg lettuce remain the two most popular vegetables in America.[46]

Finally, there has been a phenomenal increase in the use of sweeteners. Per capita consumption now exceeds 150 pounds per annum. This trend occurred despite a decline in the consumption of refined cane and beet sugar since 1972. The use of corn sweetener and noncaloric sweeteners has increased substantially.[47]

So, how well are Americans complying with recommended dietary guidelines? *Not well.* Although in recent years health conscious Americans have done better, most Americans have not. During the 1960s, the counter-culture spawned a fad for pure, natural products such as brown rice and herb teas, combined with a campaign against artificial additives. Later, similar movements promoted organic production methods and opposed genetically modified food, but the scientific basis of both, in terms of nutrition and safety, remains controversial.

In the meantime, mean per capita consumption of complex carbohy-drates has risen only slightly, while consumption of sweeteners has risen sig-nificantly. Salt consumption is still high, and fat intake exceeds recommended limits. Calorie intake has remained stable, but Americans are becoming increasingly overweight due to lack of exercise. And since 1940, there has been a marked rise in diet-related diseases like hypertension, cardiovascular disease, and diabetes. If at any time in their existence people ate simply to stock up on fuel, most researchers agree that is no longer the case. As one report put it: "From early childhood food becomes tied up with other things, with love and hate, power and control, with culture, religion, social circum-stances and personal belief."[48] Today, in the United States at least, this "new" reason to eat poses a more serious threat than the "old" reason. The old adage appears to continue to apply: Americans live to eat, rather than eat to live.

POLITICAL-ECONOMY: CHANGING OWNERSHIP AND CONTROL

Technological development and growth in agricultural productivity accompa-nied and perhaps stimulated dramatic changes in the ownership and control of food and agricultural assets—or its political-economy. We now explore the ramifications of these changes in greater depth. We hyphenate the word "political-economy" because economic and political factors are intertwined and hard to separate. Our focus here is on structures and organizations, because understanding the food system means understanding the intercon-nectedness of systems like families, farms, food companies, restaurants, gov-ernment agencies that set food policies, and transnational conglomerates that own and control food companies. Another reason for emphasizing structures and organizations is that technological and productivity change occur in them rather than in individuals.

As we noted earlier, America evolved from an early integrated "seed to the plate" food system into a multistage one with hundreds of firms competing at various stages—because of the specialization of functions in the food system that were characteristic of industrial systems. In that process the farming and food system changed from a relatively open competitive market system to a more integrated one, in which struggles for profits and market control altered the power relationships between farmers, firms, and food consumers. Outcomes were the increased concentration of economic resources, control of the food system, and the ongoing decline of smaller family farms. Overwhelming control of the system gradually passed to larger and larger farms and bureaucratic food companies dominated by a pervasive ethos of rationality.[49] In this context, *rationality* means concerns about the efficient linking of means and ends in the interest of growth and profitability.

The evolving American food system is a particular illustration of the kind of rationality that classical sociologist Max Weber argued to be basic in the evolution of modern Western societies. It promoted scientific and technological thinking, an emphasis on efficiency, and very large, bureaucratic organizations. In that historical process, "modern" social and economic social forms often swamped and out-competed more traditional systems, which had emphasized tradition, belonging, and identity. Within the American food system, such growing modernity and rationalization accelerated after the 1950s, reaching down to the level of the family farm, transforming food distribution and storage processes, and, most recently, the processes involving food preparation in homes and restaurants. Food and prepared meals came to be experienced less as products of the earth and human effort, and more as commodities standardized and packaged for sale.

DOWN ON THE FARM . . .

Like other changes in industrial societies, farms became more specialized, and the declining diversity of crops and livestock produced on farms created greatly simplified agricultural monocultures, amplified by the spread of specially produced hybrid seeds for many crops. As we noted at the beginning of this chapter, the period after World War II was a watershed period when the introduction of chemical fertilizers and synthetic pesticides (introduced as part of the war effort) combined with the spread of productive seed hybrids and with greater mechanization.

It set in motion dramatic changes in how we farm. This included "outsourcing" pieces of work farmers used to do for themselves (like saving back their own seeds, producing their own fertilizer, cleaning and packaging their harvest). But what seemed like a convenience at the time may have boomeranged. Although it first enabled a farmer to increase output, and thus profits, when all the other farmers were doing it, crop and livestock prices began to fall. Ironically, as U.S. farms became more mechanized, efficient, and productive, a self-destructive feedback loop was set in motion. Oversupply and declining crop prices cut into profits and fueled a demand for more technology aimed at protecting their shrinking profit margins. Output increased dramatically, but so did expenses (for tractors, combines, fertilizer, and seed), while food commodity prices stagnated or declined.

On a typical Iowa farm, the farmer's profit margin declined from 35 percent in 1950 to 9 percent today. To generate the same income that farm would have to be roughly four times as large today as in 1950—or the farmer would need a second job. And that's precisely what has happened in most industrial nations: fewer farmers on much larger tracts of land producing a greater share of the total food supply. In such a situation the farmer buys out his neighbor and expands, or risks being cannibalized himself.[50]

As we noted earlier, farmers now constitute less that 1 percent of the entire population. But, the declining number of operating farms has been different for different farm sizes. Most of the decline was in middle-sized farms. Among all farms, the proportion of both large and small-sized farms increased. Small-sized farms are family operations whose members usually hold full-time employment off the farm and maintain the farm after hours or on weekends (sometimes facetiously called "hobby farms").[52]

In the last several decades farmers threatened with bankruptcy sometimes continued as "contract farmers" under terms dictated by an agribusiness corporation. This is sometimes called a "new share-cropping" arrangement.[53] In *contract production* farmers and growers are required to provide the land and buildings and equip them to the contracting firm's specifications, while providing all the labor. They are, in fact, hired workers paid on a piece rate basis. If they contract to raise chickens, they never own the birds or the feed provided and have no knowledge of the genetics or the medications (growth hormones, antibiotics) used in the process. Farmers typically mortgage their

---

AN ENDANGERED SPECIES—NOT JUST IN THE UNITED STATES

In Japan, more than half of the farmers are over sixty-five years old. In the United States, those sixty-five outnumber those under thirty-five by 3 to 1, and when they retire many will leave farms to children who live in cities. In Poland, 1.8 million farms could disappear as the country is absorbed into the European Union—dropping the total number by 90 percent. In Sweden, the number of farms going out of business in the next decade is expected to reach about 50 percent. In the United States, in the states of Nebraska and Iowa, between one-fifth and one-third of farmers are expected to be out of business within two years. [51]

land to raise money to build and equip buildings (which can cost over $100,000 each), with a repayment schedule over a ten- or fifteen-year period, while the contracting firm's obligation goes from one batch of chickens to the next—about six weeks. By the time the buildings are almost paid off, they need to be replaced or modernized, and consequently, growers rarely get out of debt.

In earlier decades, when growers had access to, and bargained with, several contracting firms, they prospered. But as the number of contracting firms consolidated through buyouts, farmers rarely had such choices any longer. Moreover, because of transportation costs, firms will send trucks only 25 to 30 miles from the processing site to deliver feed and pick up poultry for processing. Very few farmers live close enough to more than one processing plant to have an option to choose between different contracting firms. It's "take it or leave it." American agricultural output produced under contract since 1980 has more than tripled, from 10 to 35 percent. In such centralized control of food production, farmers are reduced to hired hands on their own land.[54]

Confined animal feeding operations (CAFOs) also threaten independent farmers and animal producers. In CAFOs, thousands of animals (e.g., hogs, chickens, and turkeys) are crowded in specially designed buildings and, from birth to maturity, are fed specially designed commercial feed to promote rapid growth. When they are large enough to sell they are shipped to the company slaughterhouse (usually owned by the same firm) to be processed for consumers. Animals do not move freely or grow in pastures, hog lots, or barnyards. Their lives are literally spent crammed together eating and defecating. Since animal pathogens spread rapidly in such crowded and unsanitary conditions, the animals are routinely fed or injected with antibiotics, as well as growth hormones. Jane Rissler, a biological scientist, describes a trip to an Oklahoma pork producer's sow operation where "2,400 sows live, breed, and give birth to at least two litters of at least 10 piglets a year—or about 1,000 per week. Three-week old pigs are moved from sow to feeder barns, where they are confined in pens and fed for seven months or so, until they reach a slaughter weight of about 250 pounds."[55]

CAFOs and factorylike dairy farms are spreading rapidly because they are so profitable, compared with more traditional farms. The key to their success is a kind of market concentration pioneered by poultry company executive Frank Perdue. Chicken farming once involved hundreds of thousands of competing small farmers, feed mills, and processors. Today, Perdue and the other poultry titans control every phase of production, from corn and soybean mills that produce feed to slaughter houses that package broilers and fryers for sale. Contract farmers supply the land, build the buildings, raise the birds, and shoulder the risks. Billionaire chicken barons Frank Perdue and Don Tyson, like North Carolina hog tycoon Wendell Murphy, used their market power to drive a million family farmers out of business, including nearly every independent egg and broiler producer in the country. In the past fifteen years the number of hog farms in America dropped from 600,000 to 175,000. Cattle farmers, notoriously independent, have better resisted corporate takeovers, but cattle production is still very concentrated: 2 percent of the feedlots produce over 40 percent of the beef.[56]

Everywhere they are raised, CAFO animals produce cheap meat, but also serious health and environmental problems. Hog CAFOs are probably the most objectionable. North Carolina's hogs, which now outnumber people, produce more fecal waste than all the people in California, New York, and Washington combined. Many industrial pork farms produce more sewage than America's largest cities. While human wastes must be treated, hog waste, similarly fetid and virulent, is simply stored in ten-acre, open-air pits called "lagoons" (such a romantic name!). Stinking vapors from them choke surrounding communities, and tens of millions of gallons ooze into water tables and rivers, causing health hazards and degrading the environment. Such practices have created public health and ecological scenarios reminiscent of science fiction. In North Carolina the festering effluent escaping from industrial swine pens gave rise to *Pfiesteria piscicida,* a toxic microbe that thrives in the fecal marinade of North Carolina and other East Coast rivers. This tiny predator can "morph" into twenty-four forms, depending on its prey species. The "cell from hell" has killed at least a billion fish—so many that North Carolina has had to use bulldozers to bury them beneath the rancid shores of the Neuse River and Pamlico Sound. Scientists suspect that *Pfiesteria* causes brain damage and respiratory illness in humans who touch infected fish or water. In 1998 *Pfiesteria* outbreaks connected with wastes from chicken CAFOs forced the closure of two major tributaries of the Chesapeake River, and threatened Maryland's important shellfish industry. The rivers of Northwest Arkansas are similarly degraded.[57]

Ken Midkiff, a Sierra Club leader from Missouri, who grew up raising hogs on an Illinois farm, had a more earthy way of putting it. "We never worried about the environment impact because there wasn't any. The problem is that nature never intended for 80,000 hogs to shit in the same place."[58]

Massive political contributions from this tiny handful of firms and agriculture barons often allow them to evade laws that prohibit polluting ground water and water tables, and sometimes such contributions garner powerful congressional support. At the same time, across the nation, an impressive coalition of community groups, county zoning boards, health officials, and state environmental departments is emerging to regulate and stop the further expansion of such CAFOs. It will, to say the least, be an interesting political fight in the next few decades.

You would think that such concentration and corporatization among America's farmers have driven the final nail in Thomas Jefferson's vision of a democracy rooted in family-owned freeholds. It is important to note, however, that while they are much fewer and larger, family farms do survive. With the exception of the factorylike livestock and dairy sectors, most of the so-called corporate farms are family corporations rather than agribusiness buyouts, as was once suspected. Indeed, that survival needs explaining, particularly for Marxist scholars who were long curious about the "anomalous" persistence of the family farm under the expanding capitalist juggernaut. Attempting to address this "anomaly," Harriet Friedmann suggested that the flexible cost structures of family farms often enable them to compete with corporate farms having higher and more fixed costs. Her argument could be recast in ecological terms: Family farms have more "generalist" niches in both nature and the economy, while industrial farms are more "specialists." Ecologists consider generalists as more adaptive and more likely to "reproduce" in highly variable and uncertain environments. The rise of large-scale farming changed opportunities and constraints on family farms. Even so, most contemporary American farms continue with a combination of traditional family and industrial organizational characteristics.[59] In one sense, farming is not unique: like other sectors of the economy, small, entrepreneurial firms proliferate and thrive, even in the teeth of the global financial and industrial behemoths.

THE CHANGING FOOD BUSINESS: OLIGOPOLIES

Increases in the scale of production and the concentration of ownership in the American food system is certainly not new, but they have vastly accelerated since the 1950s. Such concentration is not limited to food and agriculture, but is a general trend in the economy. Beyond the farm, we note the growth of huge agribusiness, food-processing companies, food wholesalers and retailers that are the "middlemen" in the market between farmers and consumers. What is new in the post World War II era is their enormous size and growing market control across the whole spectrum of the food system. They have become the dominant players in the food system. They buy raw materials from farmers—usually on their terms. The share of your food dollar that trickles back to farmers has plunged from about 40 cents in 1910 to just above 7 cents in 1997, while the shares going to inputs (machinery, agrichemicals, seeds) and marketing firms (processing, shipping, brokerage, advertising, and retailing) continue to expand. Of the typical dollar spent on a loaf of bread, for instance, wheat farmers get about 6 cents—and you are paying about as much for the wrapper as for the wheat.[60]

Consider such growth in scale and market control, starting closest to you as a food consumer with food retailing and marketing. As large retailing chains like Safeway and Albertson's spread beyond their original locations, increasing the competitiveness of a particular market area, the number of supermarkets declined (by about 10 percent from 1980 to 1991). Increased competition, as well as customers' demands for more services, led to an increase in the size of a typical supermarket as well as the diversification of its products. As you know, such superstores now routinely include self-service and sit-down deli counters, bakeries, and ATM money machines. Some have added postal service, banking, beauty parlors, and enlarged household appliance departments, with the goal of one-stop shopping. While huge, they combine a consumer orientation with scanning technology, knowledge of customer demographics, and control over what products receive and retain shelf space, which gives them greater power in relation to food-processing companies than before.[61]

Moving from the retailers to manufacturers of prepared foods and wholesale distributors of food, you would find that while the diversity of "brands" is very real (and sometimes illusory[62]), their ownership and control is very concentrated. In fact, if you did your homework at the supermarket, you would find that probably a mere half dozen large food-conglomerate companies own, control, and profit most from the thousands of brand names available. Among these are Kraft foods (in turn owned by Phillip Morris), Beatrice, General Mills, and ConAgra.

To get a sense of how great that size and market concentration is, consider ConAgra, which had $24.0 billion in sales, 82,000 employees, and operations in thirty-two countries in 1997.[63] The company owns more than eighty brands—twenty-seven of which have retail sales of $100 million or more each year. Here are some of those brands you may recognize, produced by subsidiaries owned by ConAgra:

- *On the grocery shelf:* Hunt's (ketchup, spaghetti, tomato sauces, etc.), Hunt's Manwich (sloppy Joe's, tacos, burrito seasoning), Hunt's Snack Pack (puddings, fruit snacks, gels), Healthy Choice (prepared and canned food), VanCamp's (canned beans, chili, wieners), Texas BBQ, Peter Pan, Beanie Weenie, Orville Redenbacher's, Act II (popcorn), Chun King, LaChoy (oriental foods), Wesson (cooking oil), Rosarita, Mesa, and Chi Chi's (Mexican food and tortilla chips), Swiss Miss (hot cocoa mixes), Advantage 10 (nutrition bars and beverages), Eagle Mills (bread mixes, flour, grain snacks), Knott's Berry Farm (preserves, cookies, syrups);
- *Processed and fresh meat, including poultry and Kosher products:* Swift and Swift Premium, Armour products, Eckrich (deli products), Healthy Choice, Decker, Cook's, Butterball, Jennie-O (chickens and turkeys), Country Pride (chicken), Longmont, Golden Star, Hebrew National, Galil (Kosher);
- *Frozen foods:* Banquet, Morton, Healthy Choice, Kid Cuisine, Marie Callender's, Chun King, La Choy, Patio, Country Skillet, Inland Valley, Lamb-Weston;
- *Dairy foods:* Reddi wip (dessert topping), Country Line, (cheese), Healthy Choice, Dormans;
- *Specialty products:* Chefs Choice, Budget Buy (aluminum foil, paper

Food is increasingly marketed by huge food retail corporations. Here a supermarket cashier checks out merchandise under the watchful gaze of a young child.

Many foods today are purchased in standard packages with recognizable brand names. Here is a still life including Pepperidge Farm cookies, Dannon yogurt, Coca-Cola diet soda, Apollinaris mineral water, Birdseye green peas, Hellmann's mayonnaise, and Heinz ketchup.

plates), Fiesta (plastic wraps, lawn and trash bags), Sergeant's (pet products), Brute.[64]

In 2000 ConAgra negotiated a $2.9 billion purchase of International Home Foods Inc., a New Jersey-based food company that owns Bumble Bee Tuna, Pam cooking spray, Gulden's mustard, Chef Boyardee canned pasta and pizza kits, and various private label products. International Home Foods controlled six brands that each had retail sales of more than $1 million each year.[65] Food-industry analyst Patrick Schumann, from St. Louis, said he expected other small to mid-sized companies like International Foods to be gobbled up by bigger companies, and that, "If you don't participate in consolidation, you're going to be on the sidelines."[66]

Concentrated ownership and market control goes far beyond owning brand names of food. There are about fifty different kinds of food processors in the United States that buy livestock and crops from farmers and sell them directly to companies that process them for consumption. They include, for instance, processors that mill corn or flour, or produce crushed soybeans, or those that slaughter hogs, beef, and chickens. Though they differ in many ways, they have all been a part of the trend toward market concentration. For instance, for the entire United States in the meat sectors, the four largest firms slaughter 87 percent of beef cattle. Slaughtering hogs by the four largest firms increased from 37 percent in 1987 to 60 percent in 1998. Over half of the broiler chickens (produced for meat) are today processed by the four largest firms, and the largest (Tyson) now produces about one-third of all chicken broilers in the United States. In crop sectors, the four largest firms process from 57 to 76 percent of the corn, wheat, and soybeans in the United States.[67] To recognize the extent of the market concentration in different commodity sectors in the United States, see Table 4.1.

A few of these organizations are cooperatives (for example, Farmland Industries and Gold Kist), the rare descendants of early farmers' protest movements and legislation that encouraged farmer marketing co-ops. Ag Processors is also a co-op (marketing soybean products), but it is a co-op of grain elevator owners, not farmers. Note, however, that overall food processing market is highly concentrated. As shown in Table 4.1 the same few names appear as dominant firms in different markets (ConAgra, Archer Daniels Midland, Cargill). As of 2001, IBP is nearly bankrupt and a couple of other packing company giants, including Smithfield, are negotiating to buy it.

Here again the situation is like the narrow opening of an hourglass that controls the flow of sand from the top to the bottom is an apt metaphor. The small number of food processing firms are positioned between the thousands of producers (farmers) and the literally millions of food consumers in the United States and the world. Their control of respective markets is so great that, compared to more competitive markets, they have an overwhelming influence on the quality, quantity, type, location of production, and prices

TABLE 4.1   The Four Largest Commodity Processors and Percent of the Market They Control

- **Broilers (meat chicken):** *55 percent of production* by Tyson Foods, Gold Kist, Perdue Farms, ConAgra
- **Beef:** *87 percent of slaughter* by IBP, ConAgra (Armour, Monfort, Swift, Miller), Cargill (Excel), Farmland Industries (National Beef)
- **Pork:** *60 percent of slaughter* by Smithfield, IBP, ConAgra, Cargill
- **Sheep:** *73 percent of slaughter* by ConAgra, Superior Packing, High Country, Denver Lamb.
- **Turkey:** *35 percent of production* by ConAgra (Butterball), Wampler Turkeys, Hormel (Jennie-O)
- **Flour Milling:** *62 percent of milling* by Archer Daniels Midland, ConAgra, Cargill, Cereal Food Processors.
- **Soybean Crushing:** *76 percent of processing* by Archer Daniels Midland, Cargill, Bunge, Ag Processors
- **Wet Corn Milling:** *75 percent of milling* by Archer Daniels Midland, Cargill, Tate and Lyle, CPC

Source: Adapted from Heffernan, W. (1998). Agriculture and Monopoly Capital, *Monthly Review*, 50, 3, p. 50.

throughout the entire food system. In economic terms, it is an *oligopoly* or near oligopoly, meaning market conditions in which sellers are so few that the actions of any one of them can materially affect the prices and costs that competitors (and customers) must pay. At the very least, oligopolies limit the role of competition in free markets to send realistic signals about production costs, prices, and consumer demand—long ago discussed by Adam Smith, the founder of modern economics, supported by most Americans and particularly by the business community itself.

Economists recognize two different forms of such market control or "integration" (the technical term or euphemism for it). *Horizontal integration* is accomplished through building new facilities, acquisitions, and mergers with firms at the same level or stage of production in the food system. So far, we have discussed horizontal integration, such as processing chickens to sell or acquiring retail brands. But often firms are powerful in different sectors at the same stage in the economic process, such as processing beef, pork, chickens, turkeys, and seafood. Then they can achieve enormous advantages by cross-subsidizing products, selling some low or at a loss, while making higher profits on others. Industry spokespersons often describe this to consumers as competition between different kinds of products (pork vs. beef), when in fact the same conglomerate is using such differences for its own purposes, like building demand to raise prices in the future or driving competitors out of the market.

Another kind of market control is *vertical integration,* when firms increase control and ownership of a number of different stages of production in the food system. Feed grain, for instance, is very important to produce livestock. So Cargill, one of the world's three main traders of grain, became (in 1998) the second largest animal feed producer, and also one of the largest processors of hogs and beef.

Consider what this really means by imagining that you are a farmer. Do you want to buy seed to grow corn? If Cargill is the only buyer of corn in a hundred-mile radius, and if Cargill is only buying a particular Monsanto variety for its mills, then if you don't plant Monsanto's seed you won't have a market for your corn. Need a loan to buy seed? Go to Cargill-owned Bank of Ellsworth, but be sure to let them know which seed you'll be buying. Also let them know you are buying Cargill's fertilizer. But once the corn is grown, suppose you don't like the idea of selling to Cargill at their prices. Well, maybe you could feed corn to your pigs, then sell them to the highest bidder. No problem—Cargill's Excel Corporation buys pigs too. At some point suppose you are giving it all up to move to the city to find a better life. You will still need breakfast. Good news: Cargill Foods supplies corn flour to the top cereal makers of all the big brands of Corn Flakes, which all cost about the same price. After all, they were made in the same oligopolistic food system.[68]

Things have been tough "down on the farm" at many times, but farmers' loss of control of their fates is perhaps more complex now. To put the whole picture together, and summarize the main point we have been developing, consider, as shown in Table 4.2, the pervasive oligopolistic nature of the whole commercial American food system from the farm to the supermarket, with some mention of the world.[69] We focus in particular on the role of ConAgra, not because it is better or worse than other such firms, but because there is a lot of public information available about it, and because it grew dramatically in recent decades from a small grain company in the Midwest to one of the world's largest food conglomerates.

GOVERNMENT AND FOOD

So far, we have mainly discussed the economics of the food political economy. What about politics and government? They have, in fact, been deeply involved in the whole process. A "farmer's lobby" to stimulate government action for threatened farmers emerged from the agrarian reform movements of the late nineteenth century. Some of the market concentration described earlier has a significant history: Wilson, Armour, and Swift dominated pork and beef slaughtering at the dawn of the twentieth century. As with other sectors of the American economy like steel and oil, trends toward monopolies with market control and price fixing generated considerable protest, and a powerful political Progressive movement that elected President Theodore Roosevelt. It eventually passed antitrust legislation declaring such monopolies illegal. Opposition to exploitive labor practices and the absence of sanitary standards of the big meatpacking companies in the Chicago stockyards inspired Upton Sinclair's widely read *The Jungle* (1906) and led to the passage of the first Food and Drug Act in 1906. Moreover, their collusion to establish monopoly prices was largely responsible for the creation of the Packers and Stockyards Agency

TABLE 4.2   Food Oligopolies: Vertical Integration, Horizontal Concentration, and Global Presence

| Key: | ↓ | Vertical integration of production links, from farm to supermarket. |
| | ↔ | Horizontal concentration within a link |

INPUTS	↔	3 companies dominate N. American farm machinery mkt.
Distribution of		6 companies control 63 percent of global pesticide mkt.
Chemicals, Machinery,		4 companies control 69 percent of N. American seed corn mkt.
Fertilizer, and Seed		3 companies control 71 percent of Canadian nitrogen fertilizer. **ConAgra** distributes all these inputs and is in joint venture with DuPont to distribute its biotech high-oil corn seed.
	↓	
FARM	↔	The farm sector is rapidly consolidated as farms "get big or out," but others contract with **ConAgra** and other conglomerates to produce for them. The number of farmers rapidly declines in all industrial nations.
	↓	
GRAIN COLLECTION	↔	A proposed merger of Cargill and Continental Grain will control half of the global grain trade; **ConAgra** has one quarter.
	↓	
GRAIN MILLING	↔	**ConAgra** and 3 other firms account for 62 percent of the N. American market
	↓	
PRODUCTION OF	↔	**ConAgra** ranks 3rd in cattle production, and 5th in broiler
BEEF, PORK, TURKEY,		chickens; **ConAgra** Poultry, Tyson Foods, Perdue, and
CHICKEN AND SEAFOOD		three other companies control 60 percent of U.S. chicken production
	↓	
PROCESSING OF	↔	IBP, **ConAgra**, Cargill, and Farmland control 80 percent of U.S.
BEEF, PORK, TURKEY		beef packing; Smithfield Foods, **ConAgra**, and 3 other
CHICKEN AND SEAFOOD		companies control 75 percent of U.S. pork packing
	↓	
SUPERMARKETS	↔	**ConAgra** divisions own Wesson oil, Butterball turkeys, Swift Premium meats, Peter Pan peanut butter, Healthy Choice diet foods, Hunt's tomato sauce, and about 75 other brands.

Source: Adapted from Halweil, Brian (2000). Where Have All the Farmers Gone? *Worldwatch*, 13, 5, p. 20.

of the U.S. Department of Agriculture (USDA) in 1921 to monitor predatory practices.[70]

While actual monopolies were forever banned and oligopolies made illegal, "near oligopolies," such as those noted earlier that skirt the legal definition (control by four firms) proved much harder to regulate. The regulatory mandates of government officials proved fragile when faced with the political and lobbying clout of big companies—often major sources of taxes and jobs in local communities. Furthermore, they became less effective because of the lack of manpower in federal and state agencies to effectively monitor and regulate abuses of the antitrust and food safety laws. Although the resources for monitoring legal infractions are quite thinly spread, the costs of getting caught are quite high (both in terms of fines and bad public relations), and most food companies have incentives to avoid obvious violations that attract regulatory attention.

As the twentieth century went on, the number of farmers dwindled, and their lobby (or "Farm Bloc," as it was called) was a less coherent political force. But commodity producers' organizations, mainly representing the interests of very large producers, began to lobby effectively, as did the emerging large food-processing and agribusiness firms. The great depression of the 1930s reshaped food problems: prices were too low to make a profit and incomes too low to purchase food. But the Agricultural Adjustment Act (1933), part of President Franklin Roosevelt's New Deal, did not protect consumers, farm workers, or small farms. Price supports mostly favoring large-scale farmers were its main policy outcome, resulting from the influence of pressure by groups like the Farm Bureau. The Federal Surplus Relief Corporation was later renamed the Federal Surplus Commodities Corporation, clarifying its mission to support commodity prices and giving relief a lower priority.[71] The main thrust of agricultural legislation during the Great Depression, then, was to support farm prices, and only secondarily to provide food for the needy.

After the Great Depression ended, food producer groups continued to attempt to influence national food policies by lobbying, but also in other ways. For example, producer interests became involved in the actual mechanics of legislation for the Food Stamp Program, a response to poverty in the 1960s. Ambiguity in how to "flesh out" the legislation gave top USDA officials lots of administrative leeway, and they "considered their primary constituency to be farmers; the clientele for food stamps (poor people) were of peripheral interest to them."[72]

Each year, various food commodity legislative proposals are grouped into an annual overall "farm bill" proposed for legislative action by the president and the USDA. Such farm bills are enormously complex, containing sections about commodity price supports and production limits that support agricultural prices, soil and water conservation policies related to agriculture, and agricultural research and services related to the whole gamut of entities in the American food system, from small farmers to consumers.

All observers agree that, in spite of the rhetoric of supporting family farms, USDA policies and subsidies have overwhelmingly benefited the interests of large-scale producers and agribusiness firms rather than small farmers, the environment, or consumers. The principle was always the more bushels you grew, the more help you got. Illustrations include developing more productive seed hybrids that benefit monocrop production and encouraging the use of inputs like fertilizers and pesticides, establishing "grades" of meat and regulatory procedures that benefit meat processors, or developing tomatoes that maintain their taste while being shipped long distances. A more recent illustration includes support for, and weak regulation of, genetically altered crops, for which corporations hold patents, though most of the financial support for their development comes from private corporations.

As we noted, the Farm Bloc no longer dominates the crafting of agricultural legislation, and its power continues to decline as rural areas continue to lose population. Congressmen from farm districts increasingly rely on support from urban coalitions, which provide votes in exchange for supporting urban and consumer interests. Commodity producers increasingly protect their interests with promotional and advertising campaigns stressing the healthfulness of milk, beef, pork, and so on. More important for food policy, the economically powerful food-processing sector multiplied the number of groups attempting to influence agricultural legislation. While the decline in the number of farms and farmers continues, the number of interest groups related to food and agricultural production, processing, distribution, and consumption has continued to rise. In 1965, more than 150 groups commented on the proposed Food and Agricultural Act; by 1985, 215 organizations "expressed concerns" about the 1985 farm bill.[73] State and federal regulatory agencies can become "captured" (the term political scientists use) when they wind up representing the interest groups they were intended to regulate in the first place.

Having said this, it is important to note that departments of the executive branch of government like the FDA and the USDA do have abstract areas of legal concern—like the safety of food and drugs and agricultural problems and progress. But, in responding to public needs and congressional groups, they attempt to address so many demands of such diverse interest groups that incoherent and contradictory policy outcomes are almost certain. In crafting legislation, the USDA, for instance, attempts to include and reconcile (with limited budgets and manpower) the needs of threatened farmers, commodity producer groups, agribusiness firms, and groups representing environmentalists, labor, and consumers. Rather than a conspiratorial collusion between the USDA and particular interest groups, those with the most money and most effective mobilization get a large share of the policy benefits. Consumer groups usually have smaller budgets than producer or industry groups and have usually achieved their aims only through mobilizing public opinion or through the legal system.

While not the prime mission of agricultural policy, consumer health and food safety issues remain important. For instance, complaints by producer groups about the USDA/HHS "food pyramid" delayed its release by a year. Beef and dairy groups apparently viewed the pyramid as a threat to consumption of their products. To counter it, the Beef Council produced a poster for schools that unpacks the pyramid, placing the various food groups in simple descending order. The poster suggested that the foods at the top were of highest nutritional value. A piece of red meat sat at the top of the list! In spite of this, we now have a food pyramid, as well as nutrient labeling of prepared foods, developed over similar objections.[74]

Similarly, food safety nags at food companies and restaurants, and some fear the consequence of food-poisoning scandals for profits. In 1999 hamburgers sold to customers in the Seattle area and traced back to a packinghouse in Nebraska caused widespread painful food poisoning. A failure of routine safety procedures at the plant allowed tainted frozen meat to be shipped to the West Coast, and both the hamburger chain and the packinghouse are now out of business. Such problems are rare but important because they affect public trust in the food system. USDA industry food-safety proposals to address such problems remain controversial. Food companies and others have attempted to shift the responsibility for food safety on to the consumer, arguing that it is currently impossible for meat processors to completely eliminate the risk of food-born pathogens.[75]

Among the most current food-safety agriculture issues in the news around the nation are issues surrounding the proliferation of new, large corporate confined-animal-feeding operations (CAFOs). They involve the USDA and issues about unfair competition and price fixing of animal production, as well as the EPA and state environmental-quality agencies concerned about the prodigious amounts of pollution and wastes generated that affect air and water quality. CAFOs also involve community groups concerned about noxious odors close to residences, health officials concerned with real hazards to public health, nutritionists and physicians concerned about the routine use of hormones and antibiotics to boost animal growth, and animal rights groups concerned about the treatment of animals. The issue usually engages business groups and Chambers of Commerce promoting economic and business growth.

Similar issues surround genetically altered crops. Further examples would illustrate the same point. For governments to form coherent food and agricultural policy in the broad public interest is never simple or easy.

GLOBALIZATION : THE EVOLVING WORLD FOOD ORDER

Huge oligopolistic food organizations not only shape the American food system but also that of the entire world. As scholars use the word, *globalization* means the world is not only connected by international trade, but also by production processes that take place in different firms in different countries under the direction of an overarching parent organization. Transnational companies (TNCs) involve many different companies spread across many different countries. For example, in 1992 Klyveld Mair Goerderier, based in the Netherlands, had 498 affiliates in other nations; Citicorp, a U.S. banking firm, had 240 foreign operations.[76]

From the early modern period (in the 1500s) contacts between people around the world were politically governed as colonial relations by European and North American colonial powers. But as the colonial system ended, international relations were gradually transformed into a world market economy of trade increasingly dominated by TNCs. There are TNCs headquartered not only in the United States and Europe but also in some Asian nations like Japan and Korea. Scholars have followed the rise of TNCs with concern because of the implications of increasing oligopolistic control over the world's resources and over democratic control of national economic and social policy. Harriet Friedmann, for instance, documented the rise of a *world food order*, controlled by a small number of large-scale industries that control food reproduction, processing, and distribution.[77] Food and beverage processing is an area of much TNC activity, through such companies as United Brands, Cargill, ConAgra, Del Monte, Archer Daniels Midlands, Heinz, and Coca-Cola. Governments as well as newer multilateral treaty agreements play a "supportive role" that is sometimes regulatory, but often promotes the expansion of TNCs.

Even policies advertised as in the interests of farmers—like liberalized trade in agricultural products that increases the flow of food commodities around the world—are increasingly shaped by nonfarmers, food traders, processors, and distributors. Such groups were, for instance, among the architects of the General Agreement on Trade and Tariffs (GATT) that has been evolving since 1942, now replaced by the World Trade Organization (WTO). Before the WTO, many countries had laws and tariffs to assure that their farm-

THE GLOBALIZATION OF SUSHI

The sushi market has undergone a vast globalization. The Japanese demand for bluefin tuna now supports an industry that stretches from Japan to small-scale fisheries off New England and enormous Spanish tuna pens near the Strait of Gibraltar. The vast industry combines intense international competition and thorny environmental regulations with centuries-old practices and high technology. In the tuna farm off the coast of Cartagena the waters and workers are Spanish, but almost everything else is part of a global flow of techniques and capital. Financing is from major Japanese trading companies. Japanese vessels tend the nets with aquaculture techniques developed in Australia. Vitamin supplements from European pharmaceutical giants packed into frozen herring from Holland are heaved over the gunwhales for the tuna. Computer models of feeding schedules, weight gains, and target prices are developed by Japanese fishery technicians and scientists. The culinary demand for sushi has also become global. It's not just cool but popular. Bluefin tuna (once primarily sport fish and cat-food fodder) now brings a wholesale price of $34 per kilogram. Globalization aside, sushi remains a thoroughly Japanese undertaking, as restaurants demand "authentic" sushi chefs, and Japanese buyers worldwide instruct the locals on the "proper" culinary techniques.[78]

ers wouldn't be driven out of their own domestic markets by predatory global traders. But freer trade in agricultural commodities means that as agribusiness TNCs slide around the planet, buying at the lowest possible price and selling at the highest possible price, every farmer on the planet is (theoretically) in competition with every other one. Under the 1994 GATT agreements, for example, it was estimated that by the year 2000, U.S. corn exports would undercut Philippine corn prices by 20 percent. That would threaten a half million peasants, by reducing incomes by about 15 percent—and result in higher costs for education, increased reliance on child labor, greater nutritional problems, and increased pressure for women to work outside their homes. Comparatively speaking, the average subsidy to U.S. farmers and grain traders, is about 100 times the income of a corn farmer in Mindanao, an island in the Philippines.

Free trade agreements, like the North American Free Trade Agreement (NAFTA), mirror the WTO's consequences for farmers in the developing world. In Mexico, for example, about 2.5 million households engage in rainfed maize production producing 2 or 3 tons per hectare, compared with 7.5 tons per hectare in the American Midwest—often with the benefits of irrigation, inorganic fertilizers, and pesticides. With an estimated 200 percent rise in corn imports under NAFTA's full implementation by 2008, more than two-thirds of Mexican corn production will not survive the competition.[79] What happens to the Mexican farmers increasingly driven into poverty and bankruptcy?[80] Many will pull up stakes and move to the slums of Mexico City or, perhaps, as migrants (legal or not) to El Norte, and the cities of Texas, California, or perhaps to the meat packing plants in Omaha, Nebraska.

The U.S. government has promoted the globalization of food as well. Depression era USDA price supports of the Agricultural Adjustment Act set domestic price supports above world market prices in order to shelter local farmers from cheap overseas imports. This led farmers to overproduce, and the government tried for years to dispose of these surpluses in school cafeterias and overseas food aid "giveaways," which added to the plight of foreign farmers! The 1973 farm bill removed production constraints and encouraged commercial exports by subsidizing both farmers and exporters. Cargill and Archer Daniels Midlands prospered under this "Export Enhancement Program." In the 1950s, developing nations were importing about 10 percent of their wheat, but by the 1980s that figure had risen to 60 percent. American agriculture had, meanwhile, become highly export dependent for its viability. By 1994, U.S. agro-exports accounted for 36 percent of the global wheat trade, 64 percent of the corn, barley, sorghum, and oats, 40 percent of the soy beans, and 33 percent of the world trade in cotton. These changes have not benefited American farmers nearly as much as they have tightened the grip of the food companies, domestically and globally. In 1994, for instance, 50 percent of American grain exports where shared by two companies: Cargill and Continental.[81]

It is important that you hear what we are not saying. There is no "grand conspiracy" among agribusiness firms or governments to deliberately impoverish farmers or ruin domestic food markets in developing nations. It is, rather, a case of agencies, be they TNCs or governments representing them, using their considerable assets and power in trade negotiations and multilateral agreements to promote their own interests in an emerging global food regime. If the losers of this are the Mexican and Philippine corn growers and displaced rural migrants around the world, the beneficiaries are agroindustrial firms and, secondarily, American farmers and food consumers. Consumers benefit from the ability to purchase cheap winter vegetables, sweetener for their Cokes, or hamburgers at Burger King for bargain prices. Nor is such food globalization uniform. It proceeded rapidly in the 1960s and 1970s, but at a slower pace in the 1990s, when Third World debt and economic problems made penetration by TNCs less lucrative. In the 1990s, with the exceptions of China and Asian nations, most food company mergers, acquisitions, and profits occurred within the United States and Europe. Both Japan and Europe have invested heavily in the United States, because of its favorable monetary climate.

Even so, globalization has meant that developing nations are having a lot of trouble competing with large TNCs as they attempt to develop (or preserve) their own domestic food-producing capacity. Local farms producing for local markets are becoming unprofitable. Hunger is becoming concentrated among people and in areas that used to be poor but at least self-provisioning in terms of food. Cheap, highly subsidized, food from the United States and Europe coupled with efforts of developing nations to develop industry while ignoring agriculture is reducing the demand for local products. This combination of factors has driven many indigenous producers out of business and into work for wages in factories. Thus, in the global order, wheat has become the means of proletarianization.[82]

SO WHAT?

You may be thinking: *"What difference does all that make?"* To address that question, we start with those consequences close to us as individuals.

The technological and political-economic changes in the food system since World War II taken together are—from one perspective—a simply stunning achievement. Consider what was available to urban American families in 1939. Canning and the use of refrigeration to store and transport perishable food were well established, and frozen foods were just beginning to reach the retail level. But there were barriers, because the freezers of home refrigerators only held four ice cube trays. In cities, neighborhood food lockers, where you could keep your frozen foods in the neighborhood, were a popular small business. There was no fresh seafood more than a hundred miles from the coast.

If you observed it and abstained from meat, Lent was hell! Fresh oranges, lemons, apples, and vegetables were available only when locally in season and you enjoyed them when you could.[83]

Later on larger home refrigerators and freezers made it possible for families to keep and store significantly more perishables and frozen foods. These changes paralleled the growth in size of retail stores and the diversity of foods available. In 1916 grocery stores sold about 600 items, while today supermarkets offer thousands, as well as many nonfood items.[84] Though vegetables and fruits are still fresher and tastier in season, *seasonality* is gone, and the importance of location in marketing food is considerably diminished. Even in the "dead of winter" Americans can purchase fresh tomatoes, apples, lettuce, bananas, or oranges, far from where they are grown, and mangoes, papayas, and star fruit from even more distant and exotic places. The same is true of having fresh (or frozen) beef or chicken, as well as Gulf shrimp, Atlantic salmon, and seafood from ocean fisheries around the world. The supply and diversity of foods available without regard to season or place or origin to North Americans is truly unprecedented in human history—as it is for others around the world with sufficient income to be world-scale consumers. It is also a significant benefit that the building blocks of healthy diets are all around us, whether or not we choose to avail ourselves of them.

Furthermore, throughout this transformation, American food remained relatively cheap in relation to food in other places and times. During the twentieth century, industrialization and economic growth, though uneven, resulted in higher family incomes. As a result the proportion of family income spent on food fell, as incomes rose (known as Engel's law). Historically Americans spent about one-third of their incomes on food, but by the early 1990s food expenditures were about 20 percent of household incomes.[85]

Perhaps as important, as incomes rose the composition of our diets changed. Meat, fat, fruit, and vegetables played a more prominent role, while complex carbohydrates from grains or fibers declined dramatically. These trends occurred not only in the United States, but also around the world, as economic growth occurred.[86] As we noted earlier, Americans were eating healthier diets in 1909 than at any time since, including today. They were unwittingly following modern dietary guidelines.[87] Since then, the general trend has been one of the overconsumption of fats, sugar, and corn sweeteners and underconsumption of complex carbohydrates. Combined with more sedentary urban lifestyles, this diet has resulted in the growth of obesity as a serious public health problem—considered in the next chapter.

Beyond consumer choices, there are health concerns about industrial-style food growing and processing, in spite of oversight by government agencies. In 1998 the FDA reported that over one-third of the food that they tested had remaining pesticide residues classified as "carcinogenic." As we noted earlier, an intense controversy exists about the safety of food with such residues. They are present in small concentrations (parts per million), but their damaging effects accumulate over long periods of time. The Consumers Union reported tests of apples, grapes, green beans, peaches, pears, and winter squash having high toxicity levels—and some products from the United States tested higher than did those from other countries. Every week the media carry stories about people getting sick from bacteria in food.

It is still true that large-scale food distribution carries risks that contaminants can spread more rapidly. Even so, the detection of trace amounts of food contaminants may be overblown in the popular media (it sells newspapers). Generally, the FDA and USDA have a good record for detecting contaminants and protecting consumers. Researchers from the Centers for Disease Control (CDC) estimated that, at the turn of the twenty-first century, food-born pathogens infected about 80 million Americans and caused over 9,000 deaths. The microorganisms are passed to people from beef, poultry, or pork, and sometimes from cheese, fruit, and vegetables that are carelessly processed. Industry advocates argue that such diseases are caused by the way food is stored and handled in supermarkets and kitchens. That is undoubtedly a cause. But, a portion of food-born diseases are caused by the industrialization of animal production by big companies in CAFOs, discussed earlier, where animals are jammed together in tiny cages or on the floors of poorly ventilated buildings, covered with each other's excrement, and injected with growth-inducing hormones and antibiotics.

The median size of *E. coli* and other disease outbreaks nearly doubled from sixteen to thirty-one people per outbreak between 1973 and 1987, the same period that rapid packing concentration happened. The CDC said that reported cases of illness from *salmonella* and *E. coli* pathogens were ten times what they were two decades ago. Five hundred people die and at least 20,000 become ill from *E. coli* contamination each year. Another 2 million cases of *salmonella* poisoning occur each year, with up to 2,000 deaths. The meat industry disclaims any responsibility, maintaining that they are "natural" occurrences that can best be cleaned up during food preparation. Recent federal meat regulations simply keep contamination from exceeding current average levels.[88]

CAFOS routinely use antibiotics to keep animals disease free while they grow. Scientists know that the regular and routine use of antibiotics causes the antibiotic-resistant strains of germs to selectively survive. Consequently, antibiotics do not have their original effectiveness. Indeed, in the United States infections resistant to antibiotics have become the eleventh leading cause of death. Many reports blame doctors for overprescribing antibiotics to people, but nearly 50 percent of the antibiotics used are routinely given to animals, and we get them "second hand" through eating.

The scariest health threat, however, is the outbreak of "Mad Cow Disease" by which lethal viruses from slaughtered cattle were transmitted to humans in Britain. Scientists believe it is associated with Creutzfeldt-Jakob, a human degenerative brain disease. Cattle are thought to acquire the disease by eating commercial feed containing groundup dead animal parts—until recently a common practice in the United States also. English beef was banned on the Continent, and 4 million English cattle were destroyed because of the fear of infection. In March 1996 the E.U. livestock industry announced a voluntary and partial ban on using dead animal parts in feed, and the FDA proposed a mandatory ban. Eighty people have died from the epidemic in Britain, and three or four in France.[89] A renewed outbreak occurred in France and Belgium in 2000 that resulted in widespread concern about beef consumption.

The defenders of such concentration of ownership of land and productive assets argue that large is more efficient than small. But it may surprise you to know that a wide body of evidence shows that smaller farms are actually more productive than large ones. Every single study made by the USDA found that the most efficient farm, measured in terms of cost-per-unit of output, is a mechanized one- or two-farmer unit, not the largest operations. Any savings associated with sheer size (and there are remarkably few) are quickly offset by the higher management, supervisory, input, and labor costs of large farms. Big farm advantages are always calculated on how much of one crop the land will yield per acre. The greater productivity of smaller farms is calculated on how much total food can be produced per acre. An independent smaller farmer is more likely to polycrop (rather than monocrop)—growing corn, beans, potatoes, and squash perhaps—and using weeds as animal fodder. Such farms produce more food—whether measured in weight, volume, bushels, calories, or dollars.

A SMALL DIVERSE FARM AND PROFITS IN IOWA

Dick Thompson farms a 300-acre farm (small by today's standards) near Boone, Iowa. He rotates corn, soybeans, oats, and wheat interplanted with clover, and a hay combination that includes an assortment of grasses and legumes. The pests that plague neighboring monoculture farms have been less of a problem, because insect pests usually "specialize" in one particular crop. In a diverse setting, no single pest is likely to get the upper hand. Diversity tends to reduce weed problems, because complex cropping uses nutrient resources more efficiently than monocultures, so there is less left over for weeds to consume. Thompson also keeps weeds in check by grazing a herd of cattle, becoming a rarity on Midwestern corn farms, where most cattle are now raised in feed lots. Cattle, hogs, and nitrogen-fixing legumes maintain nutrient-healthy soil. Moreover, Thompson is making money. He profits from his healthy soil and crops, and the fact that his input costs (for agrichemicals) are almost nothing. Thompson is, incidentally, active in an organized network of Iowa farmers promoting similar farms.[90]

Food analysts Lappe and Collins examined the net income per acre ¸, farm size in the United States between 1960 and 1973 and found that in all except two of those fourteen years, modest sized family farms realized higher net income per acre than very large farms. The same pattern holds for developing countries as well.[91] Ecological research found that on average a polyculture with four or five different crop species produces higher yields per unit area than high-input monocultures—by as much as 200 to 1,000 percent greater output per unit of area.[92] Farmers on smaller farms are likely to have greater knowledge of local soil, water, and growing seasons, and their polycrops are more likely to be buffers against plant pathogens as well as the vagaries of price fluctuations of agricultural commodity markets. This goes a long way to explaining what, to some, is the surprising, or "anomalous," survival of such farms that we mentioned earlier. In sum, the taken-for-granted efficiency of large farms is questionable. The largest and most industrialized farms survive because they are often too well capitalized to fail, in spite of their inefficiencies.

Not only are smaller, more diversified farms often more ecologically and economically efficient, but without exception rural communities surrounded by smaller independent farms are economically healthier and more socially vibrant than those surrounded by large farms. Over a half-century ago Walter Goldschmidt, an anthropologist working for the USDA, wanted to see how the size and structure of farms affected the health of rural communities. He compared two communities in California's San Joaquin Valley, similar in all respects except that one was surrounded by small farms, and the other by huge farms—often operated by absentee landlords. He found an inverse relationship between the size of farms and community well-being. The "small farm" community supported more people, had lower poverty rates, more businesses and entrepreneurs (e.g., pharmacies, feed store operators) and had a more vibrant set of schools, churches, recreational facilities, and so forth. Similar findings have been repeatedly replicated throughout the United States and Europe. Sociologist Debra Bryceson, found that in sub-Saharan Africa, "as de-agrarianization proceeds, signs of social dysfunction (such as the crime, hunger, and the breakdown of family ties) accelerates." When the economic prospects of small farmers erode, so do the social fabric of rural communities, with higher rates of unemployment, alcoholism, domestic violence, infant mortality, and malnutrition.[93] Displaced rural people migrate in large numbers to the urban shantytowns with overburdened infrastructures in Third World cities, like Mexico City or Calcutta. Such social costs (usually termed "externalities" by economists) are of only slight concern for large-scale agriculture, particularly agribusiness firms, because their main concern is increasing the wealth of their stockholders.

Turning to other consequences of scale and size, you would think that the "economies of scale" that accompany huge oligopolistic firms could contribute to cheaper food for consumers. There are economies of scale, and benefits do go to consumers—particularly if they are part of a firm's strategy to protect or increase market shares or to enter new markets. But seeing only consumer benefits misses the more basic goals of large private corporations; in the long run such advantages go to company investors and to market maintenance or expansion. Over the century, the growth of real incomes and purchasing power of "middle Americans" are as much responsible for the relative affordability of food as are the advantages of large-scale production. But as things change, the past is a poor predictor of the future. How much (and for whom) will that relative affordability of food be maintained as America evolves into a postindustrial economy that does not routinely produce real increases in living standards?

As a matter of fact, like very large farms, big food processing firms are not very economically efficient without considerable government support. The oligopolization of food processing was only achieved with the acquiescence of governments, and local and state governments showered the meat-packing giants with millions in tax rebates and subsidies. When the Reagan Administration signaled to industry leaders that they could dispense with unions, a packing plant in Storm Lake, Iowa, closed when it could not reach a contract agreement with its workers. After $10 million in local tax subsidies were offered as enticements, IBP reopened the plant, replacing former well-paid workers with low-paid new immigrant workers from Laos, Mexico, and Central America. Production lines were sped up, and injury rates climbed. Although immigration is a powerful controversy in the United States, anthropologist Mark Grey, an expert on the restructured packing industry says: "No one wants to state the truth—that food processing in America today would collapse were it not for immigrant labor."[94] Ironically, as noted earlier, in 2000 IBP itself was nearly bankrupt and being bought by other packing industry giants.

A truly competitive market (with many producers and buyers) sends realistic signals about the costs of production and consumer demand. However, oligopolistic firms have the power and resources to cross-subsidize and operate with little profit or even losses for a time to gain market shares. They have the power to prevent new producers from getting into markets that are "locked up." Competition is intense among the few big players in each market in the United States and around the globe, with government regulation but also much support and subsidy. Among oligopolies, economic and political power, rather than efficiency, rules. This is an ironic consequence of processes that began by rationalizing production in the name of efficiency.

In sum, this chapter has traced the technological and structural infrastructures of the transformations in the American food system since the end of World War II, and by extension, with an emerging world food system. Some positive and negative consequences of that system for food producers and consumers, and the environmental impacts of the agroindustrial system were highlighted. Both health and environmental consequences are discussed further in later chapters. This chapter focused mainly on the American food system; the next returns more directly to eating and changes in American foodways.

SOME SUGGESTIONS FOR FURTHER READING

Atkins, P., and I. Bowler (2001). *Food in Society: Economy, Culture, Geography.* New York: Oxford University Press.

Bonnano, A., W. Friedland, L. Goviea, and E. Mingione, Eds. (1994). *From Columbus to ConAgra: The Globalization of Agriculture and Food.* Lawrence, KS: University of Kansas Press.

Bourcher, D., Ed. (1999). *The Paradox of Plenty: Hunger in a Bountiful World.* Oakland, CA: Food First Books.

Garbaccia, D. (1998). *We Are What We Eat: Ethnic Food and the Making of America.* Cambridge, MA: Harvard University Press.

Hampe, E., and M. Wittenberg (1964). *The Lifeline of America: Development of the Food Industry.* New York: McGraw-Hill.

Jackle, J., and Keith Sculle (1991). *Fast Food: Roadside Restaurants in the Automobile Age.* Baltimore: The Johns Hopkins University Press.

Kneen, B. (1999). *Farmageddon: Food and the Culture of Biotechnology.* Gabriola Island, British Columbia: New Society Publishers.

Kloppenburg, J. (1990). *First the Seed: The Political Economy of Plant Biotechnology, 1492–2000.* Cambridge: Cambridge University Press.

Magdoff, F., F. Buttel, and J. B. Foster, Eds. (1999). *Hungry for Profit: Agribusiness Threats to Farmers, Food, and the Environment.* New York: Monthly Review Press.

Ritzer, G. (1996). *The McDonaldization of Society.* Rev. Ed. Thousand Oaks, CA; Pine Forge Press.

CHAPTER FIVE

Foodways

Eating and Cuisines in America

The last chapter chronicled the recent history and transformation of the American food system that may be called a "second agricultural revolution," including the growth of modern industrial agriculture, and its consequences. Now we continue to explore these consequences, turning in more depth to the social meaning of eating with others and to the relationship between eating, cuisines, and the social order in the contemporary United States—what anthropologists call "foodways." In this chapter four topics are discussed: first, different social settings and meanings of eating with others; second, the ongoing interaction between social forces producing a similarity of cuisines and those preserving or generating diverse eating styles or foodways in the United States; third, the major transformation of foodways

---

ABOUT TERMS

Diet is a nutritional term, referring to the intake of nutritional chemicals like proteins, carbohydrates, minerals, etc., while *cuisine* is a culinary term referring to the a particular styles of cooking and food processing and preparation, along with stoves, utensils, cutlery, and so forth. *Foodways*, a derivative of the anthropological term folkways (or "customs"), refers broadly to the shared cuisines as well as the eating styles, structures, and behaviors common to a group of people. If they have a common culture, people inevitably share foodways.

---

in our times, or the commodification of eating and the emergence of the fast food industry, which sociologists dubbed the "McDonaldization" of society. This discussion is related to a significant countertrend that is its polar opposite: a cluster of food reform movements; and fourth, a discussion of overeating, a major form of "malnutrition American style," and suggestions about addressing this problem.

EATING TOGETHER

Let's start by trying to match the following eating contexts with their appropriate social meaning:

Eating Context	*Social Meaning*
A home cooked meal by candlelight	A first meeting
Sunday brunch	A casual get together
Saturday lunch	Celebration of an ongoing long-term relationship
A cup of coffee	A night of romance
Dinner in an elite restaurant	A business meeting
Lunch at McDonald's	"Getting to know you" better
Co-cooking at his or her house	A first date
Having a drink at a "nice" bar	A routine meal in an extended relationship

What's the point of this exercise? It illustrates that occasions of eating with others have social meanings in context, and that the care and luxury put into eating together symbolizes the relationships among people. Your answers should point to the relationship you associated with various eating social contexts and the degree of intimacy of a colleague/friend/or lover in a relationship. They begin with a cup of coffee (or tea, or a Coke) and progress through a romantic candlelight dinner. They may progress to a co-cooked meal, symbolizing the amount of time, money, and commitments invested in the relationship.[1]

Eating with others transforms biological hunger into indicators of social relationships. To eat together indicates openness and trust of one's fellow human beings. In fact, the word "companion," that connotes friendship, warmth, and security derives from French and Latin words meaning "one who eats bread with another." We previously mentioned the importance of sharing food in symbolizing common religious affiliation and belief, as the dietary restrictions of Orthodox Jews, or in rituals like the Christian Eucharist. On the other hand, refusing to eat with others or showing disdain for their food symbolizes boundaries and differences. These can be interpersonal or based on broader social and cultural differences. In other words, sharing food is a kind of interaction that symbolizes relationships and "in groups," while not doing so symbolizes differences, boundaries, and our definitions of "out groups."

Eating together is particularly significant in those important primary groups in any society that form, stabilize, and support the lives of individuals—families and households. Mealtime provides routine settings for family social interaction, for the coordination of family activities, the sharing of information, and the shaping of selves. Family meals can be important times to enjoy, console, and deepen relationships with others. But they provide opportunities to enact the whole range of family relationships, including making examples of "deviant" family members, infractions by household members (who may be sent away from the table for misdeeds), or demonstrating disgust and independence by refusing to eat or speak. Like most family interaction, meals are settings in which both family *integration* and *hierarchy* are enacted.

Mealtimes are particularly important for socializing young children, who begin life as asocial beings. For them, family meals are among the first settings in which they are required to learn self control and exhibit "proper" social behavior. They gradually learn what foods are tasty or disgusting, not only from their taste buds but by hearing adults comment about them. They learn how to eat (from their own plate, and with appropriate utensils, and when it's okay to eat with their fingers), and other rules of etiquette (about spitting or throwing food, rubbing it in their hair, or other creative ways that young

A family picnic. Eating is not just about getting nutrients into the body, but a setting for many kinds of human sociability.

children explore food). They learn about sharing with others, asserting independence, and about the rules of human conversation—how much to speak and what words or topics are not appropriate for meal times. Through socialization, rewards, and sanctions, families teach members how to communicate, acceptable goals, and acceptable ways to pursue goals, which prepare children to enter school and, ultimately, to function as adults. Mealtimes are ready forums for such socialization.

Some families accomplish these functions of family integration more smoothly and effectively than others. Research about mealtimes found that family meals may become opportunities to play out long-standing disagreements and for family factions to struggle for influence and control. Analyses of dinnertime conversations found that discipline was the second most frequent topic of conversation, and many people report their memories of childhood mealtimes are quite unpleasant.[2] Not all families value interaction at mealtime, some adults use their power to discourage it, and the presence of a TV set reduces interaction.[3] Even so, a study of husbands and wives whose families ate at least one meal per day as a group reported higher levels of family satisfaction, cohesion, and demonstration of affection.[4]

Because eating together has important family consequences, many social commentators have observed a widely intuitive "decline of the family meal" in contemporary America, and hypothesized that it is a cause (or symptom) of the problems of families and people. In 1929, a famous sociological community study of "Middletown" (Muncie, Indiana) observed that, "Morning, noon and evening meals eaten in the home are still the rule."[5] Though that characterization was certainly not true for all U.S. families even then, families and foodways are in the process of major transformations. Many forces combined to change the eating patterns of households, including the growth of dual income families, busy (and sometimes conflicting) schedules of household members, and innovations like microwave ovens and frozen or prepared foods. Other forces thought responsible for the decline include the expansion of the restaurant industry so that more meals are eaten away from home, the growing popularity of ethnic cuisines, and particularly the growth of the fast food industry. These transformed (some argue destroyed) frequency of shared family meals.

There is evidence to support this widely held perception. In the 1990s a national poll of 555 parents with children under eighteen found that one in five families did not have dinner together the previous evening. Another poll of 1,000 people in the Los Angeles area found that one in three households did not eat regularly as a family.[6] But the problem with such data is lack of historical evidence to see a clear trend, or to really understand the significance of these findings. Despite warnings and some evidence, we think that family meals have not disappeared or lost their significance for families.[7] The integrative functions of family meals are best observed at holiday seasons. Meals at Thanksgiving, Christmas, or Passover symbolize family solidarity and some-

WHAT *IS* FOOD?

In no known culture do people consume every potential food that would provide nutrition or calories. Beyond nursing infants, for instance, Asians do not cook with or consume much milk, because of cultural preferences, and also probably because a high proportion of Asians are genetically lactose intolerant. On the other hand, consider that ready and available sources of perfectly healthy protein, insects (locusts, grub worms, some ants, and termites) are not consumed at all by many people around the world—though they are considered delicacies by some. If people around the world consumed insects and other invertebrates like slugs and snails without limitation, and especially if modern methods canning or freezing were applied to them, as has been done to beef or chickens, a protein shortage would not exist anywhere.

times cultural roots. Recipes for turkey, stuffing, cranberry sauce, and Christmas cookies, as well as special foods for Passover and Kwanzaa celebrations fill cookbooks. But as journalist Ellen Goodman said, "The turkey is extra; we really feast on family."[8]

If eating has important consequences for symbolizing the integration and similarities of people as well as the boundaries and differences between

EDIBLE OR INEDIBLE?

One approach to this question describes the process by which people and groups determine what is considered food.

1. *Inedible foods* are not eaten because they are poisonous or because of strong beliefs or taboos. What is inedible varies culturally, and examples include cattle in India, pork among devout Jews and Muslims, and animals that have died from disease or for unknown reasons. The reasons behind food taboos are complex and often unknown.
2. *Edible by animals, but not by me* are food items such as insects (ants) and termites in the United States and corn in France, where it is used only as animal feed grain. These foods vary widely by culture.
3. *Edible by humans, but not my kind* are foods recognized as acceptable in some societies, but not one's own. Examples of such unacceptable foods in the United States are giant snails, eaten in Africa, dog meat in Asia, and horse meat and blood sausage in parts of Europe.
4. *Edible by humans, but not by me* includes foods acceptable by one's group or culture but not by the individual, because of tastes (e.g., tripe, raw oysters, squid), expense, health reasons (a low sodium diet may eliminate many traditional foods), or religious restrictions.[9]

them, what are some of the things that shape which potential foods are understood as edible or inedible by individuals and larger groupings in cultures, nations, and subcultures? To answer this question in concrete historical depth would take volumes, obviously beyond the scope of this book. See the box for one way of at least phrasing the question. More to the point here, what are the sources of similarities and diversity of cuisines among people in the contemporary United States?

AMERICAN FOODWAYS: ASSIMILATION AND DIVERSITY

All modern societies become socially differentiated, and cuisine differentiation often parallels and symbolizes social differentiation. Societies with clearer social differentiation had more differentiated foodways as well. This involves hierarchical differentiation between elites and other classes, and the emergence of elite cuisines versus common meals, dishes, and eating norms. Control of cuisines has been an aspect of the manipulation of symbols that helped to maintain class boundaries.[10] Some societies, such as India, China, and France produced a single high ("haute") cuisine that clearly separated elites from commoners, while others, like England and the United States, with fuzzier class distinctions and more decentralized political power systems, produced far fewer culinary distinctions. Other differences involve ethnicity and region. If the United States is less clearly differentiated in terms of social class than some European societies, it is more ethnically diverse as a "land of immigrants" with their own foodways.

Yet the hegemonic culture is still English in the United States.[11] Furthermore, the United States understood itself as a "unitary nation" quite early in its history, by comparison with Italy, Germany, and Canada, where the notion of a common nation and people came much later. In spite of its immigrant history and regional cuisines, America had relatively strong assimilationist pressures creating common values, behaviors, and identities. Such pressures for assimilation reflected a hegemonic culture, official policies toward immigrant minorities, and public education. Those pressures shaped food as well as other elements of culture. As noted previously, a standard American cuisine emerged. That, stereotypically, included three meals a day, with a breakfast of eggs or cereal, fruit, toast, and coffee; a light lunch of a sandwich, and soup or salad; and a substantial dinner with meat as a central entrée, potatoes and vegetable sides dishes, and a dessert of cake, pie, or ice cream.[12]

Food researchers found impressive evidence for the growth and persistence of such a national cuisine. Through a thorough analysis of American cookbooks published since 1945, Gvion-Rosenberg documented its presence, even while exhibiting the appearance of pluralism. She found that ethnic foods were assimilated or "Americanized" in several ways. Dishes were incor-

A sumptuous "American" holiday meal with roast, corn, beans, and bread on a dining room table set with silverware and china.

porated and presented as American (e.g., macaroni and cheese, apple pie). Foreign ingredients were replaced with local ones, or dishes were invented and granted a culinary affiliation not known in their supposed country of origin (e.g., chow mein, fortune cookies).[13]

Beyond cultural hegemony, structural factors facilitated the assimilation of regional and ethnic cuisines into a national cuisine. Urbanization and intermarriage often blurred ethnic and regional distinctions. Research demonstrated that the importance of ethnic affiliation declined fairly steadily by generation, and that while previous generations successfully passed on food traditions, their authenticity decreased with each successive generation.[14] The growth of national food markets, and the decline of regional ones, was as important. Connected with mass markets was the emergence of large bureaucratic food corporations (like Kraft and ConAgra), and national and regional franchise retail chain stores (supermarkets). These were made possible by innovations in food preservation, processing, and packaging. Tourism, the growth of advertising and the mass media, common socializing experiences in school cafeterias, and the proliferation of similar restaurants in different regions also promoted the emergent national foodways.[15]

Researchers found that regional differences, which were extensive until well into the twentieth century, are now in rapid decline.[16] The forces at work were the emergence of mass markets and a mass society, as well as capitalism that increasingly rationalized the forces of production for profit. Furthermore, the standardization of the American cuisine continues vigorously in the age where fast food franchises continue to sweep the nation (and the world) and comprise a larger share of meals consumed. To get a sense of how extensive this has become, ask yourself where you could go in the United States to a town of 10–20,000 people and *not* find a Pizza Hut, 7-11 Store, McDonald's, or their lookalikes?

But assimilation and the national foodway are only part of the American story, and they interact with powerful forces that maintained and created complexity, diversity, and pluralism. Complete assimilation would have meant the disappearance of each group's distinctive cuisines and foodways. On the other hand, complete separation would mean the ghettoization of cuisines, where each ethnic group would maintain its own set of restaurants, serving its own cuisine with little patronage by nonmembers.[17] Obviously, neither reflects the American reality. Perhaps more than most modern societies, the United States has become a multiethnic society of diverse subcultures held together by common political, economic, and cultural arrangements. Economic class and ethnic distinctions do not neatly coincide, and ethnic communities remain distinct but are incorporated within larger frameworks—as are ethnic cuisines. They are, to be sure, differently incorporated. Some (e.g., French) are prestigious and pricey haute cuisines, while others (e.g., Mexican and Chinese) are often lowbrow and inexpensive. Some commentators suggest that such differences may reflect the racist strains in American culture as well as the colonial experiences of people of color.

Standardized "fast food." A Burger King Whopper and wrapper.

AMERICAN FOODWAYS: ETHNICITY AND SOCIAL CLASS

Ethnicity is surely the most obvious and visible source of diversity among American foodways. It reflects the ever growing *cultural plurality* of the nation, recently driven by increasingly large numbers of immigrant Latinos and Asians.[18] Some of the same structural forces that promote assimilation are, in fact, double-edged swords. Urbanization, while normally associated with the weakening of ethnic identity, also may lead to the residential concentration of ethnic groups facilitating the maintenance of ethnic identity and cuisines. Ethnic foodways are an important part of the maintenance of ethnic identity.

Even this oversimplifies the diversity of cuisines, because "Latino" includes people from such diverse national origins as Mexico, Cuba, Nicaragua, Columbia, and the Dominican Republic. "Asian" similarly represents people from Japan, China, Korea, Thailand, Vietnam, India, and other places, and each group brings a distinctive cuisine. Many represent the "new" immigration after the 1970s, predominantly from Asia and Latin America, in contrast to the "old immigrants" of the late nineteenth and early twentieth centuries, predominantly from Europe. Nevertheless, identity and cuisines remain visible even among "white ethnics" from the older waves of immigration (e.g., Poles, Italians, and Czechs). Alba found that 85 percent of "white ethnics" could identify their ethnic heritage, and most could identify experiences that maintained it. Eating ethnic foods figured prominently.[19] Food writer John Mariani noted that

> ...the U.S.—a stewpot of cultures—has developed a gastronomy more varied than any other country in the world...In any major American city one will find restaurants representing a dozen national cuisines, including northern Italian trattorias, bourgeois French bistros, Portuguese seafood houses, Vietnamese and Thai eateries, Japanese sushi bars, and German rathskellers.[20]

Ethnic communities in the United States are not only growing in numbers and diversity, but also in purchasing power. For instance, while the total buying power of Americans increased by about 41 percent since 1990, the purchasing power of African Americans increased by over 54 percent, and Latinos by nearly 66 percent.[22] At the same time, it is important to note that these ethnic groups have proportionally the highest concentration of the poor and food-insecure people, and that some Asian groups are among the nation's poorest minorities.

With this collective purchasing power, it is not surprising that ethnic cuisines found major market niches in the national food economy. Mexican food, for instance, is the country's fastest growing ethnic food with sales running into the several billions of dollars, and tortillas now outsell bagels and English muffins.[23] To some extent, the explosion of interest in ethnic cuisines is driven by the needs of the fast food industry for market expansion. Much of the demand for tortillas, for example, derives from the fast food industry's need to expand its repertoires. Ethnic groups, particularly recent immigrants,

DIPPING INTO THE MELTING POT

The American "melting pot" never completely melted into a uniform broth. Ethnic cuisines are distinctly recognizable "chunks" in a stewpot. Try a three-way match: the name, its description, and the ethnic cuisine from which it derives:

Burritos	Chilies Rellenos	Dim Sum	Chitlins
Schmaltz	Kasha	Jicama	Grits
Kashrut	Glutinous rice	Soul Food	Chorizo
Queso blanco	Bok Choy	Matzo	Gefelte fish
Rice Sticks	Mantou	Sopa	Lox
Hominy			

1. A chopped fish mixture, unleavened bread crumbs, eggs, and seasoning.
2. A vegetable with broad white stalks and dark green leaves.
3. Roasted mild chili pepper stuffed with cheese, dipped in egg batter and fried.
4. Rice or pasta that is fried and cooked in consomme.
5. Smoked salmon.
6. Spicy beef or pork sausage.
7. Coarsely ground corn meal with the fleshy party of kernel removed.
8. Warm flour tortillas stuffed with a mixture of meat, beans, and avocado.
9. Steamed bread or rolls.
10. A term coined in the 1960s to promote ethnic pride or a particular group.
11. Cracked barely, millet, or wheat that is served as a cooked cereal or potato substitute.
12. A cracker-like unleavened bread, often eaten at religious holidays.
13. A crisp root vegetable, always eaten raw, as popular in its native country as potatoes.
14. Religious rules about which foods are fit to eat.
15. Soft white cheese made of part-skim milk.
16. Short-grained, opaque, white rice that turns sticky when cooked.
17. Chicken fat.
18. Pig intestine.

A. Jewish
B. Mexican
C. Italian
D. African American
E. Chinese[21]

represent "uncaptured" market segments. Many decisions about what foods are grown or imported, what new items are developed, how foods are marketed, even what menu items are available at public institutions and restaurants are often dependent on the preferences of the target population.

Furthermore, U.S. consumer demands for "bold new flavors" mean that

A West Indian restaurant beside a Burger King below a palmist shop at a busy corner on West 14th Street in New York City.

ethnic cuisines are growing in popularity, perhaps even becoming faddish. During the 1980s the restaurant business increased customers by 10 percent, but Italian, Mexican, and Asian restaurants increased by 26 percent, 43 percent, and 54 percent respectively. The National Restaurant Association found that in 1997 one-third of the entrées on American restaurant menus were adaptations of ethnic dishes.[24] *Fusion cuisine* that merges elements from different cuisines to create a new dish has been gaining in popularity (for instance, Mexican Pizza, drawing from both Hispanic and Italian food traditions). Some are concerned that as nationwide food companies recognize the potential of the ethnic-foods market and acquire smaller, traditional food firms, ethnic flavors will be lost or homogenized for American palates. Thus the very success of various ethnic cuisines may contribute to the evolution of a more complex national cuisine in a pluralistic setting.[25] In sum, ethnic heritage remains central for many Americans, food plays an important role in that, and "eating ethnic" is becoming more popular among many.

Social class represents the hierarchical or vertical differences in money and wealth, education, power and prestige. It is perhaps less visible than ethnicity, but it is another real dimension of foodway diversity. Social class is related to ethnicity but imperfectly so. We already noted the control of food by elites, and the emergence of elite cuisines, as distinguished from those of non-elites who had different kinds of foods. French social theorist Pierre Bourdieu argued that elite cuisines embody the "taste of luxury" with many options and choices, while non-elite cuisines embodying the "taste of necessity"—reflecting more limited class circumstances of affordability and availability. Elites viewed the taste of necessity as vulgar because it is easy and common, while portraying their own tastes and lifestyles in more aesthetic terms.[26]

Some evidence exists to support Bourdieu's characterization, but it is limited. Many researchers have used occupation as a measure to study social class, since occupation combines income, education, and social prestige. European researchers found that professional and nonmanual working classes consumed more meat, and more expensive cuts of meat than did manual workers, but—in a reversal of history—more whole grain bread and less "white bread" from refined flour (which is now cheaper, mass-produced, and less nutritious). Compared to manual workers, professional and nonmanual workers were less concerned with the price of foodstuffs and "ate out" at restaurants more frequently. In the United States, researchers found that manual workers had higher caloric intakes than did nonmanual workers, such as clerical, managerial, and sales workers. The highest food intake was found among farmers.[27]

"Class cuisines" are not as clear cut in the United States as in some European nations. For instance, Michael Lamont, who studied upper-middle class people in France and America, found that "cultivated dispositions" and the importance of displaying adequate "command of a high culture" was far less important in the United States than in France. More than their American counterparts, the French drew differences on the basis of sophistication and had rules for everything, for example, "when one uses *vous* rather than *tu*, and whether one knows at a glance the difference between a fish knife and a cheese knife."

Rather than class distinctions, Americans for whom these distinctions were important made them on the basis of what was considered cosmopolitan: an interest in other cultures via travel, language, and the culinary traditions of other cultures.[28] This is perhaps because of the strong pressures for a national cuisine that we previously noted; and "high culture" has only a shadowy existence because Americans, even elite Americans, are under great pressures to espouse egalitarian values. At any rate, cross-cutting social ties (involving class, ethnicity, religion, education, occupation, and region) insure less rigidity of group boundaries and the likelihood of exposure to a variety of cultural traditions, including cuisines. Some even argue that the social significance of eating is eroding, and they see a trend toward "dietary individualism."[29] To say the least, we are suspicious of this extreme view.

If the evidence for class cuisines in the United States is not clear cut, class differences are clearly evident in food purchase, food intake, and nutritional status. Karl Marx's collaborator, Friedrich Engels, observed long ago that as incomes increase, the proportion of household income devoted to purchasing food grows smaller (Engels' Law). Once a household reaches a sufficient level of consumption, there is little advantage to purchasing more food. Conversely, those with less money spend a greater proportion of it on food. Few exceptions have been found to these claims, and they continue to hold true in the United States. In 1988 consumer expenditure surveys reported that persons with annual incomes of less than $5,000 spent about 82 percent of it on food, those making between $10,000 and $15,000 spent 22 percent of their income on food, and those with incomes greater than $50,000 spent about 8 percent on food. Compared to those not living in poverty significantly greater percentages of both blacks and whites living in poverty consumed less than 70 percent of the Recommended Daily Allowances (RDAs) of calories, calcium, iron, and magnesium. Iron deficiency and various forms of anemia are concentrated among the poor at all age levels, including 3- to 5-year-old children.

Social class interacts with family structure to amplify nutritional impacts, because family size adversely affects the purchase and consumption of food among low-income families. Studies by nutritionists consistently found that nutritional stunting in children is particularly severe in larger, low-income families. They report significantly poorer intakes of various vitamins and minerals in children from large families, particularly "later born" children. Another structural constraint related to social class and family size was the size of household eating areas. While middle-class families had sufficient room to eat meals together, many large lower-class families had to spread themselves across several rooms to accomplish a meal. In light of this, such a constraint likely reduced the effectiveness of the socialization and supervision of children.[30]

Social class not only relates to undernutrition and stunting, but to the predominant American form of malnutrition: obesity. Sobal and Stunkard's review of about 144 studies from developed nations (including the United States) found that the vast majority reported an inverse relationship: low-income people were far more likely to be obese.[31]

Why is that so? Is it because low-income people have less nutritional knowledge about healthy diets and weight control, or have less access to medically supervised weight control foods and programs? Is it mainly because less expensive foods are generally more fattening? Is it because most "restaurants" in low-income neighborhoods are fast food outlets that offer fattening fares? Is it because the cultural pressure associating thinness with attractiveness is more powerful or realizable among more affluent people? Is there an emotional link here? That is, is overeating a generalized response to the frustrations and privations of low-income life? As you can see, explaining this correlation is complicated and involves a tangled web of hypothetical causes.

To complicate matters further, the inverse correlation between social class and obesity is about twice as strong for women and as it is for men. This suggests links between gender and food, as well.

Although often used interchangeably, the terms here are not exactly the same. "Male" and "female" relate to genetic and biological differences between men and women. By contrast, "gender" differences relate to "masculinity" and "femininity." Gender defines a basic social role that is more cultural, learned, and variable.

AMERICAN FOODWAYS: GENDER

Women have a very different relationship to food and eating than men. As well as ethnicity and social class, gender is a powerful factor defining differences between people in societies, including the control, preparation, and consumption of foods—with a multitude of ramifications. We noted this historically in Chapter 2, when discussing the "saintly women" anorexics of the middle ages who starved themselves (like Catherine of Siena).

In America, where the slim but not skinny body is the ideal, individuals with such bodies experience higher self-esteem and fewer affective disorders. But, the cultural pressure for a thin and svelte body for interpersonal attractiveness is more central for females than males. In an age where the ideal body image is so "out of whack" with what public health officials are calling the "epidemic of obesity," there are many consequences. One is a booming market for cosmetic surgery, largely among affluent women who find their bodies "misshapen" and seek breast enhancement, tummy tucks, and liposuction. Others include compulsive dieting and the industry connected with it.

A more serious consequence is the burgeoning growth of serious eating disorders: anorexia nervosa and bulimia nervosa. Anorexia means food self-deprivation to the point of wasting and cessation of menses, and is most common among adolescent females. It is one of the deadliest of psychological disorders, and 7 percent who have it die within ten years. Bulimia is more common among somewhat older populations, and involves alternatively bingeing and purging food by self-induced vomiting. Both are serious medical conditions. Bulimics are less likely to die than anorexics, but the disease takes over and wreaks havoc on their lives. They may experience serious dehydration and electrolyte imbalance, deterioration of tooth enamel, abrasions on the esophagus, kidney failure, and osteoporosis. Bulimia is at least five times more common than anorexia, and manifests itself among females in a 9 to 1 ratio over males. Eating disorders are most common among females socialized for high achievement and self-control, and they are a serious concern on most college campuses. More immediately serious than obesity, eating disorders, once they become established, are serious mental and physical health problems with a physiology and psychology all their own.[32]

Eating disorders have attracted medical attention since the nineteenth century in America. Today, there is a huge scholarly and clinical literature about eating disorders involving diverse approaches. Medical researchers have come to view bulimia as a neurological disorder involving lack of appetite control. Psychologists speculate that eating disorders stem from affective disorders, such as low self-esteem or depression. Social psychologists and others tend to treat eating disorders as a result of dysfunctional relations between adolescents and young women and at least one of their parents. Historians, sociologists, and feminist scholars emphasize the so-called culture of slimness, patriarchy, or sometimes capitalism. Some claim that in periods in which women were encouraged to compete with men as equals, women strove to look more like men, and during such periods, eating disorders were more prevalent. Others argue that the culture of slimness represents a patriarchal power discourse between males and females.[33] Bordo finds, for instance, that men idealize slimness and expect it in "their women." "Over and over again extremely slender women students complain of hating their thighs and stomachs (an anorexic's most dreaded spot) and they often express concern and anger over frequent teasing by their boyfriends."[34] Beyond the connection between gender and eating disorders, however, food and gender are connected to the social order.

As we noted in Chapter 2, food was associated with the earliest role divisions in human societies. Among early hunter-gatherers, men were associated with hunting and the consumption of meat, while women and children provided edible plants and vegetables. Indeed, "man the hunter," a figure who stalked the world, and consumed lots of meat, often characterized the conception of power and masculinity then and now.[35] We would be remiss, however, in not mentioning that in many parts of the world, particularly in developing nations, women produce most of the foodstuffs needed for subsistence, and make major contributions to cash crop production.

Not only do men usually eat more meat, but they generally have greater power in families. Many people and some scholars, however, assume that in her caring role, the wife-mother had greater authority in food-related activities about what and how the family eats, including shopping, gardening, cooking, and serving food. But, studies of American family decision making suggest a more complex picture. They found that women are responsible for food, but do not control it, and that husbands and boyfriends have considerable power over these decisions. Power over cooking and grocery shopping was not equivalent to controlling purchase and recipe choices. Husbands retained veto power over dishes served, and wives gave husbands' and children's preferences high priority, regardless of their own needs or beliefs about the healthfulness of foods. Scholars hypothesized that a woman's control of food decisions increased when her income and status equaled her husband's.[36]

Gender differences may be maintained and reproduced in households, but differences in the larger society and economy tend to disadvantage women relative to men, in terms of the access they have to wealth, power, and prestige. A patriarchal culture legitimizes such inequalities, but in turn power differences make patriarchy possible. It is no longer news that women have entered the paid labor force in large numbers, or that dual-wage families have transformed family relations—including mealtimes—in many ways. Nor is it news that women have entered occupations at all levels, including prestigious and high-paying occupations in, for instance, law, medicine, science, and management. But even professional women are concentrated in occupations that are extensions of women's nurturing, self-sacrificing, and caring social role. For example, women are concentrated in education, nursing, and social work, and even those who become medical doctors are concentrated in lower-status, less lucrative practices such as family practice and obstetrics-gynecology.[37] In a gendered world, "caring" jobs are perceived as less important than jobs requiring aggression, competitiveness, and achievement.

In spite of the growing numbers of well-educated women entering the labor force, the labor force is still relatively segregated by gender. Women are overwhelmingly concentrated in the "service sector" jobs like secretarial, clerical, and jobs in the food and beverage industry, which have lower status, salaries, benefits, and opportunities than professional jobs.[38] In fact, the fastest-growing female jobs are in food preparation and service in restaurants and the fast food industry. Today 90 percent of the "wait" personnel are women, and research literature consistently notes the low-status, low-benefit nature of this work. Men dominated the occupation at the turn of the twentieth century, before the vast expansion of the restaurant industry, when the shift to waitresses was one of the first female invasions of a male-dominated occupational structure.

Today male waiters work in more prestigious restaurants, usually under much more rewarding conditions than do waitresses, who are employed by less prestigious restaurants and coffee shops. Many "waitressing" jobs have minimum wages, poor to nonexistent benefits, few opportunities for mobility, and often sexually exploitive work environments. Waitresses benefit the food and beverage industry because they lack job autonomy, are closely supervised by owners or managers, are poorly paid, and depend on customers for tips.[39]

This varies by type of establishment, however. At one end of a spectrum are more traditional restaurants in which waitresses have considerable autonomy in relation to both management and customers. At the other end are restaurants with more centralization, formal rules, and less opportunity to develop worker cohesion. They typically have high rates of employee turnover. Those with more centralized control and formality are restaurants and fast food establishments produced by advanced modernity, where "rational" procedures dominate to achieve control over the labor process. In these establishments (McDonald's, Burger King, Taco Bell) fast food personnel interact minimally with customers, and are trained to serve them within

---

DISHING IT OUT AT THE TRUCKSTOP

Waitresses at a New Jersey truckstop used a variety of individual strategies to "make out," that is, to neutralize the exploitive nature of their work. Successful ones developed a "voice" (autonomy) in the enterprise rather than leaving. First, they learned they had much to gain but little to lose by putting customer's desires ahead of company policy. This increased tips, but not the risk of being fired. Second, the longer she had worked, the easier she was able to refuse to take on either seating areas or tasks that would reduce the opportunity for tips. Third, she might refuse to serve a customer who had a history of poor tipping, or who appeared to fit the stereotype of a poor tipper. These were individually competitive strategies, and waitresses had no interest in worker solidarity or collective action. Some research reports that waiters and perhaps waitresses engage in theft, from customers, management, or fellow wait personnel. Detection generally led to firing rather than to involving the legal system, so the consequences were not severe. Like other marginal workers, stealing may be a form of making out.[41]

---

three minutes of entering the establishment. Customers come to the counter, and workers remain at workstations. Wait personnel no longer receive tips, nor are they compensated for their loss. The lack of an enclosed kitchen means that staff have no place to which they can retreat and express frustrations about unpleasant customers. Managerial supervision is close and continuous, and employers try to specify what their employees say, their demeanors, their gestures, their moods, and even their thoughts. Worker cohesion is not really possible. The only "voice" for frustration is to leave, as many do. One study found the turnover rate at both managerial and worker level exceeded 100 percent per year, and other estimates put it higher.[40]

AMERICAN FOODWAY TRENDS: MCDONALDIZATION

Restaurants with more centralized power and formalized rules illustrate a profound social transition in modern societies, termed McDonaldization by contemporary sociologist George Ritzer. It signifies the latest phase of a broad and pervasive trend that includes American foodways and much more.

It began with a "civilizing process" that was a precursor to modernity, including the restraint of natural impulses, centralized power in organizations, and formal rules. We discussed this idea of Norbert Elias's in Chapter 2, who observed it in relation to the end of gluttony and the emergence of food etiquette in late medieval times. He saw the beginnings of this in the increasing interdependence of kings and nobility in royal courts, but its spread to other groups eventually transformed whole social configurations. As organizations and formal rules spread, individuals learned to constrain themselves, and were less prisoners of their natural impulses. This process was not an unmixed blessing, however. The civilizing of the human young, for example, is never a process entirely without pain, and often leaves scars, as we noted earlier about families eating together and the socialization of children.[42]

Famous early-twentieth-century German sociologist Max Weber described the acceleration of this process, as the Western world became increasingly rational, with huge formal bureaucratic systems, market economies, and scientific technologies. The Western world became permeated by a distinctive kind of rationality that he termed "formal rationality"— dominated by efficiency, predictability, calculability, and nonhuman technologies that control people. We are not on new ground here—Chapter 4 discussed this process in relation to the structural changes in American agriculture and food systems.[43] Western nations permeated by formal rationality grew in economic and military power, and they competed to dominate and colonize much of the rest of the world. Such rational and bureaucratic systems had many benefits, both for nations in contact with each other, and for individuals—particularly those in positions of power—who could live more predictable, healthier, and more well-nourished lives. Yet despite the advantages it offers, Weber observed that formal rationality and bureaucracy often suffer from the "irrationality of rationality." Inefficiency and "red tape," for example, are well known in large bureaucratic organizations. Weber was even more concerned by the dehumanizing "iron cage" of bureaucracy in which people feel trapped, and which denies their basic humanity. Fast food restaurants, as described earlier, can be dehumanizing places to work and to be served. They can be places in which the "self is placed in confinement, its emotions controlled, and its spirit subdued."[44]

While growing rationality and bureaucracy is certainly not new, Ritzer argues that the United States and other societies are increasingly permeated by organizations, corporations, and modes of consumption (including foodways) that are in tune with contemporary lifestyles, and "hyper-rational" in Weber's terms. Easily symbolized by the McDonald's restaurants, such hyper-rational McDonaldization has four basic dimensions:

1. *Efficiency* is the best way to get from one point to another. For customers, McDonald's offers the best way to get from being hungry to being full; particularly in a society where parents work, and where people rush from one place to another, usually by car, the efficiency of a fast food meal (perhaps "drive thru") is hard to resist. Other businesses are similarly efficient to help people lose weight, lubricate cars, get new glasses, and complete tax forms. Like customers, workers in McDonaldized systems follow steps in a predesigned process. Managers who closely supervise work make sure they do, and formal rules and regulations ensure highly efficient work.

2. *Calculability* emphasizes the quantitative aspects of products or services sold (portion size, cost, time for service) . In McDonaldized systems, quantity becomes equivalent to quality; a lot of something or its quick delivery means it must be good. In contemporary America, we tend to believe that bigger is better, as in a Big Mac, large fries, or a "super gulp" drink. Customers are encouraged to supersize an order. They feel they are getting a lot for a nominal amount of money, but that calculation misses an important point: the high profits of fast food chains mean that owners, not consumers, get the best deal. They also calculate how long it will take to drive to McDonald's to eat or get food, compared to the time required to fix food at home. Workers emphasize quantity, since the quality of their work varies little. Analogous to customers, workers are expected to work a lot, and very quickly, for low pay.

3. *Predictability* is the assurance that products and services will be the same over time and in different places. An Egg McMuffin in New York, will be, for all practical purposes, the same as one in Los Angeles or Pocatello, Idaho. People take some comfort in knowing that McDonald's offers no surprises, which is odd, considering that McDonald's is the product of a culture that honors individualism above all. Workers also behave in predictable ways. McDonaldized organizations often have scripts that employees are supposed to memorize and follow whenever various situations arise. Customers don't follow scripts, but often develop simple recipes for dealing with employees of McDonaldized systems.

4. *Control through nonhuman technology* is exerted over all who enter a McDonaldized setting. Lines, limited menus, few options, and uncomfortable seats all lead diners to do what management wants—to eat quickly and leave. "Drive thrus" are another mode of customer control, and at Domino's they never enter in the first place. Since workers are more directly and blatantly controlled than customers, they are trained to do a limited number of things in a precise order (e.g., how and in what order to assemble the bread, meat, cheese, pickles, onions, tomatoes, and mustard for a cheeseburger). But no matter how well programmed and controlled, a worker can foul up the system's operation by being unpredictable or too slow. Therefore McDonaldized firms threaten—and often do—use technology to replace human workers and skills, such as a French fry machine that lifts the basket out of the oil when the fries are crisp, or the preprogrammed cash register that eliminates the need to calculate prices or make change. Replacing workers with technology may assure customers that their products and service will be consistent.[45]

McDonaldization symbolizes a trend toward regional, national, and international franchised firms of all kinds, and there were 30,000 of them by 2000. By then, McDonald's was such an international presence that most of

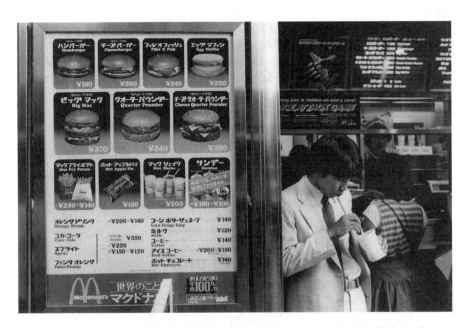

A Japanese customer at a McDonald's restaurant in the Ginza district of Tokyo. The menu sign is in both Japanese and English with pictures of hamburgers, fries, and soft drinks.

the restaurants it opened each day were outside of the United States. It's biggest competitor is Tricon, spun off by PepsiCo in 1997, which owns Pizza Hut, Taco Bell, and Kentucky Fried Chicken.[46]

Reasons why the growth of such hyperrational enterprises is such a pervasive trend, marketing food and many other products and services, are not hard to find. Corporations benefit because such hyperrational enterprises are usually more profitable than more traditional ones. For consumers, McDonaldized companies make available a wider range of goods and services to a much larger proportion of the population than ever before. They are convenient, people can satisfy their needs quickly, and getting goods and services depends less on time and location. People can do things which were previously impossible, like drive up and get a complete family meal quickly, or get money from a grocery store in the middle of the night. Such convenience is particularly important for busy people working long hours with little time to spare. They provide standardized goods of uniform quality, and quantification makes it easy to compare competing goods and services. At least some people get better goods and services than before McDonaldization. People are more likely to be treated similarly, no matter what their social class, ethnicity, or gender. In that way they are more democratic; and the most popular products in one culture are more easily spread to others.[47]

McDonaldization not only transforms institutions and provides benefits in the consumption process. Many of its settings have become some of America's and the world's cultural icons—such as McDonald's, Wal-Mart, and Disney. Structures for the new means of consumption are often enchanting "cathedrals of consumption" that Ritzer came to see as having a religiouslike quality. If they are enchanting, however, they are also profoundly disenchanting.

Max Weber's most general thesis was that the process of rationalization caused the Western world to be increasingly disenchanted; instead of a world with enchantment, magic, and mystery that people value, increasingly we have one in which everything seems clear, cut-and-dried, logical, and routine. Enchantment, magic, and mystery, which depend more on quality that quantity, are difficult to maintain in a world of hyperrational standardization—in spite of the many benefits it brings.[48]

DISENCHANTMENT AND RE-ENCHANTMENT: FOODWAY REFORM MOVEMENTS

The disenchantment flowing from hyperrationality is widely recognized, but not absolute. There are degrees of it. Disney World and Las Vegas are more enchanting than Wal-Mart or the Sears catalogue. While some settings (Sam's Club) have devolved to as colorless and starkly utilitarian and disenchanting settings as imaginable, others have gone to great lengths to engineer re-enchantment. McDonald's, for example, are bright, glitzy places, with clowns, toys, and jungle gyms that enchant children (and many adults).

If the experience of disenchantment is not absolute, neither is the homogenization of products and services, since McDonaldized firms do strive to accommodate the tastes of local and national markets, in varying degrees. In Maine you can buy anything on the Illinois menu, but also a McLobster sandwich. In Norway you can get a McLaks, a grilled salmon sandwich with dill sauce on whole grain bread; in Uruguay, McHuevos, hamburgers with poached eggs; Japan, Chicken Tatsuta sandwich, fried chicken spiced with soy sauce and ginger, with cabbage and mustard mayonnaise. In England, McDonald's adapted to the growing popularity of Indian cuisine by offering Lamb McSpicy, and during Passover in Israel it adds Chicken McNuggets with matzo meal to its menu. Still, there are limits to what can be done, and American fast food restaurants spreading around the world are often perceived as a culinary form of cultural imperialism.[49] Nor do these attempts at local adaptation and engineered re-enchantment counterbalance the reality of pervasive disenchantment and threats to social institutions and human health. For that reason, McDonaldization has spawned several food reform movements and countermovements, of which we discuss several.

Food reform movements are social and cultural movements that encompass a variety of people and organizations that promote ways of producing, preparing, and eating food contrary to the dominant pattern. A food reform movement is more than a culture of food preferences, or an alternative foodway; it is also a worldview that includes symbols about health and salvation of the body, the psyche, and society. Early in the twentieth century, food reform movements came to be symbolized by the oft-repeated slogan mentioned in our Introduction: "You are what you eat." The ideology of these movements involved a seemingly contradictory mixture of ideas from science and nonscience, along with a nostalgia for "natural" and nature, and a view of health, healing, and prevention that are only partly about food. Reacting to the growth and dominance of corporations in foodways and professionals over traditional matters, they emphasize natural foods, self-healing, and lay knowledge. Many food reform movements maintain that society is a corrupting influence, and converts learn how to criticize prevailing social values and institutions. As discussed in Chapter 3, they are not new: They have accompanied industrialization, commodification, and professionalism in the United States since the nineteenth century.[50]

The contemporary food reform movement grew rapidly in the 1960s as it connected with the counterculture of protest against "establishment" organizations and lifestyles. Their themes resonate with earlier movements about food, health, and well-being, but with some differences. Like earlier movements, contemporary health reform movements saw problems with unhealthy diets and a "medical establishment" not focused on wellness, as well the food industry and society they represented. Perceptions of government involvement, however, are different. In the nineteenth century, food consumers could not expect government protection from business—now consumers do. Currently, many have grown disillusioned about the ability and the willingness of the United States Department of Agriculture (USDA) and the Food and Drug Administration (FDA) to regulate agriculture and the food industry. Indeed, some observers suggest that consumer mistrust grew with increasing distance between them and food producers and regulators.[51]

Although some health food consumers are part of organized groups like food co-ops, most are not. To be sure, there are leaders and organizations, but a social movement is never as simple as a conspiracy of organizations and agitators. The food reform movements exist primarily as a set of values and practices disseminated from person-to-person and by other means. Important among these are health food stores, restaurants, and publications. Emphasizing the spiritual and quasi-religious nature of food reform movements, health food stores are like "temples" of the food reform movements, and their leaders are like prophets, or clergy. Its two most prominent magazines ("literature of the faith"?) are *Prevention* and *Let's Live*, founded in the 1920s and 1930s, but now having much larger subscription and readerships. If you find it strange to think of food reform and lifestyle movements as quasireligious movements, recall that Ritzer came to see the supermarkets and shopping malls in the world of McDonaldized settings as the "cathedrals of consumption" in relation to the popular American quasi-religion of hyperconsumerism.

Extending this perspective, anthropologist Jill Dubish notes that in the moral cosmology of tribal peoples, there is an opposition of forces and things. Some are good, healthy, and have beneficial power (*mana*), and some are bad, unhealthy, and have dangerous power (*taboos*). So it is, she argues, with food. Foods with mana, for instance, include those that are dark, whole, natural, raw, or crunchy, as well as specific foods like honey, yogurt, fish, stir-fried vegetables, soybeans, and fresh fruits and juices. Those with taboos include those that are white, processed, fried, salted, and flavored, as well as "junk foods" and specific foods like candy, hot dogs, Coke, overcooked vegetables, beef, McDonald's hamburgers, and potato chips. Thus dark bread is preferred over white bread, and brown rice over white rice. The real health food purists must learn to eat foods that at first are strange or exotic, and to reject many foods that are part of the standard American cuisine that fall into their list or the generally accepted category of junk food.[52]

Some people are pure health food devotees or food reform movement activists to the extent of thoroughly rejecting the dominant foodway and "toxic food environment" to adopt a different and often strange foodway. They are often easy for outsiders and opponents to dismiss as "nuts" or "food faddists." The vast majority of Americans, however, are not such health food purists. That having been said, basic food reform movement messages about eating for better health and well-being have become widely and popularly influential among consumers, as well as in the scientific and medical communities.[54] The recommendations for dietary reforms are reflected in the current recommendations and "food pyramids" of the USDA, as well as in mandatory nutritional labeling on retail foods.

On the popular level, per capita beef consumption fell by 25 percent between 1970 and the 1990s, because of the perceived health benefits of eating less red meat, as well as the relative prices for beef.[55] The shift to poultry

---

NUTRITION AS A MORALITY PLAY

"Dr. Robbins was thinking how it might be interesting to make a film from Adelle Davis's perennial best seller, *Let's Eat Right to Keep Fit*. Representing a classic confrontation between good and evil—in this case nutrition versus unhealthy diet—the story had definite box office appeal. The role of the hero, Protein, probably should be filled by Jim Brown, although Burt Reynolds would pull strings to get the part. Sunny Doris Day would be a clear choice to play the heroine, Vitamin C, and Orson Welles, oozing saturated fatty acids from the pits of his flesh could win an Oscar for his interpretation of the villainous Cholesterol. The film might begin on a stormy night in the central nervous system...."[53]

from red meat also lowered per capita grain consumption, because poultry need less grain than cattle to produce the same amount of meat. Americans believe that they *should* eat more fruits and vegetables, and fewer fried foods—whether they do or not.[56] Though a small minority of Americans are purist vegetarians ("vegans"), vegetarian menus have become a standard option at most restaurants and formal banquets—something unheard of twenty years ago. Also, over the last several decades the kinds and number of "alternative markets," like farmer's markets, urban gardening programs, health food stores, and food co-ops, have proliferated.

Though they pose no real threat to big food companies and the fast food culture, a measure of the success of the food reform movement message is the way that it is being co-opted by them (much to the chagrin of some movement activists). The fastest growing section of supermarkets includes vegetables, and in particular "organic" foods. Foods that are "Lite," Healthy, Lo-Cal, Natural, and so forth are "in." Sometimes the differences are real and sometimes only marketing ploys for the unwary. The USDA recently adopted standards for the descriptors (e.g., having a USDA certified "organic" label), but, as with nutritional labels, they have been met with howls of protest from food corporations—as well as from some food reform movement activists, who believe the certified label is watered down.

Less familiar to Americans is another type of food reform movement, a "slow food movement" that began more recently in Europe. It is a reaction to the perception of the culinary imperialism and homogenization of fast food corporations. Less about health food per se, the slow food movement is more about preserving cuisines and foodways as national and local treasures. It began in Italy where towns, from Asti in the North to Trentino in the South, took pride in local cuisines, such as styles of making sausage, cheese, and wines, and often staged profitable tourist festivals to celebrate them. They formed a "Slow Cities League."

The first McDonald's came to Rome in 1968, and "the Golden Arches" are now found just about everywhere. But in Italy fast food has not been very successful in puncturing long-standing culinary traditions, where it accounts for only 5 percent of food eaten away from home (compared with 25 percent in the rest of Europe and 50 percent in the United States). The slow food movement was founded by political leftists, who saw in it a symbolic rallying point to oppose the intrusion of multinational firms into European culture, but it has become a broad-based movement. The slow food movement wants to protect local traditions, and it particularly has lobbied against enacting standardized "hygienic rules" as the entering wedge of homogenization. It also defends the European and Mediterranean tradition of leisurely meals that can take several hours, whether in homes or in restaurants, as a social ritual and form of pleasant sociability—qualities short circuited by most fast food settings. From Italy it spread to France, to promote food as a way of maintaining tradition, family, and childhood memories. It now claims 60,000 organizations in forty-two countries.

It made little headway in the United States until 1999 when a New York office opened, and then it mushroomed around the country. Media attention and endorsements from notable chefs spawned eating groups—or "convivia" (from the Latin word for festive) as "Slow Foodies" call them. In 2000 there were thirty such groups with over 2,500 members, which sponsor meals, lectures, and trips to farms and regional food producers. In Madison, Wisconsin, for instance, the convivia had sixty members, including college students, surgeons, and farmers, and promoted fresh and local food, including the products of Wisconsin's famous small breweries and artisanal cheese makers. They held an "apple tasting" event and tried fifty varieties of apples, some of which were grown only in Wisconsin.

As the environmental movement tries to save endangered animals from extinction, the slow food movement is bent on saving endangered cuisines, as well as fruits and vegetables. It has been called the Greenpeace of gastronomy. The movement develops educational programs in grade schools to teach kids about food, and its Fraternal Tables project helps farmers in Nicaragua to recover agricultural land. While praised for promoting good food and sociability, the slow food movement has not avoided controversy. None other than University of Maryland's George Ritzer (the doyen of McDonaldization critics) alleges that its "sensual correctness" is breeding elitist appetites and needs to attract more middle- and lower-class supporters. Activists respond that the movement can appeal to all, because it is basically about enhancing eating pleasure and spreading the message to "slow down and enjoy." But surely the most elitist food reform movement is the Boston-based Oldways Preservation and Exchange Trust, which similarly promotes a return to the traditional arts of cooking food and socializing around food. It targets food consumers but in particular chefs of upscale restaurants.[57]

Both growing hyperrationality and food reform movements that preserve and revitalize tradition have been around for a long time. It is hard to imagine McDonaldization not continuing, because it is driven by powerful economic and social forces and serves the very real human needs about living in contemporary societies. But it is equally unlikely that it will unfold without being shaped and modified by continuing reform movements that react to it. Both speak to different but very real human needs. In America and around the world, people will continue to want food that is fast, commercialized, and convenient. They will continue to like food from small and local producers, and prepared "from scratch" to their particular tastes. They will value efficiency on some occasions, but more leisurely and sociable eating experiences on others. We think that for many there will be a two-tiered lifestyle, using fast and convenience foods when expedient, but at other times engaging in more creative and time-consuming meals. We believe, in other words, that the trend and its countertrends will form an ongoing dialectic of disenchantment and re-enchantment regarding an important part of the human experience.

HUNGRY FOR MORE? MAKING CONNECTIONS

Here's how you can get in touch with organizations of the food reform movement:

- *Edible Schoolyard*: plants organic gardens on school grounds to nourish the most neglected schoolroom: the cafeteria (510) 558–1335; www.edibleschoolyard.org
- *Food First*: A think tank committed to establishing food as a fundamental human right. (510) 654–4400; www.foodfirst.org
- *Local Harvest*: Great online resource for finding food grown near your home. www.localharvest.org
- *Slow Food*: An international movement celebrating the joy of eating. (877) 756–9366; www.slowfood.com
- *Community Food Security Coalition*: promotes community-based solutions to hunger, poor nutrition, and globalization of the world's food system. (310) 822–5410; www.foodsecurity.org
- *Center for Urban Agriculture*: demonstrates the economic viability of small farm operations and urban gardens, and the connections between food, land, and community well-being. (805) 683–2001.
- *Institute for Agriculture and Trade Policy*: promotes family farms, rural communities, and healthy ecosystems around the world. (612) 870–0453; www.iatp.org
- *Oldways Preservation and Trust*: dedicated to promoting the traditional culinary arts. www.oldwayspt.org

MCDONALDIZATION, NUTRITION, AND HEALTH

One reason for this ongoing dialectic is that growing hyperrationality threatens more than the nature of social institutions or people's expectations or fantasies about cuisines and diversity. It threatens their health and perhaps even lives. The McDonaldization of American foodways amplifies a historical trend we noted earlier, in which diets rich in meat, dairy products, and highly processed items supplanted those richer in whole grains, vegetables, and fruit. Consequently, USDA researchers find "the average American diet" to be seriously out of balance with the most recent food guide (as depicted by the food pyramid in Chapter 1).[58] The proliferation of high-calorie diets with lots of fats, cholesterol, salt, and sugar—widely available, heavily promoted, and served up in huge portions—has resulted in what Yale food scholar Kelly Brownell calls a "toxic food environment." The result is a virtual epidemic of obesity, high cholesterol levels, high blood pressure, and diabetes. When such eating habits combine with urbanized and more sedentary lifestyles (particularly with television saturated with food ads), people find it difficult to avoid gaining weight.

Consumers get most of their dietary cues from food companies, which spend more on advertising—$30 billion each year in the United States alone—than any other industry.[59] The most heavily advertised foods are of dubious nutritional value, and ads disproportionately target children, the least savvy consumers, to shape lifelong habits. According to the Center for Science in the Public Interest, the average American child watches 10,000 commercials each year, and most of these are for sugary cereals, candy, soda, or other "junk foods." Many studies show that these ads work by prompting children to request, purchase, and consume advertised foods, and these habits continue into adulthood. One study found that the health of many immigrant children deteriorates the longer they are in the United States, in large part because their diet comes to more closely resemble the junk food diets of American children. [60]

Americans now consume 70 kilograms of caloric sweeteners per year, the equivalent of a 5-pound bag of sugar every week-and-a-half. In the United States and Europe, fats and sugar now count for more than half of all caloric intake, squeezing complex carbohydrates and vegetables down to about one-third of total calories. In addition to promoting fatty and sweet foods that are highly profitable (and for which we have an innate liking), food portions have steadily grown in recent years. A standard serving of soda in the 1950s was a 6.5 oz. bottle. Today the industry standard is 20 ounces. "Supersizing" evolved as a marketing strategy that costs food producers little, and appears to give significant added value to consumers. But the trend skews perceptions of normal servings. The typical McDonald's meal of a Big Mac, large fries, and a shake has more than 1,000 calories, few of them of great nutritional value. Burger

---

FOOD BOOKS PITCH SNACKS TO TODDLERS

A hot selling item is a stack of children's books starring brand name candies and snacks, like Froot Loops, Cheerios, M&Ms, Pepperidge Farm Goldfish, Reese's Pieces, and Hershey's chocolates. They, for instance, teach kids to count using Taco Bell's fast foods. Publishers pay a licensing fee to food companies, who see a novel opportunity to market brand names, "taking Froot Loops from the cereal aisle into learning arenas," said a spokesperson for Kellogg's, which also provides Froot Loop book covers to schools. The Cheerios play book sold more than 1.2 million copies in the last two years. But not everybody is pleased to see brand-name snacks invading the world of children's books. Said Marit Larson, a mother of a two-year old, "It's offensive—I wouldn't let my kid near books like that." And the chairwoman of the education committee of the American Academy of Pediatrics, and professor of pediatrics at Loyola University, said "I think the whole thing is revolting, to be targeting little kids with that kind of marketing."[61]

King's Double Whopper with cheese alone has 960 calories, and 63 grams of fat. The trend toward larger portions has increased the problem. These trends, already established in the United States and other industrial nations, is spreading to developing nations as incomes rise, creating an epidemic of obesity and a largely misunderstood public health crisis. [62]

THE EPIDEMIC OF OBESITY

Ironically, at a time when thinness is potent cultural ideal, fattening food is everywhere and 55 percent of the population is officially overweight, and at least 20 percent of Americans are clinically obese, now defined as being 30 percent above the established normal body weight. Obesity jumped 60 percent during the 1990s, among all sociodemographic groups and among both men and women. It is no longer treated as an eating disorder like anorexia or bulimia, but scientists increasingly recognize it as having often-deadly consequences for individuals as well as serious and costly ones for society. Obesity is a major cause of heart disease. It may cause cancer, and it is a major risk factor in diabetes—which also surged in the 1990s. The Center for Disease Control (CDC) estimates that 300,000 Americans die each year of causes related to obesity. In fact, so many Americans have crossed the line into obesity that public health officials have launched a full-scale frontal assault on an "epidemic of obesity," as they would have done long ago for an infectious disease as widespread and as costly (more than $100 billion a year).[63] Of particular concern is the growing obesity of America's children.

The causes of the obesity epidemic are not clear. The availability of a more plentiful food supply is involved, as is lack of exercise and more seden-

AMERICAN CHILDREN ARE GETTING FATTER

In the 1960s about 6.5 percent of American children between the ages of six and eleven were overweight. By 1994 that fraction had almost doubled to 11.4 percent. "Ten or fifteen years ago, children who showed up for treatment were about 40 percent overweight," says Dr. Tomas Robinson, Professor of Pediatric Medicine at Stanford University, but now the children he treats average 80 percent overweight. The obesity epidemic has been traced to fast foods combined with massive inactivity. Studies find, for instance, that fatter children watch more television, but cannot distinguish between cause and effect. Do fat children watch more television because they are socially isolated, or is watching television making them fat? Public health officials think that the food industry and television constitute, in some combination, a culprit and an accomplice. Children who watch lots of television are inactive while being barraged with junk food advertisements.[64]

tary lifestyles. Some experts emphasize American culture and the way individuals are socialized. As previously noted, from early childhood food and eating becomes tied up with other things, with love and hate, power and control, group and sociodemographic affiliation, religion, and personal beliefs. Others find the McDonaldization of American foodways a large factor, with its fattening junk foods, gargantuan portions, and highly persuasive ads promoting overeating.

Evidence is also accumulating that, given sufficient food, overeating is biologically inherent. A trait that evolved for human survival has become dysfunctional in an era of food abundance. Thus, the search is underway for a "fat gene," while the pharmaceutical industry works overtime to brew up an "antiobesity" drug for voracious appetites.[65] Even so, it is worth reiterating, as we did in Chapter 1, that such genetic characteristics are both quite variable within human populations and subject to modification by culture and socialization. This is particularly true of food preferences and tastes, and particularly when a multimillion-dollar advertising industry systematically persuades people to overeat. If obesity has serious health consequences, so does the cultural pressure to be thin, thinner that what is normal for most humans, according to scientists. Never in human history has obesity been more common or more socially stigmatized.

THE OTHER EPIDEMIC: SLIMMING GIMMICKS

Medical quackery with misleading concoctions for weight loss is ancient. But the epidemic of obesity and the tendencies for Americans to look for medical cures has given it a boost. After being stable for years, the sales of diet concoctions have quadrupled since 1996, particularly after fen-fen (fenfluramine), a much-ballyhooed weight-loss prescription drug, was pulled from the market in 1997 for having potentially fatal side effects. The scramble for substitutes turned quick fix, over-the-counter weight loss products into the fastest-growing segment of the diet industry. Such gimmicks include soaps that slough off fat in the shower, miracle pills that get rid of pounds without dieting or exercise, plastic earplugs that curb the appetite, and even a glittering ring called Fat-be-gone that trims hips, buttocks, and thighs, just from slipping it on a finger. The surging demand for a weight-loss silver bullet fueled fraudulent advertising, giving rise to a tripling of complaints to the Federal Trade Commission (FTC). The increase in questionable advertising worries federal and state regulators, leading Andrea Levine of the FTC to exclaim, "We're in the Wild West of advertising right now. We're seeing claims being made on a whim without a scintilla of evidence, and there's such a huge proliferation of products it's very hard for the regulatory world to get hold of it." But a leader of an advocacy group for overweight people said, "I don't think it's unreasonable that we want to have a miracle. That's what we are sold everyday."[66]

A concerted public health campaign has begun to deal with the epidemic of obesity. Governments and many private organizations recognize the existence of an epidemic of overeating, and are attempting to empower people through education about nutrition and healthy eating habits. People need to be able to counter the social pressures that promote poor eating habits. In a society like the United States, where important cues about food and eating come from the media, education is critical. Mass media campaigns are important to changing long-standing nutritional habits of adults. For illustration, Finland launched a campaign in the 1970s and 1980s to reduce the country's high rate of heart disease, involving government-sponsored advertisements, national dietary guidelines, and regulations on food labeling (e.g., for heavily salted or high-fat foods). The broad, high profile campaign also advocated an end to smoking. The campaign increased fruit and vegetable consumption two-fold, and slashed deaths from coronary disease by 65 percent between 1969 and 1995. About half of that drop was credited to the lower levels of cholesterol induced by the nutrition education campaign.[67]

Experts who emphasize nutritional education for health and to avoid obesity want good nutrition to become a routine part of one's lifestyle and are upset that so many people are chronic dieters, who regain pounds when the diet ends. A national survey by the CDC reported, for instance, that two-thirds of Americans are either dieting to lose weight or watching what they eat to avoid gaining weight. But experts who emphasize a genetic inclination to overeat, like obesity researcher James Hill of The University of Colorado, think that "The only way to keep from gaining weight is to make not gaining weight a conscious activity rather than an unconscious activity. If you leave it to your physiology, you're going to gain weight. You have to have a plan."[68] It is still true, however, that experts universally condemn "fad diets" promising quick, miraculous results.

Given the growth of obesity among children, efforts to promote good nutrition should not be only for adults. It can extend to children's television programs and also to school programs. For example, the Berkley Food System Project teaches kids about healthy eating, and promotes the use of vegetable gardens in schools to help kids learn about food from the source. Kids weaned on packaged and processed foods often shy away from fruits and veggies, because they have not been properly introduced. But, said a program organizer, "when a child pops a cherry tomato that she helped grow into her mouth, then introducing a salad bar in the school cafeteria is likely to be more successful."[69]

Doctors, nurses, and other health professionals are well positioned to educate patients about the links between diet and health, and can be effective in improving eating habits. But medical systems often deemphasize the role of nutrition: In 1994 only 23 percent of U.S. medical schools required that students take a separate course in nutrition. Doctors untrained in preventative approaches to health care (e.g., nutrition, exercise, stress reduction) are likely to emphasize dealing with the consequences of foodways and lifestyles, like prescribing a cholesterol-lowering drug, or scheduling by-pass surgery. In the 1990s, the CDC found that "less than half of obese adults report being advised to lose weight by health care professionals."

Health care as a whole is beginning to integrate nutrition by recognizing obesity as a disease and covering weight-loss programs and other nutritional interventions. Insurance that covers these expenses reduce illness and patient suffering, and likely reduce health care costs. The Mutual of Omaha Company, for example, decided to cover intensive dietary and lifestyle modification programs for patients with heart disease, in hopes of reducing the need for costly prescriptions or surgery months or years down the road. A logical step would be to cover regular nutrition checkups like they now do for dental checkups as part of a basic insurance coverage.

As they have been used in the anticigarette smoking campaign, fiscal tools could also be used to promote good nutrition. Yale nutrition expert Kelly Brownell advocates creating a tax on food based on the nutrient value per calorie. Fatty and sugary foods loaded with calories but poor in nutrients could be taxed the most, while fruits and vegetable might escape most taxes. The idea is to discourage consumption of unhealthy foods and raise revenues to promote healthier alternatives, nutrition education programs, or exercise programs—in other words, to make it easier and cheaper to eat well. Such taxes are more reasonable as the cost of overeating to society grows, including direct costs (like hospital stays, medicine, treatment, and doctor visits) and indirect costs (like reduced worker productivity, missed work days, and

---

VENDING STUDY IS FOR "TWINKIE TAX" EFFORT

To get people to pick low-fat foods, "price and availability may be a lot more powerful than education," said Robert Jeffry of the University of Minnesota, in the Jan 2001 issue of the *American Journal of Public Health*. He and other researchers found that low-fat selections in vending machines became more attractive when they were cheap. To be considered low-fat, each snack had to contain less than 3 grams of fat per package, which included Nutri-grain bars, baked Lays potato chips, pretzels, and raisins. Lowering the price of these by 10 percent increased the sales by 9 percent. When the price was lowered to half of their regular price, their sales jumped by 93 percent compared to those at equal prices. Jeffry said "People are willing to buy lower fat items if it's economical and practical for them to do so...the magnitude of the effect was surprising. Maybe we should think about a Twinkie tax like the tax on cigarettes a little more seriously...[but]...the political battle to establish it would be a difficult one...." The Minnesota researchers said that one research goal should be to find a price balance that discourages high-fat habits while maintaining vending profits.[70]

disability pensions). Such costs, as we noted earlier, are estimated to be more than $100 billion per year.

And finally, authorities can encourage lifestyle changes that compliment good nutrition. In Australia, for example, various state agencies teamed up to promote a "National Bicycling Strategy," which seeks to raise the level of cycling in the country. More cycling means more exercise, an indispensable tool in the fight against obesity, but it could also mean cleaner air, less congested cities, and a cheaper transportation infrastructure. [71] Authorities could also encourage urban gardening programs, local farmer's markets, co-operative arrangements between producers and consumers that could not only produce healthy food but make it available to poorer people. Governments and authorities could also require product labeling that gives consumers real information about the health consequences of their consumer choices. If you think it not appropriate for governments to do these things, consider that historically government policies (especially those of the USDA) have supported the health of people, as well as the interests of agribusiness and large food corporations.

In sum, the far-reaching effects of foodways and nutrition make them central factors in personal as well as national development. The availability of a variety of food can have positive consequences, but the reverse is also true. To the extent that it promotes nutritional imbalances and obesity, they can be a drag on national economic activity as well as on personal health.

SOME SUGGESTIONS FOR FURTHER READING

Belasco, W. (1993). *Appetite for Change: How the Counterculture Took on the Food Industry.* Ithaca, NY: Cornell University Press.

Camp, C. (1989). *American Foodways: What, Where, When, Why, and How We Eat in America.* Little Rock, AK: August House.

Counihan, C., and P. Van Esterik, Eds. (1997). *Food and Culture: A Reader.* New York: Routledge.

Dreze, J., and A. Sen (1989). *Hunger and Public Action.* New York: Oxford University Press.

Finkelstein, J. (1989). *Eating Out: A Sociology of Modern Manners.* New York: New York University Press.

Harris, M. (1985). *Good to Eat; Riddles of Food and Culture.* New York: Simon and Schuster.

Kittler, P., and K. Sucher (2001). *Food and Culture.* 3rd Ed. Belmont, CA: Wadsworth.

Maurer, D., and J. Sobal, Eds. (1995). *Eating Agendas: Food and Nutrition as Social Problems.* New York: Aldine de Gruyter.

McIntosh, W. (1996). *Sociologies of Food and Nutrition.* New York: Plenum.

Ritzer, G. (1996). *The McDonaldization of Society.* Rev. Ed. Thousand Oaks, CA: Pine Forge Press.

Schlosser, E. (2001). *Fast Food Nation: The Dark Side of the All-American Meal.* Boston, MA: Houghton Mifflin.

CHAPTER 6

Food, Population, and Environment

arlier we discussed the great nutritional transformation of modern times, and particularly the changes in agricultural technology after World War II that resulted in a dramatic growth in food productivity. Important issues connected to this are in some ways more elemental and bio-physical—the challenge of feeding the growing numbers of people and the environmental consequences of that "second agricultural revolution." We continue to focus on the United States, but also on the consequences of glob-alization, because shared environmental resources and international connec-tions of all kinds are becoming more obvious than in the past. Having discussed the problems of being overfed in Chapter 5, we will turn in more depth to the problems of hunger and undernourishment in the second half of this chapter, which includes four food-related topics: population, environ-ment, the causes of chronic hunger, and ways of addressing hunger problems.

POPULATION GROWTH

It is important to understand that the growing numbers of people in the world have always shaped historical events, including who eats and how well. The United States is no exception. Most of the world's current 6 billion-plus people now live in poorer developing nations, not in the wealthy industrial nations of Europe and North America, Japan, and Australia. Like most indus-trial nations, the U.S. population growth rate is much lower than that of many developing nations. In the year 2000 it was growing at a rate of 1 percent a year, half of what it was in 1900. But that lower rate is being applied now to a much larger population. At the beginning of the twentieth century, it was about 76 million. Now almost 273 million, the United States adds twice as many people per decade as a century ago.[1] It is mind boggling to realize that the U.S. population has almost doubled in the last sixty years! Significantly, population now grows in the United States more rapidly than in most industrial nations. Almost alone among the developed nations, the U.S. population is growing robustly. The causes include a high birthrate (fertility), new arrivals through immigration, and increasing life expectancy. Demographers piece together ancient estimates from a variety of historical sources. In modern times, population size became one of the more accurate statistical databases, kept by all governments for a variety of reasons (like estimating taxes). Australia has a slightly higher growth rate than that of the United States, and Canada and New Zealand have only slightly lower growth rates. But since the U.S. population is so much larger, it is indeed alone among the developed nations in terms of the number of persons added per year.[2]

The story of the growth of world population is even more astounding. For thousands of years human population was relatively small and grew at a snail's pace. It took over a million years to reach the first billion people by about 1800 A.D. But then the pace quickened, adding a second billion in the next 130 years, a third billion in the next 30 years, and a fourth in just 15 years. World population started to grow exponentially after the 1600s, partly because growing agricultural productivity enabled more people to live. More important than food, the gradual spread of improvements in public health and sanitation, like pure water and control of infectious diseases, enabled more people to avoid death longer. Most world population growth now occurs in poorer developing nations of the world. See Figure 6.1.

WORLD POPULATION GROWTH

Demographers use the notion of *demographic transition* to explain the difference between the population growth rates of the wealthy industrial nations and the rapidly growing rates of poorer ones. This means that the changes associated with industrialization, economic development, and urbanization that took place over 300 years in Europe and North America gradually provided people with reasons to have fewer children, who became more expensive to raise; and many people also had the education and resources to limit family size. The theory of *demographic transition* means that, as nations change from traditional rural economies to urban industrial ones, they undergo a transition from populations with a high birthrates, large families, and shorter life spans to urban industrial ones with fewer children, long life spans, and

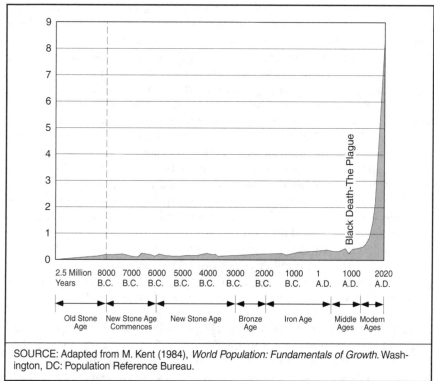

SOURCE: Adapted from M. Kent (1984), *World Population: Fundamentals of Growth*. Washington, DC: Population Reference Bureau.

FIGURE 6.1 World Population Growth Throughout History

large populations of people who live longer and have fewer children. This is a well-documented process among the nations of Europe and North America, which took place at different times and rates, beginning in the 1700s. Indeed, some European countries (for example, Germany) are no longer growing in populations and in some years do not have enough children to maintain their population, except for immigration. The United States, as noted, is an exception among industrial nations.

But things were different as the world's nonindustrial nations began the process of development, particularly after World War II. Public health and sanitation measures were relatively cheap and easy to promote by many governments and international agencies, but economic development of the kind that would encourage families to have fewer children was not. It was expensive and more difficult to promote real economic development compared to vaccinations or draining malaria-ridden swamps. Perhaps as important, such economic development in the world of developing nations was opposed by a mix of powerful forces, brought about by the legacy of exploitive European colonialism, the operation of a world market economy that benefited rich

POVERTY AND CHILDREN IN POOR DEVELOPING NATIONS

People in wealthier nations may believe that for poor people in poor countries to have many children is irrational and ignorant. But decades ago Indian scholar Mahamood Mamdani explained clearly what poor people in developing nations know. With high infant mortality rates, some may die. Beyond that, children's labor provides benefits on farms among people who could not afford to hire help when they need it, and the sale of children's labor to others may add to family income. Furthermore, as children grow, they provide a form of old-age support in nations that provide little or no retirement security. In a condition of deep poverty, young children add little to household expenses. Living in chronic poverty provides few incentives for smaller families, and thus family planning services are likely to fail.[3]

nations more than poor ones, and the prevailing patriarchal family organization in many places.

In spite of the economic forces and the disincentives to reduce family size, by the 1990s the growth rate of the world's population began to fall everywhere—for many reasons. Average fertility worldwide fell from 5 children per woman in the 1960s to 2.7 today, and the fertility in sixty-one countries representing 44 percent of the world's inhabitants is below the replacement rate of 2.1 live births per woman. Some causes of the global decline in fertility are negative, like chronic malnutrition, civil wars, and the AIDS epidemic in parts of the developing world. Others are from deliberate choices, as when family planning programs enable couples to have more control over the spacing and number of children. Importantly, decreases in fertility can result from increasing the educational and economic opportunities for women, which alter aspirations and lifestyle options. In every nation where data are available, the more schooling a woman has, the fewer children she chooses to bear, and there are no known exceptions to this generalization.[4]

In spite of the decreasing rate of growth, the huge absolute numbers of people now alive mean that the world population is still growing. By 1999 human baby number 6 billion was born, probably to a poor family in a poor nation. By mid 2000 the best estimate of the world's population was 6.06 billion. It is projected to add another billion in about thirteen years and grow to 8.9 billion by 2050.[5] Currently the two most populous nations are China and India, which each have about one-fifth of the world's population. If the United States grows at its present rate, by 2100 it will be the third most populous nation in the world, just behind China and India.[6]

The prospect of continuing such robust growth raises demands for shared resources like land, air, and water, and it increases concerns about all kinds of human problems—including the adequacy and distribution of the

PLENTY OF FOOD

In the 1990s, the world's farmers and ranchers produced enough cereal, meat, and other food products to give people the equivalent of 7.5 quadrillion calories, or about 3,800 calories per person per day. This is well above the minimum daily calorie requirements, even for people whose jobs involve hard physical labor. If all foods are considered together, enough is available to provide at least 4.3 pounds per person, including 2.5 pounds of grain, beans, and nuts, about 1 pound of fruit and vegetables, and nearly another pound of meat, milk, and eggs. Remarkably, if everyone in the world adopted a vegetarian diet and no food were wasted, current production would theoretically feed 10 billion people, more than the projected population for the year 2050.[8]

food supply. For many, the circumstance evokes a current rendition of an old and controversial scenario about human catastrophe, when population growth outstrips the resources to produce food, first formulated by English thinker Thomas Malthus in 1798.[7]

Malthusian scenarios cannot be entirely dismissed, particularly by those who observe that the remarkable productivity growth was purchased by the progressive alteration and degradation of the biological resource base. But for now, Mr. Malthus will have to wait, because the rate of growth in the world's total food supply has clearly outstripped that of population growth in the modern era. There has been famine at particular times and in some regions, and many are chronically hungry today. But the post-World War II "second agricultural revolution" was amazingly productive. Chronic hunger is down on a global basis, and American and West European farmers are so plagued with food commodity surpluses that their livelihoods are continually jeopardized. There is plenty of food to ensure food security for everyone in the world—*if* it were distributed equitably.

Aside from things that disrupt a nation's food system (like natural disasters, floods, droughts, and wars), chronic hunger has very little to do with the total supply of food.

THE ENVIRONMENTAL IMPACT OF PRODUCING FOOD

The revolution in agriculture in America and the world after the 1950s was by many measures a stunning success. Yields of wheat, corn, and rice—the world's principal crops—have risen steadily, and have outpaced world population growth during most of that period. Real food prices declined as production soared. Those achievements can be credited to technological and scientific advances in agriculture discussed earlier (new seeds, fertilizers, pest control, and extensive increases in irrigation). But, such phenomenal production increases have a dark side. Taken together, producing food and other agricultural products (like cotton) uses more soil, water, and energy resources—and causes more pollution and environmental damage—than *any* other human activity. Indeed, if our planet were a bank disbursing loans of natural resources, agriculture would be among its biggest debtors. "Industrial agriculture" often uses resources at rates well beyond their rates of replenishment—with little effort to replace them. As agricultural debts continue to mount, it borrows from resources available to future generations. Can it continue indefinitely?[9]

Soil is the basic agricultural resource containing the minerals and nutrients that grow plants that produce most of the world's food and fiber. In nature, soils slowly replace their nutrients and minerals required for the growth of living things, because then they die, they decompose, and return organic matter and nutrients to the earth. Removing these nutrients and minerals and depositing them in other places erodes soil. Eroded topsoil will not support efficient plant growth, because it lacks essential plant nutrients. Nor will it hold water close to the surface to be accessible to crops. Wind and flowing water are the natural causes of erosion, but its rate has been greatly amplified by human activities like farming, the overgrazing of livestock, deliberate burning of vegetation, logging, and urban development. All these make soil vulnerable to erosion by removing its plant cover. Erosion reduces agricultural productivity and affects the future of the world's food supply, by

- reducing the soil's ability to retain moisture,
- carrying away soil nutrients,
- degrading the physical properties of the soil, such as its porosity, and
- causing uneven soil loss, making crop management less efficient.

A reason that many farmers and governments do not make soil erosion a high priority issue is that is that it is normally slow and its effects accumulate only over long periods of time. But scientists estimate that worldwide erosion rates for agricultural lands are 20 to100 times the natural rate of soil replacement. Such rates vary significantly in different regions because of topography, rainfall, wind intensity, and the types of agricultural practices used.[10]

As we noted in Chapter 3, the United States drought in the 1930s, combined with wind and poor agricultural practices (like overgrazing and leaving the land bare between crops), caused much of the topsoil of the Great Plains to literally blow away. Thus the stage was set for massive crop and ranch failures, in the midst of the national great depression of the 1930s.[11] As a consequence of this hard environmental "dust bowl" lesson, the U.S. Department of Agriculture established the Soil Conservation Service (SCS) to protect the nation's topsoil. The SCS promoted sound conservation practices, setting up Soil Conservation Districts that gave farmers and ranchers technical and edu-

SOIL EROSION AND "THE DUSTBOWL"

Windy and dry, the vast grasslands of the Great Plains stretch across ten states, from Texas through Montana and the Dakotas. Before settlers began grazing livestock and planting crops there in the 1870s, it had deep, tangled root systems of native prairie grasses that anchored topsoil firmly in place. Plowing the land tore up these root systems, which were replaced by crops (like corn and wheat) having much less extensive root systems. After each harvest, the land was plowed and left bare for several months, exposing it to the Plains winds. Overgrazing also destroyed large expanses of grasslands. The drought between 1926 and 1934 resulted in dust clouds created by hot, dry windstorms that darkened the sky at midday in some areas, and birds often choked to death on the dust. During May 1934, a cloud of topsoil blown away from the Great Plains blanketed the entire Eastern United States, some 1,500 miles away! Journalists gave the Great Plains a new name, the *Dustbowl*. Thousands of displaced farm families migrated from Oklahoma, Texas, Kansas, Colorado, and Nebraska to California or to the industrial cities of the Midwest or East. They usually found little relief because the nation was in the midst of the Great Depression.[12]

cational assistance with agricultural practices that conserved soil. In the 1980s the SCS's Conservation Reserve Program encouraged the conversion of erodible land into grassland or woodland, and penalized farmers who didn't manage soil responsibly by denying them the benefits of government farm programs (price supports, crop insurance, and low-interest loans). By 1987, such programs helped slow U.S. soil losses significantly.

In spite of such efforts, soil on cultivated land in the United States still erodes at least eighteen times faster than it can form. Erosion rates are higher in heavily farmed areas, including the Great Plains, which has lost one-third or more of its topsoil in the 150 years since it was first plowed. Some of the country's more productive agricultural lands such as those in Iowa, have lost about half of their topsoil. California's soil is eroding about eighty times faster than it can be formed. Enough topsoil erodes each day in the United States to fill a line of dump trucks 3,500 miles long.[13] In 1995, scientist David Pimentel and his colleagues estimated the combined direct and indirect costs of soil erosion amounted to $44 billion per year in the United States alone. Direct erosion costs include such things as loss of soil nutrients with declining yields and physical damage to topsoil. Indirect costs include damaging or silting rivers, harbors, and estuaries. By comparison, the costs of erosion control measures like planting crops that protect the soil, low tillage cultivation, and contouring the land would be relatively small ($8.4 billion).[14]

As you can imagine, getting good data about the global extent of soil degradation around the world combining data from various nations and regions is a formidable task. Yet it has been done. In 1990 the United Nations

Intensive agricultural monocropping.

Environment Programme conducted a global survey of soil degradation (GLASOD) involving a team of 220 analysts from around the world, who measured soil damage from overgrazing, pollution, oversalinization, and wind and water erosion. Oversalinization occurs when soil gets too salty and crop production declines. It happens to continually irrigated land, when the water evaporates or is taken up by plants, leaving behind mineral salts to accumulate in the soils. It was probably a factor in the decline of ancient Mesopotamian river civilization. In the United States, irrigated land in California's Central Valley is plagued by oversalinization. There are treatments, such as "back flushing," using pure water to remove salts, but this is prohibitively expensive in many arid regions. GLASOD concluded that just since 1945 at least 17 percent of the world's soil has suffered human-induced degradation, caused about equally from overgrazing, poor farming practices, and deforestation.[15] In the millennium year 2000, a more comprehensive study, using satellite mapping and other techniques, was conducted by the UN- affiliated International Food Policy Research Institute (IFPRI).

It found that a whopping 40 percent of the earth's soil around the globe was seriously degraded by some combination of flooding, chemical effects such as nutrient depletion, damage from waterlogging, or compaction of soil where nothing will grow. Such damage has actually reduced per acre yields on about 16 percent of farmland worldwide, a figure that conceals vast regional disparities, ranging from 75 percent in Central America and 20 percent in Africa to 11 percent in Asia. In Asia, soil damage is mainly due to oversalinization and waterlogging from excessive irrigation. In Central America, it is from clearing and farming highly erodible hillsides, while in Africa it is from nutrient depletion. According to Ismail Serageldin, World Bank Vice President and chairperson of the consortium of international agricultural research centers, including IFPRI, "The results of this innovative mapping raise all kinds of red flags about the world's ability to feed itself in the future." But the study also notes that not all of the soil degradation is irreversible and that some—not all—could be remedied by better land management.[16]

Compared to soil problems, water problems are more pressing constraints on food production now. Like soil, water is a vast renewable resource. It cycles from the atmosphere back to land and the oceans. But fresh potable water suitable for human use or agriculture is limited and very unevenly distributed. The global consumption of this usable water has more than tripled since 1950 and is now equal to more than eight times the flow of the Mississippi River, vastly outstripping population growth. Of all water used by people, agriculture accounts for about 70 percent and is, by any measure, the most inefficient use. It takes about a million gallons of water in a growing season to grow a little more than two acres (1 hectare) of corn, and it is not unusual for 70–80 percent of that to be lost by runoff, evaporation, or seeping into the ground before reaching crops. Planners for municipalities, industry, and agriculture have met the growing demands for water by "water development projects" involving dams, irrigation systems, and river diversion schemes. But limits to this ever-expanding consumption are coming to light everywhere. Water tables are falling, lakes are shrinking, wetlands are disappearing, and rivers are often reduced to trickles as they empty into the sea (for example, the Colorado River in the United States).[18]

Since irrigation grew rapidly as a cornerstone of the second agricultural

---

WATER AND FOOD

Here is how many liters of water it takes to grow one kilogram of various foods. (A liter is about 1 quart, and a kilogram is 2.2 pounds.) [17]

Kilogram of . . .	Liters of Water
Potatoes	500
Wheat	900
Maize (corn)	1,400
Rice	1,910
Soy Beans	2,000
Chicken	3,500
Beef	100,000

revolution, groundwater supplies are particularly critical to maintaining current productivity. Groundwater stored in underground geological formations called *aquifers* is in many ways an ideal source of water for crop irrigation. Whereas river-based canal systems and reservoirs deliver water unreliably and lose much by evaporation, underground water loses none, can be tapped when needed by farmers, and requires no large government subsidies for dams or diversion projects. But currently, groundwater is being overpumped at four times its replacement rate. In the United States, pumping from the Ogallala Aquifer that underlies the Great Plains stretching from Nebraska to Texas is 130 to 160 percent above replacement rates. At these rates of consumption, much of the Great Plains, a region that now supplies 40 percent of the nation's beef and grain, may become barren. The ripple effects would be felt in "high plains" economies and communities as they begin to deal with depopulation and alternatives to conventional agriculture. Aquifer overdrafts are also critical in California's Central Valley—America's "salad bowl"—and other areas of the arid Southwest. Such overdrafts are more like "mining" a finite resource like coal than using a renewable resource.

In India, the number of groundwater wells climbed from 4 million in 1951 to 17 million by 1997, allowing the area irrigated by groundwater to climb sixfold. Irrigation overdrafts lowered water tables by 20–30 meters in the Tamil Nadu region of India during the 1970s, and for the nation, water problems became so severe that the Indian Supreme Court directed a national research center to study it. Pakistan now irrigates 80 percent of its crops from aquifer irrigation. Pumping ancient aquifers under the desert, with basically zero recharge rates drove Saudi Arabia's increase in food productivity. Around Beijing, China, water tables are declining at the rate of between 1 and 5 meters per year. Under China's northern plain, which, like the U.S. Great Plains, produces 40 percent of China's grain, projected water deficits for 2025 equals the water needed for about 14 percent of the nation's annual grain consumption. There are ways to deal with water problems: taking land out of production, eliminating a harvest or two, switching to less

AQUIFER DEPLETION THREATENS MORE THAN FOOD SECURITY

Because groundwater often supplies rivers, wetlands, and lakes, overpumping can dry out valuable wetlands, and dry up lakes and rivers when water tables drop too far. Overpumping aquifers can cause land to sink. In Tucson, Arizona, for instance, land has sunk more than seven feet. Overpumping coastal aquifers can change the zone separating the ocean and fresh water, so that seawater seeps in and contaminates freshwater supplies in coastal cities. Many towns and cities along the Atlantic and Gulf Coasts in the United States, the coastal areas in Israel, Syria, the Arabian Gulf States, and Gujarat state in India are battling the contamination of drinking water supplies by salty seawater.[20]

water-intensive crops, or adopting more efficient irrigation practices (with less waste and evaporation). But so far, these efforts pale in comparison to the scale of the problem of overpumping.[19]

Because water is so important for humans, growing shortages have amplified political squabbles everywhere. In the United States, litigation and efforts to negotiate water issues have become chronic between states that share common agricultural, industrial, and municipal water sources. Particularly included are California and other states in the arid Southwest, and Kansas, Nebraska, Colorado, and Wyoming which share water from the Missouri River basin across the Great Plains. Some of the world's historic conflicts about nationality, religion, and ethnicity are partly about who controls water. Because it is scarce in the Middle East, a "hydrological time bomb" underlies the otherwise bitter conflicts of the region between Israelis, Palestinians, Iraqis, Syrians, Turks, and others. In South Asia, the decades-long conflict between India and Pakistan over Kashmir was always partly about water—as well as the more obvious religious and nationality conflicts. India made attempts to dam up the river that ties the whole region together, and the Pakistanis feared that the Indians might turn off the floodgates in the middle of some hot summer season and parch part of Pakistan. On the Eastern border of India, the poverty-stricken Bangladeshis were afraid that the Indian project to dam the Ganges River, only miles from the border, would deny them vital water.[21]

Fertile soil and water supplies are not the only resources impacted by attempting to feed people. The world's fisheries are being overexploited, and the world's fish catch is declining. Similar to the growth of food produced on land, the global fish catch grew by an average of 5 percent per year between 1950 and 1970. But then increases in the fish catch began to decline to about 1 percent in the 1980s and 1990s. In 1993 the Food and Agricultural Organization (FAO) of the United Nations found that fifteen of the seventeen major ocean fisheries had been fished at or beyond their maximum sustainable yield for commercially valuable fish. In thirteen of these areas, fish yields have been dropping for several years, and 70 percent of the world's commercial fish stocks are fully exploited, overfished, or rebuilding from past overfishing.[22] Levels of fish catch in increasingly depleted ocean fisheries are maintained by the coordination of large fleets with sophisticated devices like sonar for finding scarcer fish, and by harvesting smaller fish and species that were considered of little commercial value a few decades ago. Examples of these include shark, torsk, pollock, and mahi mahi.

Just off shore from New England and the Atlantic Maritime Provinces of Canada, lie the North Atlantic cod fisheries (the "Grand Banks"), which have been fished by many nations over the centuries. But now catches of cod and other commercial seafood are mere fractions of their historic levels, and legal battles simmer between fishers everywhere for rights to fish the remaining stocks. Canadian provinces and American states (like New Brunswick and

Massachusetts) responded to fishery depletion by lowering the legal fish catch limits or declaring temporary moratoriums on fishing in certain areas—good strategies, but often "too little, too late." Governments also responded by subsidizing failing fishing industries with cheap business loans, social welfare, and job-retraining programs for the increasing numbers of bankrupt fishers. The decline of the North Atlantic fisheries is a significant factor in the economic problems of the New England states, and particularly in the chronically depressed Canadian Maritime Provinces. Similar problems exist in fisheries in the Pacific and around the world, used by the fleets of many nations.

As the fish catch stalled in recent decades, "fish farming," or *aquaculture,* in ocean pens or in freshwater lakes picked up the slack, growing from 8 percent of the world's seafood supply in 1984 to over 25 percent in 1998. Aquaculture, however, comes with heavy environmental impacts. Feeding carnivores like salmon or shrimp often increases pressure on ocean fisheries to deliver more food to them. Furthermore, the wastes from farmed seafood can be a source of pollution. The salmon fisheries of the Nordic nations produce nitrogen in quantities equivalent to that found in the sewage of 9.3 million people, roughly the population of Norway. Pollution often limits the useful life of operations: most intensively cultivated shrimp ponds in Asia can be used for no more than ten to fifteen years. Aquaculture can also be a source of "biological pollution," when species foreign to a region escape into the wild and dominate ecosystems in which they have no natural enemies.[24]

FISH AND CHIPS IN THE UNITED KINGDOM

The United Kingdom's distinctive contribution to world cuisine, fish and chips, could disappear unless changes are made. The World Wildlife Fund (WWF) says that fish are in desperate straits, because Irish Sea cod are at a historic low. Fishers are unable to catch their yearly quota, even though lowered 80 percent in the last year. The number of young fish being spawned is half what it was in the1960s, and over 80 percent of the immature young fish in 1997 were accidentally caught as "by-catch" with other species. Cod is now more expensive (in the United Kingdom) than farmed salmon. The WWF wants some areas of the sea to be placed out of bounds to fishing vessels, to give the fisheries a chance to recover. The WWF and the Scottish Fisherman's Federation launched a joint initiative in March 2000 calling for specific changes to local and European fisheries management. Matthew Davis of the WWF said, "Unless we take action to regenerate fish stocks, traditional fish and chips may soon become a dish of the past. This isn't just a threat to ocean wildlife; it's a threat to our cultural heritage. The commercial extinction of fish stocks could jeopardize the jobs of the 15,000 full-time and 3,500 part-time fishermen in the U.K."[23] To citizens of the United Kingdom, this is a commercial and cultural equivalent to what the threatened disappearance of hamburgers and French fries would be for people in the United States.

Such overfishing has observable consequences. Retail seafood has become very expensive in recent years, and overexploitation of ocean resources has serious implications for food security around the world, because fish provide about 15 percent of animal protein for human consumption. Over 1 billion people worldwide, most of them in Asia, rely on fish as their primary source of protein.[25]

There are more impacts of producing food. Biodiversity, the number and variety of living things on the earth, is now rapidly diminishing. In broad strokes, the causes of this decline are that the habitats of wild living things are being destroyed and fragmented as humans occupy and control more and more of the planet. More concretely, cutting forests and global warming causes shrinking biological diversity that changes the habitats of living species. Modern agriculture is also a powerful cause of the declining number and variety of species. Humans historically used thousands of plant species for food, now reduced to mainly twenty species around the world. Of these, the major ones are wheat, corn, millet, rye, and rice. People encountered these crops haphazardly at the dawn of the first agricultural revolution; they are now selectively bred into a few strains with greatly reduced genetic variability. This was, of course, the genetic basis of the second agricultural revolution and the increase in productivity it brought.

Consider some illustrations. India once had 30,000 varieties of rice, but today most production comes from only ten. In a trip to the supermarket, you can purchase perhaps five or six varieties of apples, but in North America alone there were more than a hundred varieties grown and marketed in the late 1800s. The UN Food and Agriculture Organization estimated that by the year 2000 two-thirds of the seeds planted in developing nations were from uniform strains. The same sort of reduction in genetic variability took place in the herds of cattle, sheep, horses, pigs, and other animals that humans raise.[26] Overfishing ocean and freshwater fisheries reduce complex aquatic diversity by breaking key links in aquatic food chains, as do all forms of water pollution. Importantly, we note that a number of human activities reduce biodiversity besides agriculture and fishing. Others include commercial hunting and poaching, predator control, the sale of exotic pets and plants, and the deliberate introduction of non-native species that outcompete native species.[27]

Preserving biodiversity is important for many reasons. People value diversity because it represents the ancient biological heritage of the earth, and for the sometimes-breathtaking beauty of nature. But in addition to spiritual and esthetic value is economics: products of "wild" nature such as oils, resins, spices, and fibers, are of enormous economic value. They are sources of medicines and pharmaceuticals for all kinds of painkillers and diseases. Moreover, even in an era of intensive agriculture with selective breeding and genetically engineered crops, the productivity of our food supply still depends on the diversity maintained by wilderness and traditional agriculture. Wild relatives of crops continue to be used to maintain resistance to disease, vigor, and other

COMMERCIAL CORN, WILD CORN, AND BLIGHT

By 1970, when 70 percent of the seed corn grown in the United States owed its ancestry to six inbred lines, a leaf fungus infected ("blighted") cornfields from the Great Lakes to the Gulf of Mexico, threatening the corn belt. Fifteen percent of the entire U.S. corn crop was destroyed (more than half in parts of the South) costing consumers more than $2 billion. Damage was halted using a variety of blight-resistant corn genes. Importantly, one was a "wild" genetic ancestor living in Mexico discovered and preserved from extinction just in the nick of time. Only a few thousand stalks were surviving in three tiny patches in South Central Mexico that were about to be cleared by loggers and farmers. That strain was found to have built-in genetic resistance to four of the eight major viruses that affect corn, which heretofore breeders had not been able to "breed into" commercial varieties.[28]

traits that produce billions of dollars in benefits to global agriculture. Previously we noted the vulnerabilities to predators and diseases inherent in the agricultural monocultures. We discussed the Irish potato crop failure and famine of the nineteenth century. There are similar cases of crop monocultures that have failed recently because they were particularly vulnerable to insects, blights, viruses, and other diseases. Some were saved by crossbreeding modern hybrids with wild or traditional species.

Consider a concrete example of the value of biodiversity. Both wild (feral) and managed bees and other insects fertilize crops and orchards. In the United States alone bees fertilize crops worth billions, in addition to pollinating natural plant species. Scientists estimate bees pollinate trillions of blossoms during a single summer day. There is obviously no technological substitute for such ecological and agricultural services of pollinators! But managed honeybee colonies have been declining since 1979, due to the use of pesticides. If native and wild pollinators were similarly affected, costs to the U.S. agricultural economy would be at least $4.1 to $6.7 billion a year.[29] The important point of these illustrations is that agriculture cannot prosper by depending only on a few scientifically bred livestock and crop species, however productive they are. For food production, the role of wild species is often not fully appreciated, as they are sometimes not appreciated for maintaining the earth's ecosystems.

Finally, the residues from agrochemicals that maintain or boost productivity, along with wastes from confined animal feeding operations, represent environmental and human health hazards. Inorganic fertilizers and animal wastes leave large concentrations of nitrates, phosphates, and microorganisms from animal wastes that wash into streams, rivers, lakes, and groundwater. Such increased plant nutrient levels cause algae and other water plants to grow profusely, using up most dissolved oxygen in the water. When they die, they sink to the bottom, along with many oxygen-breathing fish and other aquatic animals, leaving the body of water essentially dead—except for the few scavengers and decomposers which can live in oxygen-depleted water.

When this process, called *cultural eutrophication*, originates from a specific point (like hog confinement wastes), a river ecosystem may be degraded, only to recover miles downstream. But it is even more damaging when it does not derive from a specific point, such as the 221-square-mile Florida everglades that is being degraded by broad water flows containing nitrates and pesticides from sugar and orange groves to the north. Similarly, where the Mississippi River flows into the Gulf of Mexico there is a "dead zone" of hundreds of square miles where agrochemicals and animal wastes trigger massive algae booms that choke the oxygen supply of the water, and kill fish and shrimp.

Pesticide and herbicide pollution in surface and groundwater is widespread. In Long Island, New York, 23 percent of 330 wells tested in the early 1990s were contaminated with Aldicarb at levels that exceeded health guidelines. Aldicarb is a highly toxic pesticide once used on the region's potato

---

CONFINED ANIMAL FEEDING OPERATIONS AND POLLUTION

Factory farms or confined animal feeding operations that raise thousands of hogs, chickens, and cattle in confined spaces represent environmental and human health hazards (to say nothing of the smells!). In 1999, they produced an estimated 1.3 billion tons of manure each year, which is also infested with chemicals and antibiotic growth stimulants. This is put into open lagoons or sprayed on fields as fertilizer where it can soak into groundwater and rivers that are used by people. In North Carolina, which has a population of 9.5 million hogs and 7.4 million people, a spill from hog-waste dumped 23 million gallons of raw sewage into the New River in 1995—twice the amount of the Exxon-Valdez oil spill. Later that year, a 35-million-ton spill killed 10 million fish and closed 364,000 acres of coastal wetland. When hog confined animal feeding operations move close to residential areas, the stench and potential for groundwater contamination drive property values down as much as 7.7 percent. In 1997, chicken waste spills in the Chesapeake Bay caused an outbreak of the deadly bacteria *pfisteria*, which killed fish and caused hundreds of people to become ill. The Minnesota Pollution Control Agency estimates that daily leaks from animal waste lagoons average 500 gallons per acre, and in Olivia, Minnesota, where hog lagoons emitted high levels of hydrogen sulfide, school kids kept getting sick. In Vernon County Missouri, residents blame Murphy Farms (one of the nation's four big pig producers) for a dramatic drop in the groundwater table. Seventeen wells have dried up. Chino, California, has the highest concentration of dairy cows in the world, and their ground water has suffered. The community has been forced to build desalinization plants to treat their groundwater.[30]

McDONALD'S CLEANS UP ITS ENVIRONMENTAL ACT

In addition to the environmental impacts of agriculture, the retail food and restaurant industry generates enormous wastes that impact the environment. To many, McDonald's symbolized a consumer society run amok. Though the company was probably no worse than its rivals, it paid the sins of an industry where food was slapped into elaborate wrappers that were thrown away minutes later. McDonald's was blamed for everything from litter to traffic congestion, and there were dark rumors (never fully substantiated) that tropical rainforest land was being cleared to raise its cattle. Environmental activist groups gave it a bad public image, and some city councils banned Styrofoam burger boxes. But McDonald's turned to environmentalists for advice, and went from environmental villain to role model in a decade. McDonald's has reduced its wastes by more than 30 percent since 1990, become one of the leading buyers of recycled material, and cut its energy consumption to boot. The polystyrene "clamshell" box that held Big Macs was replaced by special lightweight paper. Napkins are an inch shorter and made of recycled newspapers. Straws are shorter, dining trays are lighter and much of its playground equipment is made of recycled plastic. Ironically, McDonald's is such a large purchaser that when it insisted on cardboard boxes made of recycled paper, box companies adopted their standards as the one for all their customers, both inside and outside the restaurant business. Fred Krupp, head of an environmental organization that helped McDonald's, said, "They've made a long series of commitments and they've hit every target." Not all of McDonald's competitors have been as responsive to public pressures and activists are trying to get the industry to clean up its environmental act. Moreover, even if the industry were waste free, problems remain because of its reliance on beef-rich menus; cattle are the most environmentally damaging kind of livestock to raise because of the food and water they consume and the wastes they produce.[31]

fields. At about the same time, studies of wells in Nebraska found that one of seven wells tested were contaminated with the herbicide Atrazine (linked to lymphatic tumors and cancers). Kansas threatened to sue Nebraska because of high Atrazine levels in the Blue River flowing between the states, which feeds into municipal water supplies in several Kansas cities, including Kansas City, Kansas. In 1987, the U.S. Environmental Protection Agency ranked pesticide residues in foods as the third most serious environmental health risk for cancer in the United States.

Health risks of contact with agrochemicals include various forms of cancer, but cancer is a complex disease and difficult to link to a particular cause. As we noted in the first chapter, agrochemical residues exist in very low concentrations (measured in parts per million in water), and their consequences materialize statistically in populations only after years of contact. Even so, the World Health Organization has estimated that each year pesticides seriously poison 25 million agricultural workers in the developing nations and kill 220,000. In the United States at least 300,000 farm workers suffer from pesticide-related illnesses each year, and at least 25 die. The effects are particularly severe among Hispanic migrant farm workers, who have very high levels of exposure. Partly because of exposure to agrochemicals, the U.S. National Institute for Occupational Safety and Health named agriculture as the nation's most hazardous occupation, ahead of construction, mining, and manufacturing.[32]

As if all this weren't bad enough, mounting evidence indicates that in the long run, pesticides do not effectively protect crops from losses. The reason is that, while insecticides may initially suppress insects, they breed and mutate rapidly and tend to develop chemically resistant strains that then require more or different chemicals to suppress them. Agrochemicals can also let more insects eventually live by killing birds and other predators that feed on them.

In sum, modern agriculture has a greater impact on the environment than any other human activity. It degrades soil fertility through erosion and nutrient loss, salinization, soil compaction, and waterlogging. It reduces biodiversity through clearing natural habitats, lowers genetic diversity by selective breeding, and overfishes the fertile breeding grounds of sea life. It kills wild species, including pest predators, by agrochemical pollution. It degrades water supplies through overusing river and ground water supplies, and is a cause of pollution by agrochemicals and dangerous microorganisms from animal confinement facilities. This produces low-level but pervasive threats to human health.

As we said earlier, the environmental impact of producing food was the "dark side" of the remarkable growth of productivity of the second agricultural revolution since the 1950s, and this increase in productivity was quite remarkable given such pervasive assaults on the resource bases that support growing and getting food. That process undoubtedly reflected the needs of a rapidly growing population in the United States and the world. But what of the future? Can the success continue indefinitely? In spite of the failure of Malthusian gloomy scenarios about the past, all analysts would agree that food security is not only a matter of productivity and the environmental resources base, but also population size and growth. In fact, there is some evidence that even as total food production continues to grow, food production *per capita* has been leveling off since the 1980s, or may have declined.[33] See Figure 6.2.

These data are controversial, but no one has been able to dismiss it completely. Less controversial is the realization that in the coming decades more food will be required, although not perhaps in North America or Europe, which have food production surpluses. But, in Southeast Asia 10 percent more food will be needed, and much more will be needed by developing nations in the Caribbean, South Asia, and parts of Africa, with their large, rapidly growing, and often undernourished populations. The world will need 40

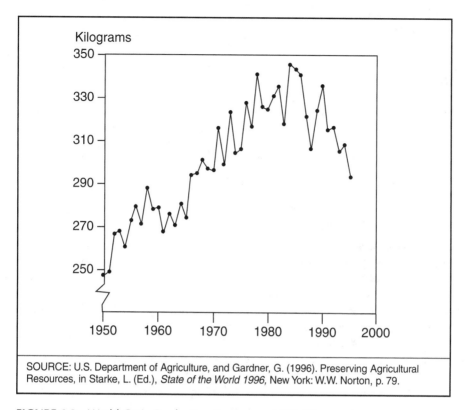

SOURCE: U.S. Department of Agriculture, and Gardner, G. (1996). Preserving Agricultural Resources, in Starke, L. (Ed.), *State of the World 1996,* New York: W.W. Norton, p. 79.

FIGURE 6.2   World Grain Production Per Person, 1950–95

percent more grain by 2020 to feed the growing world population as it approaches 8 billion. The UN Food and Agriculture Organization estimated that using the most conservative projections of world population growth to 2025, food production would need to double to meet minimum require-ments.[34] Food analysts think that this will be very difficult, because humans are degrading many of the underlying agricultural resources at rates well beyond their replenishment. Again, we ask, how can more food be produced for grow-ing populations within increasingly compromised and degraded agricultural resources?

ALTERNATIVES TO INDUSTRIAL AGRICULTURE?

The most obvious answer is to expand what has worked in the past: the indus-trial or "high-input" agriculture that began in the nineteenth century and flowered during the second agricultural revolution. It did so in conjunction with the Green Revolution (noted earlier) that produced marvelously pro-

---

TOP BANANA

The world's top banana producer, Chiquita, which grows about one-quarter of all commercially sold bananas, announced its participation in November of 2000 in the Better Banana Project, an environmental certification program requiring companies to rein in the use of toxic chemicals, reduce pollution, and conserve soil and water. Chiquita said that is has spent $20 million over the last eight years to comply with the project's guidelines, but that meeting them will actually help profits because reducing the use of chemicals will cut costs. The company said that all 127 of its farms in Latin America are now certified, and its smaller operations in Africa and Asia will meet the program guidelines soon.[35]

---

ductive rice, wheat, and corn for subtropical countries. Industrial agriculture uses large amounts of fossil-fuel energy, water from pumping groundwater or irrigation, and commercial agrochemicals to produce huge quantities of single crop monocultures. As we noted, it produces an abundance of food, and is practiced on about 25 percent of all cropland, mainly in the developed industrial nations. Plantation agriculture, a variety of industrial agriculture in developing nations, produces bananas, coffee, and cacao for sale primarily in industrial nations. The most recent extension of industrial agriculture utilizes biotechnology to genetically engineer crops, making them more resistant to pests, suitable for poorer and dryer soils, tolerant of commercial herbicides, and better able to be stored and transported.

By contrast, ancient traditional agriculture typically produced only enough crops or livestock for a farm family's survival through nonmarket means, though in good years there is a surplus to sell or to store for hard times. Shifting cultivation in tropical forests and nomadic herding also illustrate this kind of food production. In *intensive* traditional agriculture, farmers increase inputs of human and draft animal labor, fertilizers, agrochemicals, and water, enough to get a higher yield per area of cultivated land. Such yields can feed families and routinely provide income. Forms of traditional subsistence agriculture are practiced in many parts of the developing world, especially in Central Asia, Saharan and sub-Saharan Africa, and in the tropical jungles of Latin America. Intensive traditional agriculture is the dominant form of producing food in China, Southeast Asia, and India—illustrated by rice grown in paddies.

So, as we suggested, extending industrial agriculture to areas using forms of traditional farming is the most obvious strategy to address future food problems, and it is a particularly appealing strategy to agribusiness firms that would profit from its export. But, as you can see from the foregoing, the productivity of industrial agriculture has extracted an enormous price in terms of environmental degradation and resource use. In fact, the historic yield increases depend not only on having fertile soil and lots of water, but also a lot of fossil fuels to run machinery, to produce and apply inorganic fertilizers, and to pump water for irrigation. While they have yielded impressive results, at some point more inputs are of little value because a "law of diminishing returns" starts to operate. Yields plateau—and may even drop for a number of reasons. Soil erodes and loses fertility or becomes salty and waterlogged. Fertilizer is not a substitute for fertile soil and can be applied only up to certain levels before crop yields begin to decline. Underground and surface water becomes depleted and polluted with pesticides and nitrates from fertilizers. Populations of rapidly breeding pests develop genetic immunity to pesticides and genetically engineered (GE) protections. Some new land could be brought into production, but about as many acres are removed from production each year because of erosion and other damage. The net possibility means that there is not that much more arable land that can be brought into production.[36]

Institutional barriers also make the expansion of industrial agriculture difficult. Even if there were no resource problems, it is still very expensive to transplant such techniques and practices to poorer parts of the world, where food problems are likely to be most severe. As discussed in earlier chapters, GE crops are embryonic with unknown potentials, but they carry extraordinary ecological risks, and would be even more expensive for poor nations to adopt because they are being developed by private agribusiness corporations. So far, golden rice is the sole example of a GE crop that provided a distinct nutritional advantage and is cheaply available to farmers in developing nations.

SUSTAINABLE FARMING AND AGROECOLOGY

Food production that combines elements of historical traditional agriculture and scientific ecological knowledge provides an alternative. Rather than planting monocultures, traditional farmers around the world simultaneously grow several crops on the same plot of land, known as *interplanting*. This involves a variety of techniques, including:

- *Polyvarietal cultivation*, in which a plot is planted with several varieties of the same crop;
- *Intercropping*, in which two or more crops are grown at the same time— for example, a carbohydrate-rich grain that uses soil nitrogen along with a protein-rich legume that puts it back;
- *Agroforestry*, or *alley cropping*, in which crops and trees are planted together. For example, fruit trees or trees for wood can be planted in rows between rows of faster growing trees or legumes that add nitrogen to the soil;

- *Polyculture,* a more complex form of intercropping in which many different plants maturing at various times are planted together. When cultivated, they can provide food, medicines, fuel, and natural pesticides and fertilizers, on a sustainable basis.

Polycultures have root systems at different depths in the soil and are efficient in capturing water and nutrients, so they minimize the need for irrigation and fertilizer. Year-round plant coverage can protect the soil from water and wind erosion. Having a variety of habitats for pests, polycultures need not be sprayed with as many pesticides. Since weeds have trouble competing with a variety of crop plants, they can be removed fairly easily. Such diversity provides some insurance against bad weather: If one crop fails because of too much or too little water, another may survive, or even thrive.[37]

For modern farmers, planting polycultures means rediscovering the dwindling wisdom of historic traditional farmers. Whether traditional or modern, compared to industrial farming, polyculture farms are smaller; they require more human labor and specialized knowledge—about crops, livestock, and local soil, water, and growing conditions—but much less reliance on expensive mechanization or agrochemical inputs. Compared with monocultures, polycultures are more sustainable over time and do not degrade the environment. Rather than being analogous to industrial production with inputs and wastes, sustainable polycultures resemble the recycling in ecosystems. The practice is termed *agroecology* by agricultural scientists.[38] Agroecologists are likely to have greater knowledge of local soil, water, and growing seasons, and their polycrops are more likely to realize buffers against plant pathogens, as well as the vagaries of price fluctuations of agricultural commodity markets. They are also more likely to be better stewards of land, water, and environmental resources than large farms operated by absentee owners.

DIVERSITY MORE PRODUCTIVE?

"Second revolution agricultural monocultures" were developed because hybrid seeds were more productive than wild ones. But scientists are learning that in an ecological context, diverse polycultures often outperform such moncultures. Researchers from Oregon State University and Yunnan Agricultural University in China found that, where a variety of rice strains were planted, fields were far less vulnerable to rice blast, a fungus that attacks rice—the main scourge of Southeast Asian rice fields. Remarkably, these fields were 89 percent more productive than those fields where just one strain of rice was planted. This finding challenges the methods of modern agriculture that require hybrid seeds and heavy inputs of agrochemicals, or the need for genetically engineered, pest resistant crops—and argues that organic methods may be better even if applied on a commercial scale.[39]

There are experiments with agroecology in a variety of states. Iowa, for example, has an organized network of about 300 small polyculturists with their own newsletter, marketing networks, and applied research programs (who call themselves Iowa Practical Farmers). It is obvious, however, this has not been the dominant agricultural trend of the twentieth century; the dominant trend has been to drive small farmers off the land and produce the large monocultures of intensive industrial agriculture, both in the United States and around the world. These have been ecologically damaging, but more is at stake than maintaining food producing resources. We cite again (as in Chapter 4), sociologist Debra Bryceson, who found that in sub-Saharan Africa, "as de-agrarianization proceeds, signs of social dysfunction (such as the crime, hunger, and the breakdown of family ties) accelerates." When the economic prospects of small farmers erode, so does the social fabric of rural communities, with higher rates of unemployment, alcoholism, domestic violence, infant mortality—and malnutrition.[40] Displaced rural people migrate in large numbers to the overburdened urban shantytowns in third world cities, like Mexico City or Calcutta.

HUNGER IN AMERICA AND THE WORLD

Of the two main forms of malnutrition in the world today, we dealt earlier with being overfed. Now we turn to being *underfed* (or undernourished), either in terms of too few calories or micronutrient deficiencies. There is a difference between being chronically undernourished and being hungry—which may or may not be a chronic condition. Because it is more important for our purposes, we will distinguish between hunger/undernourishment and food security (or insecurity), which has to do with the risk of becoming hungry, for an individual, group or country. Before discussing the contemporary debate about the causes of hunger in America and the world, there are some factual contours about the problem that you should know.

KINDS OF HUNGER

Hunger of short duration is not necessarily debilitating to an individual (consider the ancient practice of fasting for health or religious reasons). When hunger persists for a long time it involves chronic protein-energy malnutrition with symptoms like marasmus, scurvy, pellegra, night blindness, or Kwashiorkor. Shorter-term hunger is more serious in infants and young children, however, because it stunts a physical development process not at risk in adults, which is why most agencies concerned with hunger problems emphasize starting first with hungry children.

We mentioned in several places that the incidence of world hunger has declined significantly since the 1950s. It is important to note, however, that the steepest declines were in the earlier decades, from about 30 percent to 20 percent from the 1960s to the 1980s. In the 1990s, the decline in alleviating hunger lost momentum, declining only slightly from 20 percent to 19 percent. While declining hunger rates may be cause for optimism, it is also true that in terms of absolute numbers there are more hungry people in the world and in America than ever before, because the of continued momentum of population growth. Of the world's 6-plus billion people alive in 2000, 1.1 billion people are undernourished and underweight. Hunger and fear of starvation literally shape their lives.[41] Hunger is highly concentrated in different regions. Sub-Saharan Africa has the highest rate of undernourishment (39 percent in 1996), while North Africa and the Near East have the lowest rate among developing regions (12 percent). Latin America, the Caribbean, Southeast Asia, and South Asia (particularly the Indian subcontinent) have intermediate levels (13 to 15 percent). Most countries have the best data about malnutrition among children because they are so vulnerable. In India, 53 percent of children are malnourished, in Bangladesh, 56 percent, and in Ethiopia, 48 percent. But there has been remarkable progress in some regions. In Latin America, the proportion of children who are undernourished dropped from 14 percent in 1980 to 6 percent in 2000.[42]

But because East and Southeast Asia, especially China, have much larger populations than does sub-Saharan Africa, the vast numbers of the world's hungry people are found in these regions. While East and Southeast Asia showed an impressive decline in the number of malnourished in recent decades, the rise in absolute numbers of the malnourished are accounted for by sub-Saharan Africa, the Near East, and particularly South Asia.[43]

In the United States, USDA data showed that the number of hungry people did decline during the 1990s, as the economy boomed, but that millions of people still have trouble getting enough food. In 1999, about 3 million families (2.8 percent of the nation's households) had at least one member who went hungry, down from 3.9 million in 1995. But an additional

---

DECLINING HUNGER IN CHINA

Interestingly, the single most significant national contribution to world improvement in chronic hunger was the extraordinary decline in the absolute number of undernourished people in China. From 1970 to 1990, the number of malnourished people in China shrank from 409 million to 189 million (from 46 to 16 percent of the population). As you might guess, since this took place in a Communist nation, and much of it well before the "post-Maoist" reforms, the lessons to be learned from it have been hotly debated.[44]

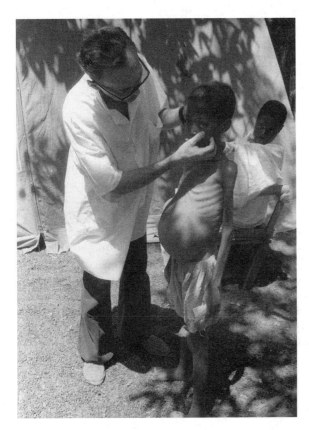

An African health worker examines a boy with an acute form of malnutrition known as Kwashiorkor. His eyes are also being checked for signs of Vitamin A deficiency. Symptoms of Kwashiorkor, caused by a deficiency of protein and calories, include stunted growth, a distended belly, and edema.

6 million households were "food insecure," that is, did not have access to enough food all the time. Among the working poor, the number of families experiencing hunger declined between 1995 and 1999, but still more than one in four households was considered food insecure. Altogether in the United States there were 27 million people, representing about 10 percent of families caring for 11 million children, who were undernourished or at least food insecure.[45]

These global data about the contours of hunger between nations and regions say little about other dimensions of the variation of undernourishment. Although food requirements vary among individuals, some studies suggest that within families, particularly in developing nations, women get less food than they need compared to men. The incidence of hunger among children everywhere is particularly severe. FAO data show that around the world, 185 million children are seriously underweight for their age. Included are nearly 100 million—comprising about one-third of all children in developing nations. In both the United States and the world, undernourishment is more concentrated in rural than urban areas. Among rural people in developing nations, one of the most consistent findings of studies is that members of rural households who own any land are better nourished than those who do not.[46]

THE CAUSES OF HUNGER

Getting a handle on the factual contours of chronic hunger is relatively easy. Trying to explain why it persists in America and the world is more complex and contentious. Some things related to the causes of hunger are matters agreed on by all observers, regardless of political and ideological differences about food issues. First, for now at least, chronic hunger is not caused by too many people or too little food. Second, problems of hunger are caused by the way food is distributed; or in other words, caused by people's lack of access to the food that exists.[47] Beyond this consensus, the causes of the perpetuation of chronic hunger are controversial. In addition to citing biophysical factors, explanations of hunger allude to things like inequality and income distributions, population density and growth, agricultural research agendas, social disruptions like wars, social welfare and insurance policies, and agricultural trade and commodity prices. In other words, explanations of hunger and how to address it, are controversial and contentious because they take us into the heart of the dominant social institutions in the various societies around the world in the twentieth century.

Within academic and food-policy circles four styles of theorizing explain why hunger exists or how to alleviate it, each with different emphases and each with some supportive empirical evidence. These approaches emphasize

1. modernization and economic development,
2. intensifying agricultural research and development,
3. ecological neo-Malthusianism, and,
4. inequality and political-economy approaches.[48]

We examine them more closely because such perspectives are not entirely academic—they also embody the interests of different groups and contain ideas for addressing the problem.

Modernization explanations focus on economic development, and in this case on the inverse relationship between per capita income in different nations and the incidence of hunger. At one level, the reason for this is perfectly obvious: poor nations have lots of poor people, who are not able to buy food. This is a dominant perspective about the causes of hunger among neoliberal economists (who promote free markets and world trade), corporate leaders, and many politicians—all of whom are likely to assume that successful modernization, or economic development, will be accompanied by increased per capita income.[49] While perhaps true, its implications for alleviating hunger are ambiguous. Saying that economic development can do this only begs that question about how it can best be achieved and why it seems to have failed miserably in large parts of the developing world (questions that are beyond our scope).

More to the point, both historical and contemporary evidence suggests that alleviating hunger everywhere depends more on alleviating poverty and redistributing income than on overall national increases in employment and income.[50] The most egregious case in point in the developing world is Brazil, in which economic growth and average incomes boomed in the last twenty years, along with growing social inequality and undernourishment. To see the limits of this style of explaining hunger among industrial nations, one need look no farther than the United States, which has one of the world's highest average per capita incomes, but also the highest levels of inequality and undernourishment among industrial nations, a situation discussed later in this chapter.

Economic growth and modernization can actually amplify hunger in two ways. Rising incomes can increase the desire for meat as a component of diets, thus taking grain to feed livestock and denying poor people elsewhere grains, vegetables, and protein, or in other words, increasing their food insecurity. This seems to be happening now in China, after its remarkable growth in the last three decades. Furthermore, modernization can exacerbate hunger by consolidating small farms, where people live partly or mostly by growing their own food ("self-provisioning"), and driving them into a market where they must earn wages to buy all food, a process anthropologists and development scholars sometimes call "depeasantization." Such a process is now rapidly taking place in developing nations, and, while it had beneficial effects on nutrition in relatively equalitarian China, Taiwan, and Korea, it has had very negative effects in highly inequalitarian Latin America and South Asia.

The related second type of theorizing about world hunger is technocratic, focusing more specifically on the need for expanded investments in *agricultural research and development* (R&D). Particularly for developing nations, it emphasizes the rapid diffusion of further increases in food productivity, and particularly the potential of new biotechnology or genetic engineering. This style of theorizing focuses on what is obvious: for people to eat there must be food, and to feed the 8–10 billion people who will certainly materialize within the next century, there must be more food.[51] This argument has enormous popular appeal, particularly among corporate leaders and researchers who develop and then benefit from developing new technologies. It is probably true that only the foolhardy would discourage investments in agriculture, but the evidence suggests that it cannot be the lynchpin to ending hunger. As we previously noted, and as all concur, the total food supply has almost no relationship to the perpetuation of hunger. If it did, there would not be a hungry person in the United States, or, for that matter, around the world. Furthermore, agricultural R&D is not all of a piece, and some increases in agricultural technology may create more hunger through the displacement and impoverishment of agricultural workers, even as it increases total food production.

The contemporary R&D argument is expressed by enthusiasm for genetically engineered crops, the newest development in biotechnology. As noted earlier in Chapter 4, some see aggressively pursuing these potentials as the key to alleviating hunger now and for a much larger world population in the future. Others, including some scholars, nongovernmental organizations (NGOs), and some consumers have formed a movement aimed at stopping genetic engineering dead in its tracks for a variety of health, ecological, and other reasons. Some NGOs that have been leaders in this anti-genetic engineering movement have also been leaders in working to alleviate world hunger (for instance, Food First and the Rural Advancement Fund). Although they oppose genetic engineering for a variety of reasons—or at best are ambivalent about it—most critical is the perception that R&D efforts devoted to genetic engineering are biased toward the needs of rich countries.[52]

Ecological neo-Malthusianism is a very different third style of theorizing about the causes of hunger. As previously noted, Thomas Malthus began the scientific study of population about two centuries ago, and first articulated fears of disaster from rapid population growth. The logic of his thought seems obvious: that the more people there are, or the faster the rate of population

---

WHO WILL FEED CHINA?

After China's remarkable progress since 1970 in feeding a growing population, alarm bells began to sound in 1994. While Chinese officials were predicting a huge grain surplus by 2025, others disagreed, observing trends like the rapid paving over of China's limited arable land for factories, roads, and housing, the diminishing returns on applications of fertilizer, and growing shortages of irrigation water. Add these strains to the context of the huge and growing Chinese population, and the growing demand for grain to produce meat for the more affluent Chinese diet. Lester Brown in a 1994 *Worldwatch* magazine article calculated that China was not heading for a grain surplus or even self-sufficiency, but rather a huge grain deficit—requiring massive imports and jeopardizing world food security by driving up grain prices. Beijing initially reacted with anger and denial, but later admitted a problem, and in Washington the National Intelligence Council appointed a prominent group of food scientists to study the Chinese food situation. They reported that if China were to turn to the world market for such massive quantities of grain, it would need to import 175 million tons of the 200 million tons projected to be on the entire world export market, and it could indeed overwhelm the capacity of grain exporting nations. That would virtually absorb most of the world grain export market, driving prices up and creating unprecedented political instability, particularly in third world cities.[53]

growth, the less food and other materials will be available to other people. But all food analysts agree, even the rapid population growth has been outstripped by total food production increases. You can see why Malthusianism, which viewed population growth as a simple and direct cause of human problems, is very much out of fashion. Neo-Malthusianism, however, which views population as an important underlying condition related to many problems, is very much alive. Population size or growth may not directly cause people to be hungry or die, but it may be a distant but pervasive factor related to more direct causes. Ecological neo-Malthusianism sees population growth in conjunction with the progressive degradation of food-producing environmental resource bases.

In its most sophisticated forms, ecological neo-Malthusianism sees environmental sustainability—the need to increase food availability while protecting the land, water, and the environmental services of living resources that make human sustenance possible—as being more important than population size/growth alone in explaining hunger. This is particularly the case in terms of future threats to food security. Scholars have documented how many gains of the second agricultural revolution in the twentieth century were achieved by environmentally threatening practices and techniques. Earlier we discussed many of these, like soil erosion, waste and degradation of water resources, oversalinization from continual irrigation, declining biodiversity, overuse of petroleum resources, and pervasive pollution from confined animals and agrochemicals. Although agricultural environmental degradation affects farmers in the United States, analysts recognize that it is particularly threatening to the food status of the poorest rural farmers around the world.[54]

In comparison to the other perspectives, ecological neo-Malthusianism is a well established but minority viewpoint with only modest influence in policy circles. Since, as the other perspectives do, its research findings cast doubt on the unique power of population growth to cause world hunger, why is its influence limited? Cross-national research, for instance, finds population size and growth rates to be less strongly related to hunger than other factors. Furthermore, the significance of population as a driver of hunger is very regionally specific. But there are other reasons why its influence in policy circles is more modest than the other perspectives. Unlike them, it does not bolster the legitimacy of prevailing institutions by providing reasons to extend Western-dominated world food trade, to "modernize" the world, or to provide technological substitutes for social reform (for example, as with genetically engineered crops). By contrast ecological neo-Malthusianism views the limits of the global resource base as constraining consumption and requiring more sustainable forms of agriculture. It would require R&D that shifts agricultural technology and practices away from those that have been successful and profitable—but environmentally damaging. And, it would limit food consumption by the affluent. You can see why it is not a dominant perspective explaining hunger.

Even with these qualifications accounting for its lack of appeal for policy makers, ecological neo-Malthusianism is compelling. Hunger is concentrated in nations and regions where poverty and population growth reinforce each other. The Indian subcontinent, for instance, is adding 21 million people a year, the equivalent of another Australia. According to UN projections, India alone will add 515 million more people by 2050, in effect adding roughly twice the current U.S. population. The subcontinent, already the hungriest region on earth, is thus expected to add another 787 million people by mid-century.[55]

Ideas about *inequality and political-economy* (I&PE) shape a fourth style of explaining hunger. It assumes that social inequality and poverty produced in the United States and in developing nations—both locally and globally—cause hunger. In a globalizing era, inequality and poverty are perpetuated, and perhaps amplified, by growing world markets for food and other traded goods. Such world markets are organized by large corporations with the support of government subsidies and international regimes like the World Trade Organization (WTO). World markets concentrate economic assets and increase the total volume of goods to be sold, but displace and disadvantage small producers and workers in many nations. Such huge markets work very well for the people with money, but not well at all for those who have little money, or who are pushed out of jobs or off their land in the process.

We have noted things earlier in many places that lend credibility to I&PE perspectives. For instance, chronic hunger is more directly related to the distribution of food than to the total supply, and hunger is a problem of *access to food* in nations where some others eat and are overnourished. Furthermore, many of the difficulties with the perspectives discussed earlier support I&PE styles of explanation, that is,

- When peasants and farmers are driven off the land by modernization and consolidation of land;
- When modernization produces more food for markets but not for displaced and poor people;
- When investing in more productive technology amplifies hunger by putting people out of work;
- When affluence encourages meat-rich diets, requiring much grain to feed animals that could support the diets of many hungry people.

Many of the illustrations about how I&PE produces chronic hunger are from developing nations. But, what about hunger in the United States? The world market economy evolved to preferentially benefit the United States and other industrial nations, through control of import taxes, prices, and money to loan or invest. But the growing world market economy impacts many Americans like it does people in developing nations. That is, it greatly benefits some—but disadvantages others. Many experience loss of livelihoods, declining real wages and living standards, and eroding health care. For the poor, it means hunger in a land of enormous surpluses. Let us be more concrete.

Since the late 1970s, the United States experienced a growing population in poverty, a deepening of poverty, and increasing social and spatial isolation of the poor. Contrary to what you might think in the growing economy of the 1990s, poverty declined only slightly; the fact was concealed that the number of those living in poverty increased (from 29.2 million in 1980 to 36.5 million in 1996). By 1996 the poorest fifth of the population commanded a smaller proportion of the national wealth than they did in 1970 (merely 4.2 percent). Even the increased impoverishment of the bottom fifth concealed more dramatic declines in the fate of those at the very bottom.[56] In spite of the reality of national economic growth and media images of affluence, poverty among the poorest fifth of Americans increased, bringing with it hunger, homelessness, and a variety of other social vulnerabilities. What were some of the causes?

In the United States, land of cultural individualism, individual characteristics are usually viewed as the most direct causes of poverty—motivation and moral problems, mental illness, substance abuse, etc. Be that as it may, there are social and political causes. From the 1980s on, the Federal Government wanted to balance budgets, and it reduced support for the poor in many ways. Aid to Families with Dependent Children (AFDC) steadily declined around the country relative to the consumer price index. Not surprisingly, poor families with children made up an increasing share of the poor (and the hungry). Government cash and food assistance declined. In the 1990s, "The end of welfare," promoted to take the poor off the government dependency roles, improved the lives of some while increasing impoverishment for others. The social safety net eroded further as affordable housing for the poor decreased. As the national population of the poor expanded, the availability of low-income housing simultaneously shrunk, creating an "affordability gap." Tax subsidies for low-income housing decreased, and rents outpaced price inflation for consumer goods. There were simply too many poor chasing too few housing units. They often made cruel choices between food, housing, and bare necessities.[57]

These four theoretical perspectives illustrate the diversity in how chronic hunger is explained. All have valuable insights and limitations. The modernization approach understands poverty as lack of capital investment and economic development, but not as something that has a generic relationship to free market institutions themselves. While agricultural R&D must be a part of alleviating hunger, it must take into account environmental sustainability. Ecological neo-Malthusianism reminds us that solutions must be developed within the limits of the biosphere and must be understood from a long-term perspective, but it overemphasizes population and environmental resources as independent causes of hunger rather than in context with the social and political factors that shape hunger. We agree with Frederick Buttel that the inequality and political-economy approach is best able to incorporate insights of the other three perspectives, while pointing to dynamics that the other three downplay—that the taproots of hunger lie most fundamentally in social relations.[58]

While going a long way toward explaining hunger, the four perspectives are very abstract and gloss over several clusters of explanatory factors. For instance, research demonstrates that *social disruptions* like wars and civil unrest are the main antecedents of famine, particularly in areas where "entitlements to food" are low. Even people in very poor countries can usually manage to avoid famine where there are no social disruptions.[59] Second, *natural disasters*, such as severe storms, hurricanes, floods, droughts, etc., are related to famine. Although natural disasters and famine are of some importance, researchers and policy circles have overemphasized them. Famines and natural disasters are estimated to cause only about 10 percent of all hunger deaths, and they are in many respects man-made.[60] Third, *local social relations*, like rural land-holding structures, ethnic stratification, class and caste relations, regional inequalities, and community power structures shape hunger.[61] Fourth, *gender relations*, gender inequality, and household power dynamics are not dealt with directly by the four perspectives. But all perspectives and scholars recognize that access to food is strongly gendered. Finally, Nobel prize-winning economist Amartya K. Sen emphasizes that hunger is related to food *entitlements*, or the ability of individuals and groups to "command food." Entitlements defined by custom, social status, and law shape who eats and who doesn't because they reflect access to social power. They reflect power relations at international, national, local, and household levels.

ADDRESSING CHRONIC HUNGER

As you can see, the "all-too-preventable-problem" is massive, complex, and intrinsically connected to social institutions in the modern world. Hunger is influenced by many social and biophysical factors, and ending hunger would require massive and fundamental changes within nations, among them, and in their existing political-economic and power relations. Even so, the important problem has been the focus of at least eleven major summit meetings and statements about ending hunger by international organizations, scholars, and nongovernmental organizations (NGOs). They contain similarities, but with different emphases.

The first such meeting, the World Food Conference in Rome (1974), urged governments to accept the goals that within the next decade no children would go hungry, no families would fear for their food security, and no human capacities would be stunted by malnutrition. NGOs around the world produced the Bellagio Declaration ("Overcoming Hunger in the 1990s") that emphasized short-term, concrete goals to alleviate hunger. These included ending famine by moving food into zones of armed conflict, ending hunger among half the world's poorest households, reducing by half the hunger among women and children by expanding maternal child health coverage, and eliminating Vitamin A and iodine deficiencies as public health problems. An assessment in 1994 found progress in all except the first goal: conflict continued to be an intractable problem. The declaration also affirmed food as a human right and insisted that progress will come only through the combined efforts and energies of grass roots and community organizations, nation states, and international organizations.[62]

In 1996 the World Food Security declaration of the World Food Summit in Rome set a goal of reducing the number of malnourished people to half their present level by no later than 2015, by eradicating poverty and promoting global and national food security. Typical of many lofty international pronouncements, it had something for everyone, illustrating the complexity of the problem. It affirmed that there is a "human right to food," stated explicitly in its plan for action (Commitment 7, objective 4). Yet, unlike the 1974 summit, the dominant messages of the 1996 summer were calls for greater private responsibility in dealing with hunger, indictments of corrupt governments in the developing world, and also calls for reforms of the dominant institutions of development and world trade.[63]

In one sense, all these global declarations and programs produced by international organizations and NGOs have amounted to little. In 1970 there were 942 million undernourished people in the developing world, by the mid-1990s there were 828 million (not counting those in affluent nations). At this rate of progress there will be many hundreds of millions of hungry people at the middle of the next century. Buttel suggests that part of the problem with such proposals and programs is their dual nature. Hunger is a big issue both in the United States and around the world, and everyone is motivated to end it for high-minded altruistic reasons. Yet proposals to address it are very specific, targeted, and technocratic (for example, agricultural R&D to increase yields, emergency feeding programs) and tend to conceal the way hunger is connected to social and institutional systems in the contemporary world. He argues that realistic, activist programs addressing hunger need to combine the big moral and political issues with more targeted technocratic and structural approaches.[64] Some consensus exists among food-policy specialists about the elements comprising real progress toward alleviating hunger. How so?

ELEMENTS OF A REALISTIC APPROACH

A first cornerstone of a realistic active approach to hunger issues is to recognize that hunger is at root a moral and political issue that ultimately requires solutions anchored in nations' and the world's moral and political institutions. Thus, concerned people, NGOs, and international organizations must emphasize—without apology—that there is an inalienable human right to food, that is of the same status as other human rights. A second cornerstone is to recognize that alleviating hunger requires substantial resources, and most of these must come from North America, Europe, and other industrialized nations. Unfortunately, because the end of the Cold War destroyed the rationale for foreign aid to developing nations, development aid has stagnated. Total U.S. overseas development aid was only $50 billion in 2000 and has declined each year in real dollars since 1980—analogous to the weakening domestic U.S. social safety nets that have exacerbated the lives of the poor and hungry in this country. Distinguish between foreign military assistance, which is much larger and goes to a few U.S. critical allies, like Egypt and Israel, and foreign development assistance, which is much smaller.

In international affairs, national interests are certainly important, but there must be a new covenant of humanitarian foreign assistance among the international community for the betterment of mankind. As with domestic humanitarian issues, NGOs and civil society groups will be important to shape and support that covenant for increasing humanitarian government aid and to monitor accountability. NGOs can work with and scrutinize the programs of international agencies (like the United Nations, but particularly the World Bank) to ensure that alleviating poverty and hunger, rural development, gender equity, and ecological sustainability are given adequate consideration. They can also work to build democracy and the self-empowerment of people in developing nations. NGOs can complement but not replace official aid programs, which still dwarf the resources NGOs get from voluntary donations by individuals, foundations, and governments. Furthermore, such voluntary aid alone is not a realistic way to transform systems of power that control access to food, particularly if such access is understood as an entitlement. Ironically, charity itself can be a barrier to the alleviation of hunger—a subject treated further in the final chapter.

There are more concrete elements that would make real progress in alleviating hunger. They are social and political reforms that promote

1. Gender-sensitive development
2. Land reform
3. A transformed agricultural R&D agenda, and
4. Reforms in international organizations, particularly those involving money and trade.

Gender-sensitive development would encourage investment in women's education and improve their social-legal status. It would not only improve the quality of life of women, but it would also enable women to make more informed choices about their own productivity as workers, the nutritional status of their children and families, and, of course, family size. Consistently, research literature finds that where the status of women is low, chronic hunger and particularly malnutrition among children tends to be higher. Another effective measure, particularly in developing nations with large agrarian populations, is land reform.

As we noted earlier, one of the most consistent findings among food researchers is that the nutritional status of families that own any land is better than those owning none.[65] Land reform redistributes societal resources, decreases rural unemployment, and makes rural families less vulnerable to price and market change. Most importantly, secure land tenure can increase the share of the population that is able to feed itself by nonmarket means (by self-provisioning). It would also be a bargain for governments. Consider a staggering bit of data: the cost of creating a nonfarm commercial job in Brazil is two to twenty times greater than the cost of establishing an unemployed head of household on farmland through land reform.[66]

In the United States and other industrial nations, similar reform policies could halt further concentration of agricultural assets that drives small- and medium-sized farmers off the land, making them "technology applicators" in an agribusiness food chain rather than independent managers of their own farms. As we noted before, smaller farms using sustainable agroecology practices would be more productive, maintaining greater biodiversity and extracting less ecological damage. And, they are more conducive to vibrant rural community life. The evidence to support this is overwhelming. That would mean, in some senses, recovering agricultural practices of not too many decades ago—using alternatives to inorganic fertilizers like manures, sewage sludge and other organic wastes, and growing nitrogen-fixing legumes in rotation. Maximum benefits of such diversity are realized when livestock animals, crops, and other resources (for example, bees) are used in good rotational patterns to optimize production efficiency, nutrient recycling, and crop protections.

As we noted earlier, the revival of such farming would slow or reverse forty-year trends in the growing concentration of agricultural assets, proliferation of industrial monocropping, and the domination of food and agribusiness oligopolies. Furthermore, USDA subsidies, research, and grants have overwhelmingly favored agribusiness and the system of industrial monoculture production. Programs have, for instance, encouraged monocultures by assuring prices for a handful of commodities (for example, corn or soybeans). The more of one supported commodity you planted, the more federal price subsidies you could get, creating a competitive disadvantage for multicropping or crop rotation. Even so, some reforms are underway. The USDA initiated a small grant program to farmers and educators to promote Sustainable Agriculture Research and Education (SARE). But the funding agenda is still unbalanced. In 1999 the USDA spent $60 million to study corn genetics benefiting mostly large monoculture cropping systems and only $8 million on SARE grants.[67]

In developing nations it might mean reform of donor dollars, grants,

URBAN GARDENING AND CLOSING THE NUTRIENT LOOP

In the industrial world, urban farming largely disappeared in the twentieth century, but in the developing world, it shows signs of resurgence. According to the most widely accepted estimate, about 200 million urban dwellers now participate in urban farming, providing 800 million people with at least some of their food. Farmers in Accra, Ghana, supply the city with an estimated 90 percent of its vegetables, including radishes, cabbage, and cauliflower. Farmers in Singapore produce 25 percent of the city's vegetables and 80 percent of its poultry. (Much of the grain needed to feed the poultry, however, is brought in from the countryside.) In Berlin, more than 80,000 gardeners lease plots on land where buildings were destroyed by bombs in World War II. The Chinese never separated farms and cities the way Europeans and American did, and Chinese urban and peri-urban farmers provide 85 percent of the vegetables and more than half of the meat and poultry consumed in eighteen of the country's largest cities (including Beijing and Shanghai).

Extensive in-city food production can also play an important role in municipal waste management. In China, human waste is treated and sold to farmers as fertilizer. In India, sewage-fed lagoons produce about one-tenth of the fish consumed by Calcutta. Techniques for safely reusing urban wastes may now make it possible to bring farming back into close proximity with people.[68]

and investments that benefit women and small landholders. Grants could encourage self-provisioning and local markets through urban gardening and community supported agriculture in both the industrial and developing worlds.

The intensity of the debates over genetic engineering is partly due to the fact that public investment in agricultural research has collapsed, domestically and globally. One of the important mechanisms of alleviating hunger is a revitalized approach to foreign aid as a moral responsibility by groups and governments in industrial nations. We do not rule all genetic engineering out of court, but if the institutional context of its development remains in the hands of agribusiness firms with their patented organisms, it is unlikely that it will ever be affordable or made freely "reproducible" by small farmers in the developing world. In that case, genetic engineering will do little to address the problems of poverty and hunger. Beyond the political-economic barriers, the uncritical promotion of genetic engineering represents a global-scale gamble that unforeseen vulnerabilities to pests, pathogens, and other ecological problems will not result from the "seed-chemical packages" that are now the highest priority of genetic engineering research.[70] We are not technophobes, but neither do we think that genetic engineering will be a painless "technical fix" for hunger problems, as some promoters argue. It is worth reiterating that the

AGROECOLOGY IN CUBA

Cuba is where ideas about sustainable agriculture and agroecology have been put to the greatest test. Before 1989 Cuba was a model industrial-style farm economy, based on enormous (state) farms using vast quantities of imported agrochemicals and machinery to produce export crops (for example, tobacco, sugar), while over half of the island's food was imported. As Cuba's socialist bloc donors collapsed, the country was plunged into the worst food crisis in its history, with consumption of calories and protein dropping by perhaps as much as 30 percent. Given the impossibility of importing either food or agrochemical inputs, Cuba turned inward to create a more self-reliant agriculture based on higher prices to farmers, agroecological practices, smaller farms, and extensive urban agriculture. As the production of small farms and cooperatives surged, the government instituted land reforms, parceling out the large (and stagnating) state farms to their former employees. The government also mobilized support for a growing urban agriculture movement involving small-scale organic farming on vacant city lots, transforming urban diets in just a few years. By 1997 Cubans were eating about as well as they did before 1989—better than most, by Caribbean and Latin American standards—even though little food and agrochemicals were being imported.[69]

problem is not now, and never has been, an actual shortage of food, around the world—and certainly not in the United States.

Agricultural R&D policies need to stress research priorities not now given adequate attention: the efficiency of water utilization by crops, nonchemical and agroecologically based means of pest control, adaptation of crop plants to stressed and marginal environments, suitable new technology for smallholder peasant farmers, and participatory approaches to research priority-setting.

The fourth part of any effective effort to alleviate world hunger is reforms in international organizations, particularly those involving money and trade. Unlike some today, we would not advocate getting rid of the World Bank, the International Monetary Fund, or the World Trade Organization (WTO), but rather selective changes or rollbacks of some of their provisions. While they have been effective in many ways, the World Bank has a track record of funding large-scale development projects that do not benefit small communities and peasant farmers, and have environmentally destructive consequences. World Bank development and International Monetary Fund loan policies often mandate "structural adjustment" that reduces the ability of Third World governments to invest in social safety nets and provide entitlements to food for the hungry. For almost any kind of development to occur in developing nations—including the kinds we advocated that would alleviate malnutrition—accumulated debts of developing nations should be partly or entirely forgiven. These accumulated debts loom very large as a barrier to any progress in many developing nations. But they are not terribly significant in terms of loans by governments and private banks in industrial nations—which lend and invest far more with each other than with developing nations. The significance of Third World indebtedness as a barrier to progress is widely recognized in financial, policy, and social justice circles. By 2000, ideas about forgiving some debts were common, along with guarantees of accountability for the money realized.

Seeking to deregulate trade, the WTO provided some benefits for developing nations, particularly for a handful of relatively affluent ones like Brazil, Chile, Taiwan, and Korea. It provided export opportunities to markets in industrial nations, access to technology, and agricultural reforms. But it subjected many other countries to significant risks. For instance, import taxes of developing nations on high-value agricultural products still exist, and those tariffs provide barriers for their production in developing nations. Furthermore, intellectual property restrictions on agricultural technology innovations restrict agricultural research and investment in developing nations, particularly patents on the much-promoted genetic engineering process and genetic material that may make them unavailable to many nations with large concentrations of the malnourished. Selective rollback, reform, and more equitable enforcement of existing programs and provisions of such international development, financial, and trade organizations would make major contributions to solve hunger problems in the world's poorest countries.

REBUILDING THE GRASSROOTS IN THE UNITED STATES

Since we earlier described the growing concentration of agricultural assets, food monopolies, and ecologically destructive practices, it is fair to mention briefly the proliferation of countermovements that have been gaining momentum in the last decades, promoting small farms, sustainable practices, and greater access to food. It is like a pervasive but decentralized jigsaw puzzle grounded in every region of the country, that encompasses agroecological farmers, farm workers, community food and hunger organizations, and environmental, consumer, and religious groups. Many of the pieces are joining together into larger national and international NGOs. We mention only a few visible nodes.

The Center for Rural Affairs, founded in the 1970s in rural Nebraska, seeks to maintain the vitality of family farms by providing technical assistance and advice to farmers about low input and sustainable farming. It funded a program of training and support to farmers and other rural residents to run small businesses and helped to found the Midwest Sustainable Agriculture Working Group, a coalition of farming and environmental organizations. The

National Farmers Union represents 300,000 farm families in twenty-four states, promotes the interests of family farmers, and generally opposes agribusiness multinationals. The National Farmers Union has formed a number of "new wave" cooperatives, like the Dakota Growers Pasta Company that buys grain from member farmers, provides directly over 200 jobs, and has investments valued at $51 million. A Wisconsin Farmers Union is forming a cheese cooperative that seeks to market a variety of premium cheeses. The Federation of Southern Cooperatives represents the struggles of black farmers to retain control of their land, and has over 20,000 member families in the Southern states. They form producer cooperatives that engage in marketing, community development, credit unions, and legal support. They help farmers move away from traditional community crops (like corn and cotton) to specialty crops, organic production, and livestock more suitable for small acreages and sales in local food markets.

Local farmers' markets have proliferated in many cities and towns, in which at designated times and places (usually Saturday mornings) local farmers bring produce, locally produced foods, and confections to sell directly to consumers. It improves earnings of local farmers while increasing the supply of fresh, nutritious food for city people. In the local market in our city, you cannot only buy all manner of fresh vegetables in season, but also range-fed chickens and grass-fed beef, trucked in fresh and frozen from a hundred miles away. In Connecticut, the Hartford Food System provides vouchers to over 50,000 low-income state residents, so that some of the produce goes to people who would otherwise not be able to afford it. The Community Food Coalition is a national network of advocacy organizations to help low-income communities become food secure. Working with the National Coalition for Sustainable Agriculture, they helped pass the Community Food Security Act in 1996, which provides training and technical assistance to groups seeking to promote community food security.

More formal than farmers' markets, community supported agriculture organizations now exist in many places, where a group of consumers form an alliance with local farmers. Members buy "shares" that enable farmers to produce, and then they are entitled to a share of fresh produce as the growing season advances. They also share the risk if crops fail. No community supported agriculture organizations are exactly alike. Some emphasize organic production and contribute to community emergency food supplies, and some require members to contribute labor to grow and harvest crops. Some provide scholarships for low-income participants. Farmers contracting with a community supported agriculture organization find that selling their food directly to people with whom they have a long-term relationship makes their lives more predictable, and often more satisfying.

The Rural Development Center in Salinas, California, educates and trains farm workers to become independent farmers. After completion of a course about agricultural production, farm management, and marketing, participants can use the Center's land, water, and equipment for up to three years, saving some proceeds to purchase or lease land. Since 1985, seventy to eighty families have participated in the program, and about 85 percent have become independent farmers. Finally, the Land Institute in Salina, Kansas, conducts research about sustainable agriculture based on renewable water and energy technologies. Its founder, Wes Jackson, and colleagues seek to develop perennial grains from native grasses, and thus avoid the need for destructive plowing or aquifer pumping on the Great Plains. Jackson argues that food is a cultural rather than an industrial product and rails against the "commodification of nature." Originally regarded with skepticism (or worse), the institute's work is taken much more seriously today, with the impending farm crisis of the Great Plains.[71]

IN SUM . . .

Similar movements are underway around the world, and it is fair to say that reform efforts are directed at all of the elements of alleviating hunger we mentioned earlier. But we are under no illusion that achieving gender-sensitive development, land reform, a transformed agricultural R&D agenda, and reforming international organizations will be easy. But if hunger is indeed a paramount "all-too-preventable problem" in a world of vast food surpluses—as all persons and organizations claim—it is important to try. We conclude by reiterating the hopeful and positive. If many millions are still hungry, the proportion of hungry people in the world declined since the 1960s. Many nations and regions made progress in addressing hunger, including Korea, Taiwan, Sri Lanka, China, Costa Rica, Chile, Cuba, Iran, Zimbabwe, and Kuwait among developing nations. So too did the United States. This progress was achieved by a number of technical and social means, and in the future alleviating hunger is likely to involve multiple paths. Within these, however, hunger is a political and moral problem that cannot be dealt with by technical innovations alone. Finally, virtually every solution to chronic hunger and food security would improve other kinds of human social well-being and the performance of social institutions, by improving human equity, health, labor productivity, and human rights.[72]

SOME SUGGESTIONS FOR FURTHER READING

Atkins, P., and I. Bowler (2001). *Food in Society: Economy, Culture, Geography.* New York: Oxford University Press.
Alteiri, M. (1995). *The Science of Sustainable Agriculture.* Boulder, CO: Westview Press.
Bender, W., and M. Smith (1997). Population, Food, and Nutrition. *Population Bulletin,* 54 (4). Washington, DC: Population Reference Bureau.

Brown, L. (1996). *Tough Choices: Facing the Challenge of Food Scarcity.* New York: W. W. Norton.

Brown, L., and H. Kane (1994). *Full House: Reassessing the Earth's Carrying Capacity.* New York: W. W. Norton.

Bryson, R., and T. Murray (1977). *Climates of Hunger: Mankind and the World's Changing Weather.* Madison, WI: University of Wisconsin Press.

DeRose, L., E. Messer, and S. Millman, Eds. (1998). *Who's Hungry? How Do We Know? Food Shortage, Poverty, and Deprivation.* New York: United Nations University Press.

Lappe, F., J. Collins, and P. Rosset, Eds. (1998). *World Hunger: Twelve Myths.* 2nd ed. New York: Grove Press.

Livernash, R., and E. Rodenburg, Eds. (1998). Population, Resources and Envrionment. *Population Bulletin, 53(1).* Washington, DC: Population Reference Bureau.

Magdoff, F., F. Buttel, and J. B. Foster, Eds. (1999). *Hungry for Profit: Agribusiness Threats to Farmers, Food, and the Environment.* New York: Monthly Review Press.

Miller, G. (1998). *Living in the Environment.* 10th ed. Belmont, CA: Wadsworth. See especially Chapters 18, 19, 20, 22, and 23.

Postel, S. (1992). *Last Oasis: Facing Water Scarcity.* New York: W. W. Norton.

Sen, A. (1981). *Poverty and Famines: An Essay on Entitlement and Development.* New York: Oxford University Press.

The State of Food and Agriculture. (1998). Rome: Food and Agriculture Organization, United Nations.

Thompson, P. (1995). *The Spirit of the Soil: Agriculture and Environmental Ethics.* New York: Routledge.

CHAPTER SEVEN

Food, Ethics, and Social Justice

W e have discussed the evolution of the modern American food system as well as many problems with it and the foodways connected to it. These problems raise many ethical and social justice issues. While discussing factual matters we hinted at such issues, but now we address them directly. Ethical issues have to do with right and wrong, and principles of moral choice. They are strongly connected to social justice concerns about fairness and equity among people who participate in the common social worlds. While ethical and social justice issues are always contentious, controversial, and complex, they are also paramount human concerns.

We have noted a whole cascade of issues that would provide fertile grounds for raising ethical and social justice questions. They include, for instance, issues about food safety, such as the residues of pesticides and chemicals in food production (or conversely, of *not* using chemicals to preserve food and increase productivity). They would certainly include the many human and ecological issues surrounding the spread of the new biotechnology, and issues about animal welfare—particularly about how animals are raised in the new factorylike, confined animal-feeding operations. There are a number of environmental and ecological issues related to the impact of industrial agriculture, which measurably degrades ecosystem resources like soil and water, and reduces the earth's biodiversity. In a globalizing world with a huge and growing population and increasing interdependencies, the just (or unjust) distribution of these resources available to people around the world becomes particularly salient, as is the resource adequacy for the world inherited by your children and grandchildren.

Other ethical and social justice concerns surround the transformation of contemporary foodways, such as the progressive weakening of family meals and the promotion of "junk food on the go," whereby eating becomes a more physiological act and less an occasion for ritual and sociability. It is an ethical issue because the deliberate policies of economic institutions systematically degrade some important bases of social interaction, solidarity, and conviviality. Connected to this is the growth of prepared and fast foods that attend the growth of a "toxic food environment" and the epidemic of obesity. Though overeating of fattening food may be a human genetic propensity, it is also promoted by prosperity and mammoth marketing and advertising industries that often overwhelm healthy nutritional choices for the unwary (like children), as well as consumer rationality in a more general sense. There is something ethically suspect about nations that spend huge amounts of money to promote profitable (but sometimes unhealthy) food, while they spend much smaller amounts promoting healthy diets and nutritional literacy.

Ethical and social justice concerns surround the political-economy of food and the progressive domination of America's (and the world's) food system by a handful of oligopolistic firms. Such transnational firms and their public subsidies produce a greater volume of food and introduce scientific agriculture around the world, but they also bankrupt farmers, ruin traditional food markets, and degrade the character of rural life. They increase migration from rural to urban areas, and the flows of refugees from bankruptcy and landlessness.

Ethical and social justice issues growing from factual matters—particularly from change—are complex, and contentious, and they defy oversimplification. They should not be ignored. Rather than getting the "right answers" that satisfy everyone, raising such concerns is useful because it can stimulate more informed discourse and reflection. It is obvious that one could easily write volumes about the ethical and social justice concerns that surround any one of those on the list we just mentioned, and obvious that we cannot do justice to the profusion of such questions in the last chapter of a short, integrative book. We therefore focus on just one.

Of the issues we raised, it seems to us that the most important surround malnutrition. Malnutrition has a special moral status for two reasons. If people are malnourished, they exist in a condition that undermines the possibility, or at least the likelihood, of their achieving other aspects of human well-being—including enjoyable activities, relatively little suffering, and the exercise of choices. Second, malnutrition has a special moral status as evil, because unlike many ethical problems, it flows from conditions that all observers agree are avoidable.[1] One form of malnutrition flows from eating too much and making the wrong choices from an abundance of available food, and the other derives from not getting enough food, when normally there is plenty of food in the world to adequately feed every person alive.

It may well be that both forms of malnutrition are preventable problems, but you can see from the last two chapters just how difficult it would be to effectively address them. Discussing ethical and social justice issues about overeating among Americans and the world's relatively affluent people and about making wrong food choices from plentiful food resources is important. It's an important concern because the lifestyle results in impaired human capacities, a host of degenerative diseases (like late-onset diabetes and cardiovascular problems), and a shorter life span than possible. Powerful social and economic forces reinforce that lifestyle, but it is theoretically within our control as individuals. It is the unintended consequence of "eating too well."

But the other kind of malnutrition—including hunger, undernutrition, and food insecurity—has an even more powerful moral status as evil. It does so because the people it affects in both America and the world (including children) are far less likely to have the capacities to make choices regarding the sources of their suffering. Furthermore, that suffering is more concrete, severe, and immediately present. Therefore, we focus on the ethical and social justice concerns surrounding hunger, prolonged undernutriton, and food insecurity.

ETHICAL AND SOCIAL JUSTICE PERSPECTIVES

A number of ethical perspectives can be applied to malnutrition issues. The famous philosopher Immanuel Kant thought that anything was unethical if it undermined a defining human quality—the development of human reason and rationality. Prolonged hunger among the poor and powerless certainly does so. This is important, but does not account for other evils that attend hunger—like sheer physical and emotional suffering, disease, and shortened life expectancy, which are also inherently wrong.[2]

Peter Singer famously suggested benevolence as an ethical principle related to malnutrition: "If it is in our power to prevent something bad from happening without sacrificing anything of comparable importance, we ought, morally, to do it."[3] This is the well known utilitarian principle: One ought to reduce human ills (including hunger) so long as this does not sacrifice something of comparable moral significance. If, for example, one is reasonably well fed, healthy, and affluent, then spending money on the needs of one's self is unconscionable compared with contributing to the needs of the poor, ill, and hungry. This statement is useful because it understands that ethical behavior involves the complex balancing of outcomes or how the behavior contributes to the overall good one can do in the world. But it locates the focus of moral duty in the balance of "overall good," not in helping people because they need help. Critics of such an approach to ethics and social justice suggest that it results in a "robust zone of indifference, where much of what we do is neither morally required nor morally forbidden."[4]

Scholars of development led by famous Indian economist and Nobel Prize winner Amartya Sen articulated a contemporary approach to ethics with assumptions reminiscent of the ancient Greek philosopher Aristotle. They argue that what is ethical is what contributes to the development of a whole range of *human capabilities* and *appropriate functioning*. This includes not only being bodily healthy, but also the exercise of reason along with practical skills, sociability and the ability to live with and for others, and autonomy in one's social and physical environment. Alleviating hunger would make it even possible for most other human capabilities to exist.[5] In Chapter 6 we noted Sen's concept of missing "entitlements," or the absence of normal social and economic expectations in life in relation to having food. This approach emphasizing the basic elements of the abilities of people to function in their social worlds supplements that narrowness of both the Kantian and utilitarian approaches. It does not require equality in how resources are distributed, since that varies by individuals and situations, but it does provide a way of understanding why we should care for others. If we belong to the same human community as others, then we will have reason to care for them. The question naturally arises: Why should we care for the well-being of distant people who do not belong to our nation or society? The answer is easier in a globalizing world. To the extent that all people today live in an interconnected global system or world order, they have mutual moral obligations—in other words, they are connected by world citizenship.[6]

Two additional ethical and social justice perspectives illustrate this global dimension. Today much political discourse focuses on human rights, meaning rights that flow from basic human nature rather than from the norms, culture, or laws of particular groups or nations. If there are such universal human rights that derive from human nature, then we clearly have a reason to promote or protect them. Henry Shue suggested that there are three basic socially universal rights: rights to subsistence, security, and liberty.[7] A right to food is obviously an important component of these, and particularly of subsistence. Such rights are basic because they are necessary for the existence of more complex rights. This universal rights approach makes little sense without a global framework of obligations like that previously noted. Shue does not, however, advocate a radical redistribution of resources from affluent to poor nations, because it raises the issue of "how much" redistribution is necessary to create the optimum balance of goods for all concerned, a concern raised by utilitarian perspectives. Even so, a widely recognized human rights approach should put pressure on governments and individuals to recognize moral obligations to aid the hungry and deprived on a global scale.

In *A Theory of Justice*, John Rawls provides a powerful social contract argument for social justice in societies with a system of coherent political authority. Seeing such authority as a scheme of cooperation among people who agree about a distribution of benefits and burdens, Rawls argues that a set of principles that would be fair as an ideal social contract would include commitments to equal liberty and to what he calls a "difference principle." This means that only those differences in resources and wealth are justified that enable the least well off to be better off than under other arrangements. Though he allows for differences in wealth to ensure incentives for productivity that would benefit everyone, the tenor of his argument is about fairness.[8] Rawls's theory is attractive because his general conception of social justice argues that it is reasonable for any person, as a member of society, to expect that society to protect their basic rights (in Shue's sense).

Others have adapted his ideas to fit a global perspective. If a globalizing world with its market integration, multilateral political institutions, and contact between people, is coming to resemble a "world society," then there exists a global difference principle, and thus a powerful argument in the name of social justice for the redistribution of resources on a global scale. This is an important extension of Rawls's theory. It suggests, for instance, that social justice applies to the whole world and that aid to the suffering (including food aid) might be seen as a sort of global income tax. We have an obligation to heal others if we see ourselves as part of a reciprocating program of social interaction and dependency.[9] Yet, if Singer and the natural rights perspective has some validity, our moral obligations to others do not depend entirely on such arrangements of reciprocity. They rest partly on our capacity to affect their well-being—for good or ill.

Obviously, the world is a long way from realizing any of these ethical perspectives, on either a national or global level. Even so, they provide powerful ideal goals and visions of just national and global moral communities. Such models are useful and informative but very abstract. We continue more concretely by examining how hunger has been addressed in the United States and then around the world.

DEALING WITH HUNGER IN AMERICA

After fading as a public issue from World War II to the 1960s, hunger is once again on the American problem agenda. Not since the Great Depression have the hungry been as numerous and visible, along with the proliferation of soup kitchens, shelters, food pantries and other agencies to serve them. This is a cruel irony, loaded with ethical and social justice questions, because America produces too much rather than too little food to feed its citizens adequately. To make matters worse, Americans waste food in spectacular quantities. A 1995 USDA study estimated that between production and consumption, more than 25 percent of the food produced in the United States goes to waste. Taken together, the food wasted on farms, during transportation, among wholesalers, retailers, supermarkets, restaurants, and households—from fields planted but not harvested to the food spoiling in kitchens or tossed in the garbage—totaled a startling 96 billion pounds; at least a pound a day for every person in the nation.[10]

A similar situation existed in the Great Depression of the 1930s, then described as "bread lines, knee deep in wheat." The current proliferation and visibility of hunger really began in the 1980s, with a sharp recession that accelerated long-term trends toward unemployment and job security among a segment of Americans. This coincided with steep cutbacks in Federal social spending producing a long-term decline in the purchasing power of public assistance. Homeless people became increasingly visible in many large cities, and they often turned for help to churches and union locals.

Existing kitchens and food pantries found themselves with ever-longer lines at their doors, and programs were hastily organized to help meet the need. "Emergency food," originally meaning food for household emergencies, came to mean food for an urgent societal emergency. Charitable emergency food programs proliferated, and food banks that receive donations of unsalable food from corporations to pass along to kitchens and pantries multiplied. Food rescue programs that redistribute perishable and prepared foods were not even invented until the early 1980s, and by 1990 there were enough such programs to form a national association called Foodchain.

But, when the economy improved for many Americans, it left behind a layer of people who continued to rely on private charitable assistance to get by. Nor did private emergency food programs wither away. For the hungry this situation was made worse by the passage of popular "welfare reform" legislation, The Personal Responsibility and Work Opportunities Reconciliation Act of 1996 (PRWORA), which resulted in significant reductions in both cash and food assistance. Consequences of this national legislation are now visible in the form of longer lines at the nation's thousands of private charitable soup kitchens and food pantries, and as a rising proportion of unmet demand at the food banks that supply these frontline "emergency food" providers.[11]

In popular American discourse, hunger is almost always portrayed as hunger amid plenty and waste, and it is virtually the only kind of hunger that Americans have known in the twentieth century. This situation is widely perceived as an ethical scandal, outrage, embarrassment, and something for which there is "no excuse." These sentiments are expressed not only by national leaders but also among most people. The intense moral discomfort that Americans express when confronted with evidence of hunger in their midst is not difficult to understand. Hunger is a painful and common human experience, not a rare or exotic disease. On some level, everyone has experienced it. Then there is the activism in American values—"Don't just stand there, Do something!"

In terms of ethics and justice, there is an underlying desire for what is fair—a limit on our appetite for inequality that is complex and subtle. Huge differences in income and wealth may be tolerable, but the idea that some people are going hungry, while others are overeating and spending billions each year trying not to show it, is offensive. Finally, there is the issue of waste. America is not a thrifty society. In fact, waste as planned obsolescence is a

building block of our economy. We waste lots of paper, time, and money—
sometimes with great gusto. But food is something else. For those who are religious, religion ups the ante. Religious ritual reinforces the sanctity of food
and the scriptures of most religions urge us to "share our bread with the hungry" (*Isaiah*, 58) and to feed "the least of our brethren."

Given the pervasiveness of such feelings and the mutually reinforcing
nature of our guilt about wasting food and not sharing it, it is no wonder that
claims about hunger amid plenty and waste make people uncomfortable and
deeply offend their sensibilities about what is ethical and just.[12] They also stimulate widespread concern and participation in efforts to do something about
the problem.

Fighting hunger has become like a national pastime. Millions of Americans are
involved. In 1992, a polling firm hired by Kraft General Foods on behalf of a
declaration to end hunger in America surveyed 1,000 randomly selected voters to gauge public attitudes in the United States. Three-fifths of those surveyed thought that hunger was a "very serious problem," and 90 percent
agreed that there are "significant numbers of people in the U.S. who are hungry and don't have enough to eat." However, the most significant finding was
that 79 percent said "yes" when asked if they had personally done anything to
help the hungry in their community, like volunteering at a soup kitchen, contributing to a distribution center, etc.

That is a remarkable finding, whether you believe it or not. But the pro-
liferating opportunities to contribute increase its credibility. These include,
for instance, contributing to a food drive—by a religious congregation, the
Boy Scouts, Postal Service letter carriers, at the supermarket checkout
counter, or in conjunction with a holiday party. Giving to food charity has
been made so easy and convenient that a large number of Americans have
contributed. They may even have had fun doing it, since recreation and entertainment are often added to antihunger projects. You can walk for hunger. As
bikers you can peddle against hunger and as film buffs attend "Canned Festivals," getting reduced-price tickets for bringing canned food. If you can afford
it, in more than 100 communities you can attend a Taste of the Nation buffet,
where top-ranked chefs offer samples of their work and donate the food, their
work, and the admission price to hunger relief. In 1994 the program raised
$3.7 million. A spin-off called Taste of the National Football League began
inviting people attending the Super Bowl to sample the fare of chefs in the
host city. In 1997 it raised $400,000. But not all participation is so glamorous.
For example, a survey of the emergency food system in New York City found
that more than four-fifths of people working in soup kitchens and food
pantries were volunteers, and they contributed the majority of the hours
worked. Some volunteer regularly while others do so only occasionally, but
even the occasional volunteer, like the occasional donor, contributes to the
overall size of the phenomenon and its capacity to touch the life of the larger
society.[13]

Soup kitchens have become an important part of the American food system. Here food is ladled into the bowl of an impoverished man.

To accommodate such popular interest and activity, the proliferation of soup kitchens, pantries, and other charitable emergency food institutions has been rapid and remarkably sustained. There is no good national baseline data; we don't know how many organizations there were before the 1980s, or exactly how many there are now. Consider, however, their growth in America's largest city alone, New York. There were thirty emergency food providers known before 1980, 487 in 1987, and 730 in 1991. By 1997 a large food bank was serving nearly 1,000 pantries and kitchens.[14] The growth in New York City was probably extreme, but similar growth rates have been reported by other cities.

"Second Harvest," the national organization of food banks, has grown from obscurity to become one of the nation's largest recipients of charitable contributions—among the top five in each of the past five years, bringing in more in the value of donations than the American Red Cross or Harvard University. This is a *big* charity, and corporations are among its largest donors.

CORPORATE PARTNERS OF SECOND HARVEST, 2000

Among the corporate partners of Second Harvest are Bestfoods, The Clorox Company, Coca-Cola, ConAgra, Del Monte Foods, General Mills, Hershey Chocolate Company, Johnson & Johnson, Kal Kan/Uncle Ben's, The Kellogg Company, K Mart Corporation, Kraft Foods, The Lipton Division of Unilever, The Minute Maid Company, Nabisco, Nestle USA, The Pillsbury Company, Procter & Gamble, Quaker Oats, SYSCO Corporation.[15]

Critics of such donations allege that, given their huge profits, corporations can easily afford such donations, and that they are motivated by public relations and tax write-offs. This may be true, but it misses an important point: Simply put, corporations are among the largest bankrollers of the America's emergency food system. Government is another huge "silent partner" in that system. It has successfully cultivated an image of reliance on private sector donations and volunteerism, but government at all levels has been more involved than the image suggests, providing both food and money as well as crucial policy supports. For example, a late 1980s study by the U.S. Conference of Mayors found that over half of the twenty-seven cities surveyed used local public funds for emergency food, and about 25 percent received state grants.[16] While programs of charitable emergency food for the hungry have become massively established in our time, it is important to note that there have been strategies based on other assumptions.

Sociologist Janet Poppendieck has argued that there are essentially 6 strategies to address hunger in America.[17]

SIX STRATEGIES TO ADDRESS HUNGER IN AMERICA

A hunger-fighting strategy can:

1. Acknowledge the hunger, but convince itself that the people who suffer deserve it or will somehow benefit in the long run;
2. Deny that hunger is real, call it a myth, or ask for more studies;
3. Reduce the abundance and get rid of the surplus;
4. Match up symptoms and transfer some of the excess to those in need;
5. Try to protect diets from poverty by setting a floor under food consumption or creating nonmarket access to food, or;
6. Redistribute income, wealth, and power so that no one is poor enough to be unable to purchase food.

The United States has tried them all in the twentieth century, and they have all left "fingerprints" on current programs.

The first can be called a "victim-blaming" strategy. It was dominant in the nineteenth century when a harsh diagnosis of poverty argued that it was rooted in the personal faults of the poor, replacing the older idea that poverty was inherent in the nature of the world. It argued that assistance to the poor would destroy whatever character they had and make them permanent paupers. Hunger was the spur that would cause them to change their dissolute ways, become hard-working citizens, and take advantage of the opportunities around them. It was unpleasant but good for them, and the nonpoor would only make things worse by "indiscriminate giving." The advocates of this strategy were not very successful in persuading the kind-hearted from helping. But, they were very successful in insisting that aid should be given "in-kind," as food, clothing, and fuel, rather than as cash—to assure that the assistance not be wasted on pleasure, alcohol, drugs, or gambling. They were also successful in promoting a preference for private rather than public charity, because the poor were less likely to consider it a "right" and become dependent on it. This view was reinvigorated by Social Darwinist thinking in the 1870s and 1880s and was reflected in the writings of charity organizers in both America and Europe. Recently it reappeared in the writings of conservatives like Charles Murray and Marvin Olansky and was recognizable in the politics of Newt Gingrich and the Republican majority in the U.S. House of Representatives, who authored the "Contract with America" in the mid-1990s.

The second strategy, "the denial of hunger," has been called the Herbert Hoover strategy, after President Hoover's often repeated assertion in the depths of the Great Depression that "No one has starved." The denial strategy did not work well for Hoover, and his reluctance to use Federal resources in relief contributed greatly to his political defeat by Roosevelt in the 1932 election. According to Hoover biographer Harris Warren, "No matter how often he denied it, people *were* starving in the midst of plenty."[18] The denial strategy reappeared in the Reagan Administration in the 1980s, when presidential advisor Ed Meese told the press that people were eating at soup kitchens because it was easier than preparing a meal at home, and that the reports of hunger were "all anecdotal stuff." When a *New Republic* reporter mentioned long soup lines as evidence, Meese responded that "people go to soup kitchens because it is free, and that's easier than paying for it." A presidential task force charged with investigating allegations of widespread hunger after the administration's cuts in food stamps, AFDC, and other safety net programs found that there were no reliable quantitative data—no national hunger count. It found that hunger was less serious than clinical malnutrition, and probably could not be reliably measured.[19]

The third strategy, "getting rid of the surplus," also derives from the Great Depression, when the juxtaposition of hunger with plenty became more visible, as enormous agricultural surpluses were literally piling up and becoming a problem. There was not only enough, but too much food. The resulting Agricultural Adjustment programs involved a number of approaches to limiting output—marketing agreements, quotas, bonuses, and so forth. But they are best remembered for attempting to forestall an impending market glut by plowing under a quarter of the country's cotton crop and slaughtering six million baby pigs so they could not grow up to be big hogs. This may have made immediate economic sense, but it did little for the hungry, and it was a public relations disaster for the Roosevelt administration. Such policies, attempting to strike a balance between excessive production and consumer demand, were resurrected in the 1980s with the addition of an ecological rationale. Soil bank and "set aside" programs gave farmers USDA subsidies for taking land out of production, particularly ecologically fragile land, allowing it to lie fallow.

The Great Depression also gave rise to the fourth strategy, that of "transferring food surpluses to hungry people." It began as a series of voluntary initiatives to harvest crop surpluses and distribute them to families in need, but the accumulation of huge stores of food and fiber in government hands led to demands for public sector action. Political controversy was intense, with many in government and congress arguing that there was not enough hunger and malnutrition to justify actions that might weaken food prices and undermine the principle of private responsibility for relief. The decisive argument proved to be the demonstration that storage and insurance charges, along with rats, mice, mold, dampness and weevils, were rapidly destroying the value of stored surpluses. In 1932 Congress released 45 million bushels of grain to the Red Cross for distribution to the hungry, which proved to be the entering wedge of a food entitlement program in the United States. The Roosevelt administration hastily organized a Federal Surplus Relief Corporation (FSRC) to purchase farm surpluses and distribute them through state emergency relief organizations. In dollar terms, the FSRC procured and redistributed only a tiny portion of the surplus and provided only a tiny increment to the diets of the unemployed. But it was apparently enough to relieve the moral anxieties of the affluent about the paradox of want amid plenty. What they got was a highly visible symbolic process that eased their discomfort.

By the late 1930s, economists of the USDA were looking for a more efficient way to transfer the nation's abundance into the hands of the needy, and they created an innovative food stamp program. Some stamps would be purchased (at deep discounts) and redeemed for any grocery store item, and other stamps were given free to be used to purchase any items designated by the USDA as surpluses. The program was enormously popular with consumers because it reintroduced consumer choice lacking in the surplus commodity distribution approach; it was popular with administrators because it eliminated the logistical problems with commodity purchase and distribution; and it was popular with retailers because it subsidized consumption through the "normal channels of trade." As surpluses disappeared during World War II, both surplus food distribution programs and food stamps disappeared.

In the 1980s surplus commodity distribution gained a new lease on life, with a superabundance of dairy products stored in government warehouses.

The USDA's cheese was rotting in the underground caves and warehouses in which it was stored, and doing so in the midst of a severe recession. In uncanny echoes of Hoover's fiasco, the Reagan administration found itself accused of sponsoring waste at public expense while withholding food from the needy. The federal government began shipping cheese to state Emergency Distribution organizations. What was supposed to be a one-time distribution turned into a regular affair with the creation of The Emergency Food Assistance Program (TFAP).

But by the 1980s, the rise of the fourth strategy was not primarily a public sector phenomenon. Paralleling the return surplus commodity distribution was the proliferation of the vast private system that we discussed earlier: food banking and charitable "emergency food" pantries and kitchens. They have become major features of the hunger-fighting landscape in the United States.

A fifth strategy attempted to "divorce hunger and undernutrition from poverty." Programs spawned by this strategy involved 14 separate federal nutrition programs and a host of state and local initiatives. These included school meals, congregate and "meals on wheels" for senior citizens, food subsidies or day care and recreation programs, and the Women's, Infant's, and Children's program (WIC) for new mothers and babies. But the heart of this effort since the 1960s was the resurrected Food Stamp Program, no longer tied to farm surpluses. It was revived to "strengthen the agricultural economy and improve levels of nutrition among the needy through normal channels of trade."[20]

The new Food Stamp Program (FSP) had many restrictions and relatively low benefits, and the "rediscovery of hunger" in the 1960s that put hunger again on the public agenda revealed its shortcomings. Subsequently, activists promoted its reform and expansion until the FSP became America's floor under food consumption intended to provide an adequate diet. It was based on the same set of assumptions that underlie federal "poverty-line" indexes: that households normally spend about one-third of their income on food and that families who could not afford that should be helped.

That may have been reasonable for the poor in the 1960s, but since then increases (particularly in energy and housing costs) have meant that the poor were caught in a "heat or eat" dilemma in which they cannot afford to allocate 30 percent of their income on food. For the elderly, that dilemma often became "medicate or eat." By the 1980s, the Food Stamp Program no longer filled the gap between food purchasing power and even the government's minimum Thrifty Food Plan. While this strategy undoubtedly helped the hungry and has much potential, it could not work effectively as inequality rose. As the poor fell further and further from America's median income, they were less and less able to purchase the unassisted part of their diet.

The sixth strategy, "making sure that all members of society have enough income to purchase an adequate diet," has been around since the beginning of the twentieth century, but has always been elusive. For instance,

Progressive reformers at the beginning of the century pursued protective legislation that reduced the likelihood of poverty by protecting workers from the most outrageous industrial hazards and dreamed about a program of comprehensive social insurance. It took the Great Depression to create the political readiness for even the most basic old age, disability, and unemployment benefits. Contemporary rhetoric stresses work as the solution to poverty (and hunger), but the large public works programs that rescued families from the depression are nowhere to be seen. The growth of inequality (partly due to changes in the tax code) means that this strategy now seems farther from implementation than at any other time in recent history.[21]

EFFECTIVENESS, ETHICS, AND JUSTICE

While all of these strategies left their imprint on America's attempt to fight hunger, and some undeniably helped, all had powerful limitations. Victim-blaming and the denial of hunger combat hunger only by morally defining it away, or by saying that hunger is only highly impressionistic "observations." Transferring food to hungry people and getting rid of food surpluses did create programs of food entitlement, but they were tied to economic hard times or other objectives, like getting rid of farm surpluses. Programs that tried to divorce nutrition from poverty, like school meals, WIC programs, and food stamps, undoubtedly made significant differences in the well-being of poor households, but the idea that people can stay poor but eat has been more a planner's fiction than a reality. It was limited by the growth of inequality. Furthermore, deep cuts in both child nutritional programs and food stamps and the "end to welfare" (PRWORA) significantly weakened this strategy. The growth of inequality and cuts in the social safety net have made the last strategy, that of addressing hunger by promoting equality, even more unrealistic in contemporary times. So what has emerged as the dominant strategy as others failed has been transferring food to hungry people, particularly in the private system of food banks, soup kitchens, and emergency food.

Why is practicing charity easier than entitlements? Both democratic governments and citizens are reluctant to spend taxes to support the poor. Charity has the sweet aroma of private benevolence, while entitlements carry the odors of taxes, welfare, and dependency. Charity is kinder, but less just. The growth of such charitable kindness and the declines in social justice are intimately related. It has both costs and benefits for the hungry as well as for the social institutions and people who generously participate in the emergency food system.

Charity is, for example, a way for corporations (and governments) to get rid of embarrassing food surpluses without depressing market prices. It also garners good public relations. It is very beneficial to religious and private groups that build elaborate emergency food infrastructures and reinforce their core teachings. Those who participate in such a system do so partly for a variety of rewards that Janet Poppendieck terms the "seductions of charity." They do so because participation in food organizations and food drives often carries its own social reward. They may do so for religious obligations ("it is better to give..."), or to alleviate guilt. They may give generously to fight hunger, a clear and familiar moral evil, while being reluctant to combat poverty, which is more abstract as well as clouded with moral and political ambiguity. Feeding the hungry is participating in something that is unambiguously good and perhaps one of the few such efforts that one can really trust today.[22]

Indeed, Americans have responded to hungry people as they usually do for people in urgent need of help, with energy and compassion. While undoubtedly helping people, however, such charitable generosity serves to relieve pressure for more fundamental solutions. It is a symptom (and possibly an on-going cause) of our failure to deal with the erosion of equality. On a cultural level it works as a sort of "moral safety valve" that reduces the discomfort evoked by destitution in our midst—by hunger in the midst of plenty.[23]

Returning to the more general ethical perspectives discussed earlier, how are we doing in combating the evils of hunger? Not well enough by most of them, with the possible exception of the utilitarian perspective. A utilitarian ethicist might argue that we don't do any better than we do fighting hunger because we are protecting other important values. But are those things we are protecting really the moral equivalent of human hunger? Or, could we cut a new utilitarian "moral deal," both personally and politically? It is certainly not enough from ethical perspectives like those of Rawls that emphasize the reciprocities and moral obligations among people who participate in connected social worlds.

DEALING WITH WORLD HUNGER:
THE ETHICS OF TRADE AND AID

Earlier chapters discussed globalization and the last chapter, in particular, ended with a focus on hunger among people in the poorer developing nations and ideas and strategies to address it. As in the foregoing, we discuss the major ways that hunger—now world hunger—has been addressed, as well as ethical and social justice issues surrounding these efforts. They boil down to ideas and strategies about trade and aid. Both trade in foodstuffs and food aid are ways to get food produce in one nation to the hungry in other nations. Of the two, the volume of food traded around the world vastly outstrips the volume of food transferred in aid programs. It is important to note that the driving forces of trade and aid are very different. Trade is driven by attempts of people and nations to maximize the value of the food they have. Food aid reflects a mixture of humanitarian and political motives involving governments, international institutions, and voluntary organizations. Because trade is largely a self-serving activity, it might appear less ethical and moral than aid, which embodies altruistic motives. In actual practice, however, complications make it clear that neither trade nor aid are wholly virtuous activities.

The contemporary rationale for viewing trade as a virtuous activity is rooted in classical economic thinking. The value of something (like food) is shaped by individual preferences and tastes reflected in how they spend money. Economic improvement means that they are able to choose a bundle of goods and services that they value more than other choices. Markets are central to such improvement because they enable people to exchange some goods and services for others. By their high degree of specialization, modern economies enable people to concentrate on a limited range of activities in which they have special skills or efficiencies. Exchanges in such markets enable them to consume far beyond what they would if they had to produce everything themselves. People become richer in their ability to consume. Extending such markets increases benefits by creating greater opportunities for specializing in those products for which individuals and nations are best fitted. These benefits do not require improvements in technologies or increased natural resources, but stem from the trade process itself. In the long term, this is a potent way of raising income levels (and thereby...nutritional adequacy). Each nation, the thinking goes, should pursue its own "comparative advantage" by producing what it does most efficiently in trade relationships with others.

This is not only theory (termed neoliberal economic thinking), but it has informed economic policy making since the 1940s. During the closing months of World War II, the world's bankers, finance ministers, and leaders gathered at Bretton Woods, New Hampshire, to consider how to avoid a repeat of the three tragedies of the twentieth century (two world wars and a great world depression). They concluded that economic nationalism and legal trade barriers were major driving forces of such events, and they urged the world's nations to embark on policies that reduced trade barriers and encouraged a vast expansion of mutually enriching international trade. That historic meeting spawned the "Bretton Woods institutions" that are with us still (the World Bank, and International Monetary Fund, and the successive "rounds" of talks to negotiate a General Agreement on Trade and Tariffs — now formalized as the World Trade Organization [WTO]).

Combined with innovations in agricultural productivity, transportation, and information technology (like computers and the Internet), such neoliberal thinking that reduced trade barriers did work to accelerate international trade, which grew more rapidly than did the economies of separate nations in the post-WWII period. World economic resources, including food, grew more rapidly than did the human population. But has international trade helped to alleviate world hunger since the 1950s?

The most reasonable conclusion would be that it has—in combination with the multitude of safety net, development, and targeted food-aid programs of governments and international agencies and private organizations (INGOs). Officially, since the 1960s, world hunger has declined from about 30 percent to about 20 percent of the world population. But, most of that progress came in the early decades, in the 1970s rather than the 1990s. Even so, 942 million were undernourished in developing nations in 1970 and 828 million still were in the mid-1990s (not counting those in the wealthier nations of Europe and North America). This is indeed modest "progress," given the resources available to address the problem. At this rate, there will be many hundreds of millions of hungry people at the middle of the twentieth century.[24] For addressing world hunger, those results and deep flaws and contradictions in the international trade provide reasons to question the claims made for it. How so?

WHAT GOES WRONG?

There are many factual, ethical, and social justice problems that surround using international trade to address hunger. A simple "free trade model" assumes relatively full employment. When competition from imports causes enterprises to fail, they move to other forms of production. The additional output is added to the real income of a nation's whole economy. Thus, the benefits of trade happen only when such "structural adjustments" are complete. But, in the real world, such adjustments are not quick, painless, or cost free.

Trade in agriculture and food was always connected with substantial structural change. In the nineteenth century, in Europe and the United States, it resulted in the bankruptcy of many small farmers and rapid migration to urban areas. Governments devised policies to protect smaller independent "family" farmers and ranchers from slow but steady decline, but without much success. They are still popular with people and governments, in spite of the costs on taxpayers and consumers, and they appeal to values other than free trade—like family survival, community, economic equity, and ecology.

This structural adjustment process of leaving unprofitable farms is being repeated around the world. Cities in developing nations are awash with displaced rural people, but it is important to note a very large fraction of the world population still grows food, or lives in rural areas and is dependent upon farmers who do. They still represent about 40 percent of the population of the developing world, vastly different from the United States where only a small proportion of the population still farms. Thus, international food trade makes large rural populations poorer, and a nation's ability to produce its own food less profitable. The spread of intensive industrial agriculture replaces human labor with capital and technological inputs. To reiterate, free trade is mutually enriching under conditions of full employment. When this is not the case, global trade can widen the gap between the rich and the poor within the same economy, and between nations, amplifying problems of equity and social justice.

Trade may make matters worse, particularly when food is scarce. As we noted in Chapter 6, famines typically occur not just because supplies are scarce, but because the hungry have too few entitlements (or money) to bid for the food that is available. Faced with food shortages, richer people may be able to pay more. In the depths of famine, food may even be exported by poorer nations, while some starve, as it was during the infamous Irish potato famine.

Government policies often exacerbate these effects. Where more food is produced than can be sold or consumed at home, countries have promoted and subsidized exports. The Bretton Woods institutions have been rather successful in getting nations to reduce barriers, but less successful in getting nations (particularly industrial nations) to abandon such subsidies.[25] The result is that major food exporters may engage in competitive dumping, further depressing world market prices. And food import policies usually focus on the need to hold food prices down (benefiting urban people), rather than to support rural incomes.

The same kinds of oligopolistic trends we described in the United States are now visible in the world market system. Commodity food trade, particularly in grains and oilseeds, are now dominated by a small number of international traders, and multinational food companies dominate markets in processed foods (for example, coffee, sugar). Such companies are investing in low-income countries to build vertically integrated markets linking production with the final point of sale, usually in higher-income countries. The result is to make low-income nations more dependent on cheap commodity imports while eroding their capacity to feed themselves. But such import dependency may be unreliable and may expose people to the fluctuations of a world pricing system. It surely corrodes a basic mission of all modern governments. Few willingly abrogate national food self-sufficiency.[26]

Finally, there are ecological problems surrounding increasing international food trade and particularly the global diffusion of industrial-style agriculture. Such production usually requires greater inputs of irrigated water, pesticides, and other agrochemicals than does traditional production. These "externalities" that degrade the biotic wealth of nations do not show up on trade balance accounts, nor does the reduction in worldwide genetic diversity in seed crops and livestock varieties. The global spread of such specialized agriculture encourages monocrop production with its greater vulnerability to crop failures caused by drought, pests, and disease. Furthermore, the intrusion of modern agriculture erodes the last vestiges of traditional agroecological knowledge of producers who had farmed more or less sustainably for decades.

Our point is that global trade in foodstuffs may exacerbate problems and is not an unmixed ethical and moral blessing, as enthusiastic neoliberal economists often imply. Having said that, it is important to note that trade can be an essential part of any long-term solution to world poverty, and therefore of the solution to world hunger.[27] This is particularly true in the dense urban nations without surrounding rural areas, such as Singapore or Hong Kong, which could not achieve food self-sufficiency under any imaginable scenario. They depend upon manufactures and their skilled and disciplined labor forces to buy food on international markets. But that is not the situation in other relatively "hungry" areas of the world, such as India, sub-Saharan Africa, or Latin America. They might look to the Chinese, who made agriculture profitable and protected farmers from predatory trade. The Chinese achieved a remarkable—if tenuous—food security in several decades in the world's largest relatively poor nation, a nation not particularly well endowed with agricultural resources. China, with a booming export economy of manufactured goods, also illustrates the positive potential of trade on long-term economic development, showing that it depends more on income than on food production in and of itself.

FOOD AID

In contrast to trade, food aid is often viewed as a wholly altruistic activity—to help people who are hungry. As in domestic politics, governments and aid agencies find it easier to give aid as food than money. But while food aid may genuinely indicate altruism on the part of governments or their electorates, other motives intrude. Evidence suggests, for instance, that the volume of food aid depends more on the extent of surpluses than on the needs of recipients.[28] Food aid may be a convenient and popular way of getting rid of ruinous surpluses at home. Food aid may be given to recipients in exchange for supporting the strategic interests of donor nations, or as a part of trade contracts with donor nations. Aid may be linked to the provision of military acquisitions (air bases, docking facilities, etc.). Aid may deliberately be used to help donor country firms and farmers out-compete Third World suppliers and locally based producers. It may, in other words, be used as the "entering wedge" to build an export market. Such justifications may "make sense" in terms of global power politics or domination of the world market food economy. But they are far removed from the ethical perspectives discussed earlier, particularly the human rights theories and the Rawlsian approach that would allocate food based on the needs of the least fortunate.

To illustrate these points, consider the checkered career of U.S. food aid. About two-thirds of U.S. food aid has gone under Title I of Public Law 480 (PL 480). Under its provisions, foreign governments take out long-term loans from the U.S. government to purchase America's surplus agricultural commodities.

The bulk of what is called "food aid" is actually purchased by foreign governments to do with as they please. Generally, the food is sold on the local market, meaning that those who can pay for it get it. While the $30-plus billion worth of food shipped abroad as "aid" since 1950 clearly represents the genuinely humanitarian impulses of ordinary Americans, the actual mechanisms and motive underlying the program are something else. Public records unequivocally demonstrate that policy makers viewed the food-aid program as:

- Ridding the United States of price-depressing domestic surpluses;
- Opening new markets for commercial sales of U.S. farm products and offsetting trade deficits;
- Pressuring foreign governments to support U.S. economic and military interests and supporting U.S. military interventions in the Third World;
- Extending the reach of U.S. agribusiness corporations.[29]

PL 480 originated during the 1950s, when India requested grain to stave off famine precipitated by monsoon failure. But since World War II, India had embargoed monazite sand containing thorium, a material necessary for the production of nuclear weapons. The U.S. government seized the threat of famine to have the embargo lifted. Congressman Charles Kersten (R-Wisconsin) put it bluntly: "In return for the wheat we are asked to give India, the very least we should ask of India is that it permit the United States to buy some of these strategic materials...."[30] The result was the India Emergency Food Act, the precursor to PL 480, later called the "food for peace" program. Only in 1966 was the humanitarian intent even written into its preamble.

Some argue that if you give people food, they will not want to grow food. The unvarnished fact is that dumping large amounts of low-priced American grain in developing nations makes it economically impossible for the small domestic producers to compete. Such displaced farmers often have no alternative but to sell their land and become landless (and often jobless) laborers.

South Korea, for example, is the second largest recipient of U.S. food aid and has purchased more U.S. agricultural goods than any other nation. That, combined with direct $13 billion in direct economic and military assistance to Seoul since the end of the Korean War, has produced a low-paid, "disciplined" labor force for export-oriented multinational companies that now dominate the South Korean economy. It enabled the South Korean government to maintain a "cheap food" policy that undercut many Korean farmers. Not surprisingly, Korea's rural population declined from about half of the total population in the 1960s to one-third in the mid-1970s. While pressure from the remaining farmers forced some increases in the government's mandatory (low) price for rice, the Korean Catholic Farmers Association found that prices still fell below production costs. Korean farmers who dared circulate a petition asking the government to pay a fair price for their rice were harassed, arrested, and beaten. Former U.S. Assistant Secretary of Agriculture Clayton Yeutter opined that, "South Korea is the greatest success story worldwide of the Food for Peace Program (PL 480) in terms of contribution to the growth of that nation."[31]

Similarly, Colombia imported over a million tons of wheat from 1955 to 1971—wheat that could have been produced locally—and the marketing agency of the Colombian government fixed the price so low that it undercut domestic producers. Most of the 407,550 acres pushed out of wheat production were not replanted. Most were converted into cattle grazing, and such ranching operations were abetted by PL 480 loans that went to subsidiaries of U.S. transnational companies like Ralston Purina, Quaker Oats, Pfizer, and Abbot Laboratories to produce feed and veterinary drugs. Large landowners now prosper by growing beef, flowers, and vegetables—mainly for the export market.[32] This kind of "development" means the growth and prosperity for one social strata alongside the increased landlessness, marginal employment, or destitution and hunger for another—and usually much larger—social strata. In the ensuing social instability and chaos it is not surprising that as the last defense of becoming landless, Colombian farmers often turned to growing a very lucrative crop for export, cocoa leaves. Meanwhile, democratic institutions are beset by a virtual civil war with the "drug barons" who organized that cocaine export market, and as we write, the United States is becoming progressively drawn into the quicksand of military interdiction to try to suppress the drug trade—most of which is with North America. In fact, by 2000, a greater share of Colombia's real export earnings came from cocaine than from coffee, cattle, flowers, oil, and other exports combined.

In brief, trade and aid are not as clearly different in fact and consequence as they are in ideal and legal conception. Furthermore, the same ethical and moral flaws beset them. This "trade-aid" system came to be practiced in the world market system by using cheap subsidized agricultural goods as the lever to drive people to cities, where Western private investments would stimulate the manufacture of cheap export goods (clothes, Nikes, computers, etc.) by a low-wage and highly disciplined workforce. This system was often enforced by "friendly" but authoritarian regimes. In terms of equity, it was—and is still—a very unequal bargain between the more-developed and the less-developed nations.

So far, we have focused on *government* food aid. What of *private* food aid efforts? In one sense, they are similar. Dumping lots of cheap—or free—food has the impact of making local agriculture less profitable. But private aid agencies (NGOs like the Red Cross, Oxfam, Bread for the World, The Heifer Project, Catholic World Service, and United Methodist Committee on Relief, to name a few) are nimbler than government aid, and can respond more quickly to targeted needs. Furthermore, they can more successfully short-circuit dealing with state ministries and food marketing boards that routinely pilfer or misallocate emergency food.

At their best, such NGOs like Oxfam and the Heifer Project focus more on development programs that encourage food self-sufficiency and less on emergency relief. They attempt to put the old saying into practice: "Give a man a fish and he eats for a day; teaching him to fish and he will eat for a long time." That idea—about sustainable development from the "bottom up"—is not lost on modern governments and international agencies like the World Bank, but they find it much more difficult to practice, given their other agendas. NGOs such as these provided food aid *without additional agendas*, like disposing of agricultural surpluses, creating "overseas" markets, creating a hungry urban labor force from displaced peasants, or enhancing military and national geopolitical objectives.

We quickly add, however, that—at their worst—private NGOs can also be unaccountable scams. In the 1970s, for example, there was an intriguing organization called "The Hunger Project," predicated on promoting the idea that ending hunger was an "idea whose time has come." This "project" it turns out, was sponsored by a U.S. religious movement (Werner Erhard's "est"), which solicited donations. It produced some glossy literature, and perhaps "raised the consciousness" about hunger, but it never contributed a single bite of food or dollar or development aid to a hungry person anywhere on the planet. Perhaps more importantly, no matter how ethical or virtuous, NGOs have minuscule resources compared to those available to governments and multilateral agencies like the World Bank or the UN Food and Agriculture Organization; they are, therefore, very inadequate resources to address the needs of the world's hungry in a meaningful way.

Finally, there is a more fundamental problem with the whole notion of food aid. Food is a relatively inefficient form of aid for the hungry. Considering all its subsidies, it often costs more to produce and transport around the world than if it had been produced locally. Food is bulky, perishable, and expensive to transport and distribute. The infrastructures for doing this are particularly scarce and fragile in hungry regions (usually rural areas) in poor nations, where communication is poor, and roads, warehouses, and transportation may not exist. Food is very likely to be wasted or stolen before it reaches its intended consumers. It would be more efficient in several senses to contribute money rather than food or other "in kind" services, particularly since the root cause of hunger is poverty. But, as in the United States, enlarging "aid" programs from food to money suffers political liabilities. Food aid is popular, but not "foreign aid" in general.

REFORMING FOOD TRADE AND AID

Having exposed these ethical, moral, and social justice warts and ambiguities that cloud the virtues of international trade and aid, do we advocate their abolition? *Indeed not.* We will not linger over the considerable practical and political difficulties for completely dismantling both systems, which purist critics of both world trade and aid sometimes entertain—except to note that doing so would be as morally bankrupt as the ways trade and aid are currently practiced.

There is, for example, an on-going need for real "emergency food" to be provided in "rapid response" by the international community (from both public and private agencies) under conditions of natural or social disasters. Near current illustrations include Hurricane "Mitch" that devastated Central America in 1999, ruining farms and food supplies, and the disastrous flood in Mozambique in 2000, driven by an Indian ocean typhoon that destroyed a rebounding agricultural capacity after a decade of civil war. Similarly, such need is illustrated by the earthquake in Gujarat state in India that killed over 15,000 and devastated homes, farms, and food supplies in early 2001. Such aid should be intense and episodic.

The benefits of ongoing attempts to increase trade by reducing trade barriers on food and other things, as well as long-term food development aid programs, are actually long-term benefits, even though perhaps quite disastrous in the short term (where people live and go hungry). At minimum, trade and aid programs that displace rural self-provisioning people should be accompanied by investments providing real "living wage" nonagricultural employment, and which also support the crumbling and overburdened infrastructures of Third World cities. In other words, free trade needs to be accompanied by support for declining economic sectors that still account for the life and livelihoods of 40 percent of the world's population, as well as greater respect for environmental integrity. Even if this is attainable, the ultimate consequence of this "neoliberal" economic vision implies a world of gargantuan cities with prosperous full employment that is specialized in a global division of labor. They would similarly be surrounded by depopulated hinterlands where, similarly, a few landlords and perhaps transnational corporations conduct specialized high-tech production in agricultural monocultures. This does not seem to us a viable social vision, either in terms of social or ecological sustainability.

Moreover, reforming food trade and aid requires divorcing them from other national agendas, like disposing of domestic surpluses, or supporting national strategic, military, and geopolitical objectives. That is a tall order, but it is not unthinkable. A worldwide "conscience constituency" could emerge among democratic electorates, policy makers, networked global NGOs, and multilateral agencies in which a global food entitlement (guaranteed by all signatories to the Charter of the United Nations) is part of a more encompassing sustainable development vision.

We are more hopeful for the growing role of NGOs to provide the moral vision for such a transformation. That moral vision could demonstrate that providing assistance is in the interests of donor nations, as well as of recipient countries. Beyond that, rather than just dumping bags of wheat or soybeans in poor nations, efforts of food-related NGOs to promote development food aid, from the "bottom up," and to create greater economic viability and self-provisioning capacities among rural people are impressive.

Even apart from such efforts, existing models abound that enable the poor to build successful enterprises. The state of Kerala in India has a legendary history of such development, with resulting longer-life expectancy, low infant mortality and fertility rates, and a virtual end to hunger—compared with other Indian states. Cuba's new emphasis on agriculture demonstrates that small farmers and urban gardeners relying mostly on sustainable agriculture, rather than agrochemicals and genetically engineered crops, can feed a nation's population. The "landless worker movement" in Brazil has demonstrated that it is indeed possible to force land reform "from below" and create successful enterprises run by the poor. In the United States, the Community Food Security movement demonstrates how poor communities can take over abandoned spaces in their neighborhoods and turn them into productive urban gardens that generate jobs and provide food for low-income families. Indeed, thousands of small farmers around the world, including in the United States, have increased their production and incomes through agroecological alternatives such as the ones described in Chapter 6, and in many cases they are spreading these initiatives through their own efforts and organizations.[33] Such alternatives, we think, show more promise for ending world hunger than do the runaway free trade policies and the slashing of safety nets everywhere that displace working people—whether computer programmers or small farmers—in a global "race to the bottom." Moreover, we think such bottom-up efforts are far less likely to be ethically corrupted than is trade and aid "business as usual" from the top down.

Are such reforms really possible? Yes, and they could be driven by two reciprocal forces. One is that the growing concentration of assets, power, and food in the hands of a few may become so visible, destabilizing, and "dysfunctional" that global elites and policy makers themselves intervene. For example, the World Bank now recognizes that malnutrition is largely the result of rural poverty, and it is replacing its long-standing agricultural development strategies that were centered around high-tech monocropping on large estates with rural development strategies that use a much broader approach. Bank planners now envision systematic approaches to eradicating rural poverty—approaches that embrace agriculture but also the enhancement of human capital, infrastructure, and community development into a broad strategy for rural development. One advantage of encouraging investment in the countryside by agriculture and other industries is that it in turn encourages breadwinners to stay in the countryside, keeping families and communities intact. Indeed, in the absence of such strategies, rural poverty simply becomes urban poverty.[34]

On the other hand, there is a related driving force to build broad-based popular movements where ordinary people in civil society networks join together to promote such reforms. At the turn of the twenty-first century, misgivings about the roles of the World Bank, as well as popular protests surrounding WTO meetings, could illustrate the beginnings of such reforms.

Building a popular and mobilized "conscience constituency" involves dispelling some myths about hunger that are immobilizing. Like what? Following Peter Rosset, we think there are four. First, that nature is to blame. Second, that we need a technological fix (in a world awash with surplus production). Third, that there are no real alternatives to the present circumstances; and fourth, that meaningful change is impossible.

SOME SUGGESTIONS FOR FURTHER READING

Aiken, W., and H. Lafollete, Eds. (1995). *World Hunger and Moral Obligation.* 2nd ed. Upper Saddle River, NJ: Prentice Hall.

Bourcher, D. (1999). *The Paradox of Plenty: Hunger in a Bountiful World.* Oakland, CA: Food First Books.

Mephamn, B., Ed. (1996). *Food Ethics.* New York: Routledge.

Poppendieck, J. (1998). *Sweet Charity? Emergency Food and the End of Entitlement.* New York: Viking.

Tefler, E. (1996). *Food for Thought: Philosophy and Food.* New York: Routledge.

Thompson, P. (1995). *The Spirit of the Soil: Agriculture and Environmental Ethics.* New York: Routledge.

Notes

INTRODUCTION

1. Boyle, M. (2001). *Personal Nutrition.* 4th ed. Belmont, CA: Wadsworth, p. 4.
2. Associated Press (April 28, 1999). Public Interest Groups Quit Food-Safety Panel. *Omaha World Herald,* p. 2.
3. Associated Press (May 23, 2000). Report: 40% of Farmland "Seriously Degraded." *Omaha World Herald,* p. 2.
4. Postel, S. (2000). Groundwater Depletion Widespread. In L. Brown, M. Renner, and B. Halweil (Eds.), *Vital Signs 2000: The Environmental Trends that are Shaping the Future.* New York: W. W. Norton; Sampat, P. (2000). Groundwater Quality Deteriorating. In Brown, Renner and Halweil (Eds.), *Vital Signs 2000,* pp. 124–125. See also Postel, S. (1992). *Last Oasis: Facing Water Scarcity.* New York: W. W. Norton.
5. Los Angeles Times (August 16, 1998). Companies Work Overtime To Find a Weight-Loss Drug. *Omaha World Herald,* p. 5A.
6. United States Conference of Mayors. Cited in Despite Strong Economy Many Still Go Hungry. *Population Today,* 27 (3), pp. 4–5.
7. Boyle, M. and G. Zyla (1996). *Personal Nutrition.* 3rd ed. St Paul, MN: West, p. 1.
8. Gardner, G., and B. Halweil (2000). Nourishing the Underfed and Overfed. In L. Starke (Ed.), *State of the World 2000.* New York: W. W. Norton; G. Gardner and B. Halweil (2000). Escaping Hunger, Escaping Excess. *Worldwatch,* 12 (4), p. 28.
9. Postel, S. (1994). Carrying Capacity: Earth's Bottom Line. In L. Starke (Ed.), *State of the World 1994.* New York: W. W. Norton, pp. 8–12.
10. McIntosh, E. (1995). *American Food Habits in Historical Perspective.* Westport, CT: Prager, p. 112.

11. A *monopoly* is control of a particular market by one firm. An *oligopolistic market* is one where decisive control of the market is shared by four or five large firms. Some world food oligopolies have become household words, such as Archer Daniels Midlands, ConAgra, Nestle, Cargill, and Beatrice Foods.
12. Ritzer, G. (2000). *The McDonaldization of Society.* New Century Edition, Thousand Oaks, CA: Pine Forge Press.

CHAPTER ONE

1. Farb, P., and G. Armelagos (1980). *Consuming Passions: The Anthropology of Eating.* Boston, MA: Houghton Mifflin, pp. 34–35.
2. Boyle, M. and G. Zyla (1996). *Personal Nutrition.* 3rd ed. St. Paul, MN: West, pp. 4, 25–33; McIntosh, E. (1995). *American Food Habits in Historical Perspective. Westport, CT: Praeger,* pp. 6–7.
3. Boyle and Zyla, (1996). *Personal Nutrition,* p. 62.
4. Boyle, M. (2001). *Personal Nutrition,* pp.110–116.
5. Boyle, M. (2001). *Personal Nutrition,* p. 180.
6. Enzymes are proteins that act as catalysts to boost the chemical reactions of the body.
7. McIntosh, E. (1995). *American Food Habits,* p. 13.
8. McIntosh, E. (1995). *American Food Habits,* pp. 3–5; Boyle and Zyla (1996). *Personal Nutrition,* pp. 197–198.
9. Boyle (2001). *Personal Nutrition,* p. 167.
10. Boyle (2001). *Personal Nutrition,* p. 42; McIntosh, E. (1995), *American Food Habits,* pp. 10–11.
11. Jaret, P. (2000). How to Eat Better and Still Eat All the Foods You Love: Italian, Mexican, Chinese.... *Remedy,* 7 (3), p. 30.
12. Jaret, P. (2000). How to Eat Better, pp. 30–38. For more about food plans and pyramids, see Boyle (2001). *Personal Nutrition,* pp. 38–64; Schlosberg, S. (1999). A Smart Way To Eat. *Shape,* Nov. pp. 105–113.
13. U.S. Public Health Service (1995). Screening for lead exposure in children. *American Family Physician,* (51), pp. 139–143.
14. Boyle (2001). *Personal Nutrition,* p. 391.
15. Gerth, J., and T. Weiner. (September 1997). Imports Swamp U.S. Food Safety Efforts. *New York Times,* pp. A1, A8; National Academy of Sciences, National Research Council (1993). *Pesticides in the Diets of Infants and Children.* Washington, DC: National Academy Press.
16. Platt, A. (2000). *Phasing Out Persistent Organic Pollutants.* In L. Starke (Ed.), *State of the World 2000.* New York: W. W. Norton.
17. Platt, A. (2000). *Phasing Out Pollutants,* pp. 89–90, citing E. Carlsen, et al. (1992). Evidence for the Decreasing Quality of Semen During Past 50 Years. *British Medical Journal,* 12 (September), pp. 89–90; and Pesticides Report: How Safe is Our Food? *Consumer Report* (March, 1999).
18. The American Academy of Pediatrics, The American Medical Association, and the American Cancer Society, cited in Boyle (2001). *Personal Nutrition,* p. 395.
19. Mellon, M. (1998). Prescription for Trouble. *Nucleus,* 27 (4), pp. 1–3.
20. Boyle (2001). *Personal Nutrition,* pp. 16–17; Pelto, G. (1981). Anthropological contributions to nutrition education research. *Journal of Nutrition Education,* 13,

S4, cited in P. Kittler and K. Sucher (2000). *Cultural Foods: Traditions and Trends.* Belmont CA: Wadsworth, p. 11.

21. Woznicki, D., and A. Case (1994). *Nutritional Accuracy in Popular Magazines.* New York: American Council on Science and Health, Inc., cited in Boyle and Zyla (1996). *Personal Nutrition,* p. 15.

22. Woznicki and Case (1994). *Nutritional Accuracy.*

23. Cohen, D. (January 18, 1999). Introduction to Nutrition. Lecture, Creighton University, Omaha, NE; Fox, N. (January 18, 2000). Nutrition Basics. Lecture, Creighton University, Omaha, NE.

24. Gardner, G., and B. Halweil (2000). Nourishing the Underfed, pp. 59–78.

25. Data from the World Health Organization, the *International Journal of Obesity,* and the International Food Policy Research Institute, summarized by Gardner and Halweil (2000). Nourishing the Underfed, p. 59.

26. Gardner and Halweil (2000). Nourishing the Underfed and Overfed. In L. Starke (ed.), *State of the World 2000.* New York: W.W. Norton, pp. 59, 62.

27. Associated Press (September 11, 2000). Report: As Fewer Families Go Hungry, Woes Linger. *Omaha World Herald,* p. 4. See also Poppendieck, J. (1998). *Sweet Charity.* New York: Viking; and Young, E. (1997). *World Hunger.* London: Routledge.

28. Gardner and Halweil (2000). Nourishing the Underfed, pp. 60–65.

29. Gardner and Halweil (2000). Nourishing the Underfed, pp. 67–68.

30. Blundell, J., and J. MacDiarmid (1997). Fat as a Risk Factor for Overcomsumption: Satiation, Satiety, and Patterns of Eating. *Journal of American Dietetic Association,* 93, (July); Supplement 7, pp. 63–69.

31. Boyle (2001). *Personal Nutrition,* pp. 176–180.

32. Boyle and Zyla (1996). *Personal Nutrition,* p. 226; McCullough, M. (2000). Cold Heart Facts: The health benefits of antioxidants are still unclear. *The Philadelphia Inquirer.* In *Omaha World Herald,* January 3, 2000, p. 29.

33. Carey, A. (2000). Cold Heart Facts: The prognosis is grim for your average American, professor says. *The Philadelphia Inquirer.* In *Omaha World Herald,* January 3, 2000, p. 29.

CHAPTER TWO

1. King, M. (2000). *Western Civilization: A Social and Cultural History.* Upper Saddle River, NJ: Prentice Hall, pp. 4–5.

2. King (2000). *Western Civilization,* p. 5. See also: Leakey, R. and R. Lewin (1992). *Origins Reconsidered: In Search of What Makes Us Human.* New York: Doubleday.

3. Dahlberg, F. (1981). Introduction. In F. Dahlberg (Ed.), *Woman the Gatherer.* New Haven: Yale University Press, pp. 1–33.

4. Gordon, K. (1987). Evolutionary Perspectives in Human Diet. In F. Johnson (Ed.), *Nutritional Anthropology.* New York: Alan R. Liss, pp. 3, 9; Beals, R. and H. Hoizer (1971). *An Introduction to Anthropology,* 4th ed. New York: Macmillan Company, pp. 222–223; Yesner, D.R. (1987). Life in the "Garden of Eden": Causes and Consequences of Adapting of Marine Diets by Human Societies. In M. Harris and E. Ross (Eds.), *Food and Evolution.* Philadelphia: Temple University Press, pp. 286–291, 295, 304.

5. Associated Press (June 13, 2000). Neanderthal Diet Likely Meaty. *Omaha World Herald*, p. 6.
6. Mellaart, J. (1975). *The Neolithic of the Near East.* New York: Scribners.
7. McIntosh, E. (1995). *American Food Habits in Historical Perspective.* Westport, CT: Praeger, pp. 30–34; Morey, D. (1994). The Early Evoluation of the Domestic Dog. *American Scientist*, 82 (4), p. 339.
8. King (2000). *Western Civilization*, p. 608; Leakey, R. (1981). *The Making of Mankind.* New York: E. P. Dutton, pp. 92–95.
9. Food in History: You Ate It, Ralph. *The Economist* (November 4, 2000), p. 94.
10. Diamond, J. (1987). The Worst Mistake in the History of the Human Race. In A. Podolesfsky and P. Brown (Eds.), (1999). *Applying Anthropology: An Introductory Reader*, 5th ed. Mountain View, CA: Manfield Publishing Company, p. 100.
11. Diamond (1987). Worst Mistake, p. 101.
12. Diamond (1987). Worst Mistake, p. 101.
13. Whit, W. (1995). *Food and Society: A Sociological Approach.* Dix Hills, NY: General Hall, Inc., p. 168; Diamond (1987). *Worst Mistake*, pp. 101–102.
14. Diamond (1987). Worst Mistake, p. 100.
15. Diamond (1987). Worst Mistake, p. 102.
16. King (2000). *Western Civilization*, p. 11.
17. King (2000). *Western Civilization*, p. 11.
18. King (2000). *Western Civilization*, p. 14.
19. King (2000). *Western Civilization*, pp. 17–19. See also: Lerner, G. (1986). *The Creation of Patriarchy.* New York: Oxford University Press.
20. King (2000). *Western Civilization*, pp. 20–22, 24.
21. King (2000). *Western Civilization*, pp. 27–32. See also Cross, F. (1973). *Canaanite Myth and Hebrew Epic: Essays in the History of the Religion of Israel.* Cambridge, MA: Harvard University Press.
22. King (2000). *Western Civilization*, pp. 64, 66.
23. King (2000). *Western Civilization*, p. 71.
24. King (2000). *Western Civilization*, p. 71. See also Cohen, E. (1992). *Athenian Economy and Society.* Princeton: Princeton University Press.
25. Hanson, V. (2000). Agricultural Equilibrium, Ancient and Modern. *The Journal of the Historical Society*, 1 (1), pp. 101–105.
26. Hanson (2000). Agricultural Equilibrium, pp. 107–108; Finley, M. (1982). *Economy and Society in Ancient Greece.* New York: Viking Press, pp. 102–133.
27. Hanson (2000). Agricultural Equilibrium, pp. 109–112.
28. Hanson (2000). Agricultural Equilibrium, pp. 111, 114.
29. King (2000). *Western Civilization*, p. 69.
30. Hanson (2000). Agricultural Equilibrium, p. 111.
31. See Blundell, S. (1995). *Women in Ancient Greece.* Cambridge, MA: Harvard University Press.
32. Tannahill, R. (1973). *Food in History.* New York: Stein and Day, p. 71; McIntosh (1995). *American Food Habits*, p. 46.
33. McIntosh (1995). *American Food Habits*, pp. 46–47.
34. Hanson (2000). Agricultural Equilibrium, p. 119.
35. Tannahill (1973). *Food in History*, p. 82; Lowenberg, M., et al. (1979). *Food and People*, 3rd ed. New York: John Wiley and Sons, p. 31.

36. Hanson (2000). Agricultural Equilibrium, p. 131 Note 14.

37. King (2000). *Western Civilization*, pp. 156, 162, 170–171. See also MacMullen, R. (1988). *Corruption and the Decline of Rome.* New Haven: Yale University Press.

38. Lowenberg et al. (1979). *Food and People*, p. 49; McIntosh (1995), *American Food Habits*, p. 49.

39. Whit, W. (1995). *Food and Society: A Sociological Approach.* Dix Hills, NY: General Hall, pp. 149–150.

40. Carcopino, J. (1940). *Daily Life in Ancient Rome: The People and the City at the Height of the Empire.* New Haven: Yale University Press, p. 39.

41. King (2000). *Western Civilization*, p. 256.

42. Duby, G. (1968). *Rural Economy and Country Life in the Medieval West.* Columbia: University of South Carolina Press.

43. King (2000). *Western Civilization*, p. 258.

44. King (2000). *Western Civilization*, p. 258.

45. King (2000). *Western Civilization*, p. 258, 260.

46. King (2000). *Western Civilization*, p. 260. See also Duby (1968). *Rural Economy and Country Life.*

47. McIntosh (1995). *American Food Habits*, p. 51.

48. King (2000). *Western Civilization*, p. 262.

49. Quoted in Whit (1995). *Food and Society*, p. 150.

50. Bell, R. (1985). *Holy Anorexia.* Chicago: University of Chicago Press, p. 146; Bynum, C.W. (1997). Fast, Feast, and Flesh: The Religious Significance of Food to Medieval Women. In C. Counihan and P. Van Esterik (Eds.), (1997). *Food and Culture: A Reader.* London: Routledge, pp. 139–140.

51. Douglas, M. (1997). Deciphering a Meal. In Counihan and Van Esterik (1997). *Food and Culture*, pp. 44–45; Soler, J. (1997). The Semiotics of Food in the Bible. In Counihan and Van Esterik (1997). *Food and Culture*, pp. 55, 58, 64–65; Harris, M. (1997). The Abominable Pig. In Counihan and Van Esterik (1997). *Food and Culture*, pp. 67–69, 71, 75.

52. Boyle, Marie A., Personal Nutrition, 4th edition (Wadsworth, a division of Thompson Learning, Inc., 2001), p. 245. Cited with permission.

53. Littlewood, R. (1995). Psychopathy and Personal Agency: Modernity, Culture, Charge, and Eating Disorders in South Asian Societies. In *The British Journal of Medical Psychology*, 68 (1), pp. 57–59; Polinska, W. (2000). Bodies Under Siege: Eating Disorders and Self-Mutilation Among Women. *The Journal of the American Academy of Religion*, 68 (3), p. 576.

54. Bynum (1997). *Fast Feast and Flesh*, pp. 138–139, 146–147; Bynum, C. (1987). *Holy Feast and Holy Fast: The Religious Significance of Food to Medieval Women.* Berkeley: The University of California Press, pp. 191, 200, 207, 210–212.

55. King (2000). *Western Civilization*, p. 263.

56. King (2000). *Western Civilization*, p. 263; see also Lopez, R (1971). *The Commercial Revolution of the Middle Ages, 950–1350.* Englewood Cliffs, NJ: Prentice Hall.

57. King (2000). *Western Civilization*, pp. 263–265; The Black Death: Plague and Economics. *The Economist* (December 31, 1999), pp. 33, 36.

58. Bryson, R. and T. Murray (1977). *Climates of Hunger.* Madison, WI: University of Wisconsin Press., pp. 20–21.

59. King (2000). *Western Civilization*, pp. 274–276; see also Lopez (1971). *The Commercial Revolution.*

60. Elias, N. (1939). *The Civilizing Process*. Vol. 1 of *The History of Manners (1978)*. Oxford: Basil Blackwell, pp. 117–122; Mennell, S. (1997), On Civilizing the Appetite. In Counihan and Van Esterik (1997). *Food and Culture*, p. 317.

61. Mennell, S. (1985). *All Manners of Food: Eating and Taste in England and France from the Middle Ages to the Present.* Oxford: Basil Blackwell, pp. 319, 321, 324–328; Elias, N. (1939), *The Civilizing Process*. Oxford: Basil Blackwell, p. 11.

62. King (2000). *Western Civilization*, pp. 322, 333, 386. See also: Bynum (1987). *Holy Feast and Holy Fast.*

63. See, for example, Hugill, P. (1993). *World Trade Since 1431: Geography, Technology, and Capitalism.* Baltimore: Johns Hopkins Press.

64. Schivelbusch, W. (1992). *Tastes of Paradise: A Social History of Spices, Stimulants, and Intoxicants.* New York: Pantheon, p. 6.

65. King (2000). *Western Civilization*, pp. 322, 333, 386. See also Burke (1987). *The Italian Renaissance*; Wallerstein (1974). *The Modern World System: Capitalist Agriculture and the Origins of the European World-Economy in the Sixteenth Century.* New York: Academic Press.

66. Milton, B. (1999). *Nathaniel's Nutmeg: Or the True and Incredible Adventures of the Spice Trader Who Changed the Course of History.* New York: Farrar, Straus, and Giroux, pp. 3–5.

67. Food in History (2000). p. 95.

68. Kurlansky, M. (1997). *Cod: A Biography of the Fish that Changed the World.* New York: Walker and Company, pp. 17–29.

69. Thornton, R. (1987). *American Indian Holocaust and Survival: Population History Since 1492.* Norman: University of Oklahoma Press; Ubelaker, D. (1992). North American Indian Population Size. In J. Verano and D. Ubelaker (Eds.), *Disease and Demography in the Americas.* Washington: Smithsonian Institution Press.

70. Beck, H. (1967). On Migration Across the Bering Land Bridge in the Upper Pleistocene. In D. Hopkins (Ed.), *The Bering Land Bridge.* Stanford, CA: Stanford University Press, pp. 373–408.

71. Viola, Herman J. (1991). Seeds of Change. In H. Viola and C. Margolis (1991), *Seeds of Change.* Washington, DC: Smithsonian Institution Press, pp. 11–16; Crosby, A. (1972). *The Columbian Exchange: Biological and Cultural Consequences of 1492.* Westport, CT: Greenwood Press, pp. 21, 165.

72. Jerome, N. (1981). The U.S. Dietary Pattern from an Anthropological Perspective. In *Food Technology*, 35 (2), p. 38. See also Josephy, Alvin M. (Ed.), (1993). *America in 1492: The World of the Indian Peoples before the Arrival of Columbus*, 2nd ed. New York: Knopf.

73. Crosby (1972). *Columbian Exchange*, 108; McIntosh (1995). *American Food Habits*, p. 66. See also Crobsy, A. (1993). *Ecological Imperialism: The Biological Expansion of Europe 900–1900.* Cambridge: Cambridge University Press.

74. Vavilov, N. (1951). *The Origin, Variation, Immunity, and Breeding of Cultivated Plants.* New York: Ronald Press.

75. Crosby (1972). *Columbian Exchange*, pp. 185–186.

76. Vavilov (1951). *Origin, Variation*, pp. 30–43.

77. Crosby (1972). *Columbian Exchange*, pp. 170, 175–177, 185–187.

78. McNeill, W. (1991). American Food Crops in the Old World. In Viola and Margolis (1991). *Seeds of Change*, pp. 43–44.

79. Crosby (1972). *Columbian Exchange*, 106–107; McIntosh (1995). *American Food Habits*, p. 65; Crosby, A. (1991), Metamorphosis of the Americas. In Viola and Margolis (1991). *Seeds of Change*, pp. 70–89.

80. Crosby (1972). *Columbian Exchange*, pp. 165–168; "Like Herrings In a Barrel." In *The Economist* (December 31, 1999), pp. 13–14; McNeill, W. (1991). American Food Crops in the Old World. In Viola and Margolis (1991). *Seeds of Change*, pp. 43–59.

81. King (2000). *Western Civilization*, pp. 503–504; McNeill (1991). *American Food Crops*.

82. Messur, E. (1997). Three Centuries of Changing European Tastes for the Potato. In H. Macbeth (Ed.), *Food Preferences and Taste: Continuity and Change*. Providence: Berghahn Books, p. 109.

83. See Mintz, S. (1996), *Tasting Food, Tasting Freedom*. Boston: Beacon Press; Messur (1997). Three Centuries of Changing Tastes, p. 107.

84. Messur (1997). Three Centuries of Changing Tastes, p. 106; Salaman, R. (1985). *The History and Social Influences of the Potato*. Cambridge: Cambridge University Press, pp. 136, 189–190, 251; Crosby (1972). *Columbian Exchange*, pp. 182–183.

85. Messur (1997). Three Centuries of Changing Tastes, pp. 107, 109.

86. Messur (1997). Three Centuries of Changing Tastes, p. 103; Crosby (1972). *Columbian Exchange*, pp. 183–184. See Salaman (1985). *History and Social Influences*; Hobhouse, H. (1986). *Seeds of Change: Five Plants that Transformed the World*. New York: Harper and Row.

87. Crosby (1972). *Columbian Exchange*, pp. 185–186, 205 Note 42.

88. Crosby (1972). *Columbian Exchange*, pp. 192–193.

89. Crosby (1972). *Columbian Exchange*, pp. 198–201.

90. Hawke, D. (1988). *Everyday Life in Early America*. New York: Harper and Row, p. 38.

91. Root, W. and R. DeRochemont (1976). *Eating in America*. New York: Ecco Press, pp. 29, 38, 40; Jones, E. (1990). *American Food*, Rev. Ed. Woodstock, NY: Overlook Press, p. 8.

92. Lowenberg, M., et al. (1968). *Food and People*. New York: John Wiley and Sons, pp. 66–67.

93. Lowenberg et al. (1968). *Food and People*, pp. 67–68.

94. Lowenberg et al. (1968). *Food and People*, pp. 68–69.

95. Bradford, W. (1981). *Of Plymouth Plantation 1620–1649*. New York: The Modern Library, p. 100.

96. Included in Bradford (1981). *Of Plymouth Plantation*, p. 100.

97. McIntosh (1995). *American Food Habits*, p. 72; McMahon, S. (1985). A Comfortable Subsistence: The Changing Composition of Diet in Rural New England, 1620–1840. In *The William and Mary Quarterly*, 42 (1): pp. 22–65; Lowenberg et al. (1968). *Food and People*.

98. Hawke (1988). *Everyday Life*, pp. 38, 75.

99. Hawke (1988). *Everyday Life*, pp. 39, 74–75.

100. Hawke (1988). *Everyday Life*, pp. 75–76.

101. Van Syckle, C. (1945). Some Pictures of Food Consumption in the United States: Part I, 1630–1860. In *The Journal of the American Dietary Association*, 21 (8), p. 508.

102. Root and de Rochement (1976). *Eating in America*, p. 356; McIntosh (1995). *American Food Habits*, p. 75; Hawke (1988). *Everyday Life*, pp. 78–80.
103. Hawke (1988). *Everyday Life*, p. 79; Jerome, N. (1981), The U.S. Dietary Pattern from an Anthropological Perspective. *Food Technology*, 35 (2), p. 39; Van Syckle (1945). *Some Pictures of Food*, pp. 21, 509.
104. Hawke (1988). *Everyday Life*, p. 77; Levenstein, H. (1988), *Revolution at the Table*. New York: Oxford University Press, p. 6.
105. Jerome (1981). U.S. Dietary Pattern, p. 39; McIntosh (1995). *American Food Habits*, p. 212.
106. Dick, E. (1937). *The Sod-House Frontier, 1854–1900*. New York: D. Appleton-Century Company, p. 275; McIntosh (1995). *American Food Habits*, pp. 213–214.
107. McIntosh (1995). *American Food Habits*, p. 214.
108. Rorabaugh, W. (1979). *The Alcoholic Republic*. New York: Oxford University Press, pp. 20, 232, 272.

CHAPTER THREE

1. Jefferson, T. (1954). *Notes on the State of Virginia*. Chapel Hill: University of North Carolina, pp. 164–165.
2. See Miller, C. (1988). *Jefferson and Nature: An Interpretation*. Baltimore: The Johns Hopkins University Press; Marx, L. (1964). *The Machine in the Garden: Technology and the Pastoral Idea in America*. New York: Oxford University Press.
3. McIntosh (1995). *American Food Habits*, pp. 87, 97; Jerome (1981). U.S. Dietary Pattern, p. 40.
4. Schlereth, T. (1991). *Victorian America: Transformations in Everyday Life, 1876–1915*. New York: HarperCollins, p. 141.
5. McIntosh (1995). *American Food Habits*, p. 79.
6. Norton, M. B., et al. (1998). *A People and a Nation: A History of the United States*, 5th ed. Boston: Houghton Mifflin Company, pp. 495–496; Berthoff, R. (1971). *An Unsettled People: Social Order and Disorder in American History*. New York: Harper and Row, p. 308.
7. McIntosh (1995). *American Food Habits*, p. 88.
8. Norton et al (1998). *A People and a Nation*, pp. 492–493.
9. Norton et al (1998). *A People and a Nation*, p. 496. See also Worster, D. (1985). *Rivers of Empire: Water, Aridity and the Growth of the American West*. New York: Pantheon Books.
10. McIntosh (1995). *American Food Habits*, p. 89.
11. Norton et al (1998). *A People and a Nation*, p. 492; Fogel, R. (1964). *Railroads and Economic Growth*. Baltimore: The Johns Hopkins University Press.
12. Norton et al (1998). *A People and a Nation*, p. 491; Berthoff (1971). *An Unsettled People*, p. 308; Degler, C. (1970). *Out of Our Past: The Forces that Shaped Modern America*. Rev. Ed. New York: Harper and Row, pp. 320–323.
13. Norton et al (1998). *A People and a Nation*, p. 491.
14. Norton et al (1998). *A People and a Nation*, p. 496.
15. Norton et al (1998). *A People and a Nation*, p. 197. See also: Atherton, L. (1961). *The Cattle Kings*. Bloomington: Indiana University Press.
16. Alpert's invention was stimulated by Napoleon, who had offered a monetary

prize to anyone who could invent a way of preserving food to feed his army during his campaign on Russia in the Napoleonic war.

17. McIntosh (1995). *American Food Habits*, p. 89; Jerome (1981). U.S. Dietary Pattern, p. 40.

18. Lowenberg, M., et al. (1979). *Food and People*. 3rd ed. New York: John Wiley and Sons, p. 79; Norton et al (1998). *A People and a Nation*, p. 526.

19. McIntosh, W. (1996). *Sociologies of Food and Nutrition*. New York: Plenum Press, p. 22.

20. McIntosh (1995). *American Food Habits*, pp. 84–85, 92; Cummings, R. (1970). *The American and His Food*. Rev. Ed. New York: Arno Press, p. 77; Fogel, R. and S. Engelman (1982). Exploring the Uses of Data on Height. *Social Science History*, 6(4), pp. 415–417.

21. McIntosh (1995). *American Food Habits*, pp. 82, 92–93; Levenstein, H. (1988). *Revolution at the Table*. New York: Oxford University Press, p. 44; Higgs, R. (1975). Mortality in Rural America, 1870–1920: Estimates and Conjectures. *Explorations in Economic History*, 10(2), pp. 177–195; Meeker, E. (1972). The Improving Health of the United States, 1850–1915. *Explorations in Economic History*, 9(3), p. 353; Cummings (1970). *The American and His Food*, pp. 12–13, 86–88.

22. Williams, S. (1985). *Savory Suppers and Fashionable Feasts*. New York: Pantheon Books, pp. x, 1; McIntosh (1995). *American Food Habits*, pp. 93–94.

23. Williams (1985). *Savory Suppers*, pp. 5, 10.

24. Schlereth (1991). *Victorian America*, pp. 143, 145.

25. Schlereth (1991). *Victorian America*, p. 163.

26. Schlereth (1991). *Victorian America*, p. 163.

27. McIntosh (1995). *American Food Habits*, p. 97.

28. Norton et al (1998). *A People and a Nation*, p. 538; Green, H. (1993). *The Uncertainty of Everyday Life, 1915–1945*. New York: Harper Perennial, pp. 40–41.

29. Norton et al (1998). *A People and a Nation*, p. 541; McIntosh (1995). *American Food Habits*, pp. 98–99.

30. McIntosh (1995). *American Food Habits*, pp. 99, 108; Williams (1985). *Savory Suppers*, p. 14.

31. McIntosh (1995). *American Food Habits*, p. 99.

32. McIntosh (1995). *American Food Habits*, pp. 99–101; Ross, E. Patterns of Diet and Forces of Production: An Economic and Ecological History of the Ascendancy of Beer in the United States. In E. Ross (Ed.), *Beyond the Myths of Culture*. New York: Academic Press, pp. 181–225.

33. McIntosh (1995). *American Food Habits*, p. 102.

34. Root and deRochement (1976). *Eating in America*; McIntosh (1995). *American Food Habits*, p. 102.

35. Norton et al (1998). *A People and a Nation*, p. 543; Levenstein (1988). *Revolution at the Table*.

36. McIntosh (1995). *American Food Habits*, p. 102.

37. McIntosh (1995). *American Food Habits*, p. 105.

38. McIntosh (1995). *American Food Habits*, p. 112.

39. Gabaccia, D. (1998). *We Are What We Eat: Ethnic Food and the Making of America*. Cambridge, MA: Harvard University Press, pp. 67–68.

40. Gabaccia (1998). *We Are What We Eat*, p. 69.

41. Gabaccia (1998). *We Are What We Eat*, pp. 105,121.

42. Gabaccia (1998). *We Are What We Eat*, pp. 121, 139; Green (1993). *The Uncertainty of Everyday Life*, p. 156.
43. Gabaccia (1998). *We Are What We Eat*, pp. 123, 125–126, 131–132.
44. Gabaccia (1998). *We Are What We Eat*, p. 138.
45. Gabaccia (1998). *We Are What We Eat*, pp. 150–151.
46. Palmer, J. (October 27, 1999). A Century of Food. *Omaha World Herald*, Living Section, pp. 45, 48.
47. Palmer, (1999). A Century of Food.
48. Palmer, (1999). A Century of Food.
49. Walter, Ronald (1978). *American Reformers*, 1815–1860. New York: Hill and Wang, pp. 147–152.
50. Billington, R. and M. Ridge (1949). *Westward Expansion*. New York: Macmillan Co., p. 526.
51. McIntosh (1995). *American Food Habits*, pp. 101, 105.
52. McIntosh (1995). *American Food Habits*, pp. 105–106; Green (1993). *The Uncertainty of Everyday Life*, pp. 155, 157.
53. Green (1993). *The Uncertainty of Everyday Life*, pp. 159–160.
54. McIntosh (1995). *American Food Habits*, p. 101.
55. McIntosh (1995). *American Food Habits*, p. 106; Levenstein (1988). *Revolution at the Table*.
56. McIntosh, E. (1995). *American Food Habits*, Ch. 6.
57. Norton et al (1998). *A People and a Nation*, p. 530.
58. Degler, (1970). *Out of Our Past*, p. 332; Norton et al (1998). *A People and a Nation*, p. 584.
59. Berthoff (1971). *An Unsettled People*, pp. 309–310.
60. Degler, (1970). *Out of Our Past*, pp. 322, 327; Berthoff (1971). *An Unsettled People*, pp. 310–311.
61. Norton et al (1998). *A People and a Nation*, pp. 585–586.
62. Norton et al (1998). *A People and a Nation*, pp. 586–587.
63. Norton et al (1998). *A People and a Nation*, pp. 588, 594–596; Degler (1970). *Out of Our Past*, pp. 330, 333; Billington, R., and Ridge, M. (1949). *Westward Expansion*, New York: Macmillan Co, pp. 588–589.
64. Degler (1970). *Out of Our Past*, pp. 333, 337; Norton et al (1998). *A People and a Nation*, p. 597; see alos Goodwyn, L. (1976). *Democratic Promise: the Populist Movement in America*. New York: Oxford University Press.
65. Green (1993). *The Uncertainty of Everyday Life*, p. 42; Norton et al (1998). *A People and a Nation*, pp. 696, 722; McIntosh (1995). *American Food Habits*, p. 106; Degler (1970). *Out of Our Past*, p. 379.
66. McIntosh (1995). *American Food Habits*, p. 108; Norton et al (1998). *A People and a Nation*, pp. 723, 733–734. See also Gregory, J. (1989). *American Exodus: The Dust Bowl Migration and Okie Culture in California*. New York Oxford University Press.
67. Steinbeck, J. (1977). *The Grapes of Wrath*. New York: Penguin Books, p. 6.
68. Norton et al (1998). *A People and a Nation*, pp. 728, 731–732; Degler (1970). *Out of Our Past*, p. 385.
69. Degler (1970). *Out of Our Past*, p. 385.
70. McIntosh (1995). *American Food Habits*, pp. 109–110.
71. Quoted in Green (1993). *The Uncertainty of Everyday Life*, p. 41.
72. Green (1993). *The Uncertainty of Everyday Life*, pp. 41–42.

73. Green (1993). *The Uncertainty of Everyday Life*, p. 42.
74. Green (1993). *The Uncertainty of Everyday Life*, pp. 160–161.
75. McIntosh (1995). *American Food Habits*, p. 110.
76. McIntosh (1995). *American Food Habits*, p. 112. See also Kessler-Harris, A. (1982). *Out to Work*. New York: Oxford University Press.
77. McIntosh (1995). *American Food Habits*, p. 112; Levenstein (1988). *Revolution at the Table*.
78. McIntosh (1995). *American Food Habits*, p. 113.
79. Jackle, J. and Keith Sculle (1999). *Fast Food: Roadside Restaurants in the Automobile Age*. Baltimore: The Johns Hopkins University Press, pp. 21, 23; Erenberg, L. (1981). *Steppin' Out: New York Nightlife and the Transformation of American Culture, 1890–1930*. Westport, CT: Greenwood Press, p. 35.
80. Erenberg (1981). *Steppin Out*, pp. 35–40; Jackle and Sculle (1999). *Fast Food*, p. 21.
81. Jackle and Sculle (1999). *Fast Food*, pp. 27–30.
82. Sengupta, S. (December 1, 1998). Food as Ritual, Restaurants as Theater. *The New York Times*, p. A25.
83. Jackle and Sculle (1999). *Fast Food*, p. 34.
84. Jackle and Sculle (1999). *Fast Food*, pp. 36–37.
85. Quoted in Jackle and Sculle (1999). *Fast Food*, p. 27.
86. Jackle and Sculle (1999). *Fast Food*, p. 39; Lynd R. and H. Lynd (1929). *Middletown*. New York: Harcourt Brace and Company, pp. 153–154.
87. McIntosh (1995). *American Food Habits*, pp. 117–119.
88. McIntosh (1995). *American Food Habits*, p. 119.
89. McIntosh (1995). *American Food Habits*, p. 117; Bernstein, I. (1970). *The Lean Years*. Baltimore: Penguin. See also Desrosier, N. (1963). *Food Preservation*. 2nd ed. Westport, CT: Avi Publishing Company.
90. McIntosh (1995). *American Food Habits*, p. 120.

CHAPTER FOUR

1. *Dietary Levels of Households in the United States: Household Food Consumption Survey, 1955* (1957). Washington, DC: United States Department of Agriculture/United States Government Printing Office; McIntosh (1995). *American Food Habits*, p. 122; Jerome (1981). U.S. Dietary Pattern, pp. 37–42; Hampe, E., and M. Wittenberg (1964). *The Lifeline of America: Development of the Food Industry*. New York: McGraw-Hill.
2. McIntosh (1995). *American Food Habits*, p. 119.
3. Boggs, M. and C. Rasmussen (1959). Modern Food Processing. *Food: The Yearbook of Agriculture, 1959*. Washington, DC: United States Department of Agriculture, pp. 418–433.
4. McIntosh (1995). *American Food Habits*, pp. 119–120, 127; Downes, T. (1989). Food Packaging in the IFT Era: Five Decades of Unprecedented Growth and Change. *Food Technology*, 43(9), pp. 228–240; Sacharow, S., and A. Brody (1987). *Packaging: An Introduction*. Duluth, MN: Harcout Brace Jovanovich; Lund D. (1989). Food Processing: From Art to Engineering. *Food Technology* 43(9), pp. 242–247.

5. McIntosh (1995). *American Food Habits*, p. 122.

6. McIntosh (1995). *American Food Habits*, p. 122.

7. McIntosh (1995). *American Food Habits*, p. 123.

8. McIntosh (1995). *American Food Habits*, p. 123.

9. Atkins, P., and I. Bowler (2001). *Food in Society: Economy, Culture, Geography*, London: Arnold, pp. 220–225.

10. Hord, B. (November 23, 2000). Drought Tests Family Farms. *Omaha World Herald*, pp. 1, 8; Hord, B. (November 23, 2000). Home, Home on the Farm. *Omaha World Herald*, p. 10; Busch, L. et al. (1991). *Plants, Power and Profit*. Cambridge: Basil Blackwell, p. 23.

11. Fitchen, J. (1997). Hunger, Malnutrition, and Poverty in the Contemporary United States: Some Observations on their Social and Cultural Context. In Counihan, C., and P. Van Esterik, Eds. (1997). *Food and Culture*, p. 385.

12. McIntosh (1995). *American Food Habits*, pp. 126–127; O'Hare, W. (1985). Poverty in America: Trends and New Patterns. *Population Bulletin*, 40(3): June 1985. Washington, DC: Population Reference Bulletin, p. 10; Fitchen (1997). *Hunger, Malnutrition, and Poverty*, p. 386.

13. Fitchen (1997). *Hunger, Malnutrition, and Poverty*, p. 386; *1961–1975 Food Stamp Program* (1976). Washington, DC: Food and Nutrition Service. United States Government Printing Office.

14. Fitchen (1997). *Hunger, Malnutrition, and Poverty*, pp. 386, 388.

15. Fitchen (1997). *Hunger, Malnutrition, and Poverty*, pp. 385, 396.

16. Fitchen (1997). *Hunger, Malnutrition, and Poverty*, p. 396.

17. Douglas, M. (1984). *Food in Social Order: Studies of Food and Festivities in Three American Communities*. New York: Russell Sage Foundation, p. 3; Jerome, N. (1969). American Culture and Food Habits: Communicating through Food in the USA. In J. Dupont (Ed.), *Dimensions of Nutrition*. Fort Collins: Colorado Dietetic Association, pp. 223–234; Fitchen (1997). *Hunger, Malnutrition, and Poverty*, p. 394.

18. McIntosh (1995). *American Food Habits*, p. 131; Etherton, T. The New Bio-Tech Foods. *Food and Nutrition News*, 65(3), p. 13.

19. Harlander, S. (1989). Food Biotechnology: Yesterday, Today, and Tomorrow. *Food Technology*, 43(9), pp. 196–206.

20. Paarlberg, R. (2000). The Global Food Fight. *Foreign Affairs*, 79(3), p. 226.

21. Paarlberg (2000). The Global Food Fight, pp. 25–26.

22. Harper, C. (2001). *Environment and Society*. Upper Saddle River, NJ: Prentice Hall, Ch. 5.

23. Anderson, J. (October 16, 1999). Budding Invasions Costly. *Omaha World Herald*, pp. 1–2; for an example of the defenders of genetically engineered crops, see Boettscher, B. (January 7, 2001). Myths Cloud Farming. *Omaha World Herald*, p. 10B.

24. Associated Press (2001). "Frankenfood" Has Key Role. *Omaha World Herald*, July 9, p. 4; Doyle, J. (2001). Millions Need Bioengineered Food. *Omaha World Herald*, February 10, p. 9; McGovern, G. (2001). *The Third Freedom*. New York: Simon and Schuster.

25. Nash, M. (2000). Grains of Hope. *Time* (July 31, 2000), p. 40.

26. Quoted in Whit (1995). *Food and Society*, p. 89.

27. Kloppenburg, J. (1990). *First the Seed: The Political Economy of Plant Biotechnology, 1492–2000*. Cambridge: Cambridge University Press, pp. 92, 117; Whit (1995). *Food and Society*, p. 270.

28. Whit (1995). *Food and Society*, pp. 172, 173, 176; Giesler, G., and Popper, F. (1984). *Land Reform American Style*. Totowa, NJ: Roman and Allanhald, p. 8; Busch, (1991). *Plants, Power, and Profit*, pp. 3, 23.
29. Whit (1995). *Food and Society*, pp. 184–185.
30. McIntosh (1995). *American Food Habits*, p. 120.
31. *Read the Label, Set a Better Table* (1975). Rockville, MD: United States Department of Health, Education, and Welfare.
32. Jackle and Sculle (1999). *Fast Food*, pp. 165–166; Ritzer, G. (1996). *The McDonaldization of Society*. Rev. Ed. Thousand Oaks, CA: Pine Forge Press, p. 30.
33. Ritzer (1996). *McDonaldization of Society*, p. 30.
34. Ritzer (1996). *McDonaldization of Society*, pp. 30–31.
35. Bolaffi, M. and D. Lulay (1989). The Foodservice Industry: Continuing into the Future with an Old Friend. *Food Technology*, 43(9), pp. 258–266; Graham, E. (August 15, 1991). McDonald's Pickle: He Began Fast Food But Got No Credit. *The Wall Street Journal*, pp. A1, 10; Shield, J., and E. Young (1990). Fat in Fast Foods—Enduring Changes. *Nutrition Today*, 25(2), pp. 32–35.
36. McIntosh (1995). *American Food Habits*, p. 136; Shields and Young (1990). Fat in Fast Foods, pp. 32–35.
37. McIntosh (1995). *American Food Habits*, pp. 130, 136.
38. McIntosh (1995). *American Food Habits*, pp. 136–137; Schlosser, E. (2001). Why McDonald's Fries Taste So Good. *Atlantic Monthly* (January 2001), p. 50.
39. Bolaffi and Lulay (1989). Foodservice Industry, pp. 258–266; Kirkegaard, P. (1989). Fat Substitutes: Taste Great—Less Fattening. *Hazelton Food Science Newsletter*, 3(31), p. 1 (Madison, WI: Wisconsin Hazleton Laboratories of America, 1989); Institute of Food Technologists (1990). Food Substitute Update. *Food Technology*, 44(3), pp. 92–97; Erdman, J. (1989). Nutrition: Past, Present, and Future. *Food Technology*, 43(9), pp. 220–227.
40. Erdman (1989). *Nutrition*, pp. 220–227; Mansen, E. (1989). The 1980s: A Look at a Decade of Growth through the Pages of the Journal. *Journal of the American Dietetic Association*, 89(12), pp. 1742–1746; O'Neill, C. (1990). Communicating the Concepts of Food Nutrition in the 1990s. *Journal of the American Dietetic Association*, 90(3), pp. 373–374; Wallingford, J. (1994). Nutrition Labeling: Help or Hindrance? *Nutrition and the M.D.*, 20(1), pp. 1–3.
41. Jerome, N. (1981). The U.S. Dietary Pattern, pp. 37–42; Gabaccia, D. (1998). *We Are What We Eat*, pp. 213–224. See also Kittles, P., and K. Sucher (1989). *Food and Culture in America*. New York: Van Nostrand Reinholdt.
42. Fortune Cookie History is Far From Venerable (January 3, 2001). *Omaha World Herald*, p. 33.
43. Senauer, B., et al., (1991). *Food Trends and the Changing Consumer*. St. Paul, MN: Eagan Press, p. 14; Putnam, J. (1989). *Food Consumption, Prices, and Expenditures, 1966–1987*. (State Department Bulletin #773). Washington, DC: United States Government Printing Office.
44. McIntosh (1995). *American Food Habits*, p. 218; Smith, B., et al. (1990). *Milk Consumption and Consumer Concerns about Fat, Cholesterol, and Calories*. University Park: Pennsylvania State University Marketing Research Report 7.
45. Hiemstra, S. (1968). *Food Consumption, Prices, and Expenditures* (Agriculture Report 138). Washington, DC: United States Department of Agriculture; Putnam (1989). *Food Consumption... 1966–1987*; Putnam, J. (1990). *Food Consump-*

tion, Prices, and Expenditures, 1967–1988. (U.S. State Department Bulletin 804). Washington, DC: United States Department of Agriculture, Economic Research Service/United States Government Printing Office; Smith, B., and Yonkers, R. (1990). *The Importance of Cereal to Fluid Milk Consumption.* University Park: Pennsylvania State University Marketing Research Report 8; Putnam, J. (1991). Food Consumption, 1970–1990. *Food Review,* 14(3), pp. 2–12.

46. Heimstra (1968). *Food Consumption*; Putnam (1989). *Food Consumption... 1966–1988*; Putnam (1990). *Food Consumption... 1967–1988*; McIntosh (1995). *American Food Habits,* p. 219.

47. Senauer et al. (1991). *Food Trends,* p. 28; McIntosh (1995). *American Food Habits,* p. 219.

48. McIntosh (1995). *American Food Habits,* pp. 220–221; Science Asks Why People Eat, Eat, Eat. (November 5, 2000). *Omaha World Herald,* p. 9A.

49. Heffernan, W. (1998). Agriculture and Monopoly Capital, *Monthly Review,* 50 (3), pp. 46–47; McIntosh, W. (1996). *Sociologies of Food and Nutrition,* p. 61.

50. Halweil, B. (2000a), Who Needs Farmers? Think Twice About Letting Big Ag Take Over Global Food production. *Worldwatch,* 13 (5), pp 15–16;

51. Halweil, B. (2000a). Who Needs Farmers?, pp. 16–17.

52. Senauer, B., et al. (1991). *Food Trends*; Santon, B. (1993). Recent Changes in Size and Structure in American Agriculture. In A. Hallam (Ed.), *Size, Structure, and the Changing Face of American Agriculture,* Boulder, CO: Westview Press.

53. "Share cropping" was a historic way of American farming, when farmers worked small plots or rented land, with seed or livestock provided by an investor or landlord, who was entitled to a large "share" of the produce, leaving the remainder for the farmer and his family.

54. Halweil, B. (2000a). Who Needs Farmers?, pp. 19–20; Heffernan, W. (1998). Agriculture and Monopoly Capital, pp. 54–55. Don't confuse contract production with "forward contracting" in which a contract is made between a producer and a buyer involving an agreed upon price or other terms of sale to be carried out at some future date. This arrangement makes it possible for investors to invest in commodity "futures markets."

55. Rissler, J. (1999). Bright Lights, Pig City. *Nucleus,* 21 (1), pp. 8–9.

56. Silverstein, K. (1999). Meat Factories. Reprinted from *Sierra,* January/February, 84 (1); Kennedy, R. (2000). Free-range at Last, Free-range at Last. *Grist Magazine,* November 20, www.gristmagazine.com.

57. Kennedy, J. (2000). Free-range at Last.

58. Cited in Silverstein, K. (1999). Meat Factories.

59. Friedmann, H. (1978). World Market, State, and Family Farm: Social Bases of Household Production in the Era of Wage Labor. *Comparative Studies in Society and History.* 20 (4), pp. 545–586; Friedmann, H. (1981). The Family Farm in Advanced Capitalism: Outline of a Simple Commodity Production in Agriculture. Presented at the annual meeting of the *American Sociological Association,* Toronto, Canada; McLaughlin, P. (1998). Rethinking the Agrarian Equation: The Limits of Essentialism and the Promise of Evolutionism. *Human Ecology Review,* 5 (2), pp 25–37; McIntosh, W. (1996). *Sociologies of Food and Nutrition,* p. 85.

60. Halweil, B. (2000a). Who Needs Farmers?, p. 17.

61. McIntosh, W. (1996). *Sociologies of Food and Nutrition,* pp. 86–87.

62. Sometimes the diversity is illusory—witness the pervasiveness and market success of the low budget "house brands" of canned vegetables, soaps, toothpaste, cereals, etc.

63. ConAgra (1997). ConAgra at a Glance. Omaha, NE: ConAgra Inc.

64. ConAgra, (1996, 1998). ConAgra's U.S. Grocery Products Shopping Guide. Omaha NE; ConAgra Inc.

65. Even this buy was not as big that year as international giant Unilever's $24.3 billion purchase of Bestfoods.

66. Taylor, J. (2000). ConAgra Adds Big Brands to Larder. *Omaha World Herald,* June 24, pp. 57, 59.

67. Heffernan, W. (1998). Agriculture and Monopoly Captital, pp. 49–51.

68. Halweil, B. (2000a). Who Needs Farmers?, p. 19.

69. Except restaurant and Fast Food chains, which would add many other dimensions of complexity to the table.

70. The Swift and Armour brand names exist today, but they were bought by ConAgra, as well as were Monfort and Miller.

71. Poppendieck, J. (1986). *Breadlines Knee-Deep in Wheat: Food Assistance in the Great Depression.* New Brunswick, NJ: Rutgers University Press.

72. Berry, J. (1984). *Feeding Hungry People: Rule-making in the Foodstamp Program.* New Brunswick, NJ: Rutgers University Press, p. 37.

73. Brown, W., and A. Ciglar, (1990). *U.S. Agricultural Groups: Institutional Profiles.* Westport, CT: Greenwood Press, p. xxii ; McIntosh, W. (1996). *Sociologies of Food and Nutrition,* p. 204.

74. It is important to note, and the food pyramid, though a significant nutritional improvement over earlier "recommended foods" could be considerably improved, according to many nutritional experts. The same can be said of nutrient labeling for prepared foods.

75. McIntosh, W. (1996). *Sociologies of Food and Nutrition,* pp. 95, 205.

76. Dicken, P. (1992). *Global Shift: Industrial Change in a Turnabout World.* 2nd ed., pp. 1–30.

77. Friedmann, H. (1990). The Origins of Third World Food Dependence. In Bernstein, B., B. Crow, M. McIntosh, and C. Martin (Eds.), *The Food Question: Profits vs. People,* New York: Monthly Review Press, pp. 13–31.

78. Bestor, Theodore C. (2000). www.foreignpolicy.com/issue_novdec_2000/essay-bestor.html

79. Watkins, K. (1996). Free Trade and Farm Fallacies: From the Uruguay Round to the World Food Summit. *The Ecologist,* 26, pp. 244–255; McMichael, P. (1998). Global food politics. *Monthly Review,* 50 (3), August, p. 109.

80. Such rural people still constitute about half of the world's people.

81. McMichael, P. (1998). *Global Food Politics,* pp. 102–104.

82. Friedmann, H., (1990). Origins of Third World Food Dependence.

83. Hall, R. (1989). Pioneers in Food Science and Technology, "Giants in the Earth." *Food Technology,* 43 (9), pp. 186–195.

84. McIntosh, E. (1995). *American Food Habits,* p. 122.

85. Poppendieck, J. (1998). *Sweet Charity? Emergency Food and the End of Entitlement.* New York: Viking Press, p. 53.

86. Caliendo, M. (1979). *Nutrition and the World Food Crisis.* New York: Macmillan; McIntosh, W. (1996). *Sociologies of Food and Nutrition,* p. 111.

87. McIntosh, E. (1995). *American Food Habits*, p. 220.
88. Cooper, M., P. Rosset, and J. Bryson (1999). Warning! Corporate Meat and Poultry may be Hazardous to Workers, Farmers, the Environment, and Your Health. In Boucher, D. (Ed.) *The Paradox of Plenty: Hunger in a Bountiful World*. Oakland, CA: Food First Books, p. 159; Meeker-Lowry, S., and J. Ferrara (1997). Meat monopolies: Dirty Meat and the False Promises of Irradiation, *Food and Water Report*, p. 18; Turning Point Project (1999). Three Ways Industrial Food Makes You Sick. Washington, DC: www.turningpoint.org.
89. Turning Point Project (1999). Three Ways Industrial Food Makes You Sick.
90. Halweil, (2000a). Who Needs Farmers?; Halweil, B. (1999). The Emperor's New Clothes, *Worldwatch*, 12 (6), pp. 21–29.
91. Baily, W. (1973). The One Man Farm, USDA/ERS-519. Washington, DC: Government Printing Office; McDonalds, A., (1975). The Family Farm is the Most Efficient Unit of Production. In P. Barnes (Ed.), *The Peoples' Land*, Emmaeus PA: Rodale Press; Lappe, F., and J. Collins, (1999). Why Can't People Feed Themselves? In Bourcher, D. (Ed.). *The Paradox of Plenty*, p. 66.
92. Halweil, B. (2000b). Where Have All The Farmers Gone? *Worldwatch* , 13 (5) September/October, p. 26; Miller (1998) Op. Cit., p. 600.
93. Halweil, (2000b) Where Have All The Farmers Gone?, pp. 21–22.
94. Cooper, M. (1997). The Heartland's Raw Deal: How Meatpacking is Creating a New Immigrant Underclass. *The Nation*, Feb 3.; Cooper, Rosset, and Bryson (1999). Warning! Corporate Meat and Poultry may be Hazardous, pp. 157, 160–161.

CHAPTER FIVE

1. Whit, W. (1995). *Society and Food*, pp. 140–142.
2. Cited in McIntosh, W. (1996). *Sociologies of Food and Nutrition*, p. 65.
3. Charles, N., and M. Kerr (1988). *Women, Food, and Families*, Manchester, UK: Manchester University Press; McIntosh, (1996). *Sociologies of Food and Nutrition*, p. 65.
4. Coopock, M., and W. McIntosh, (1991). The Relationship of Family Mealtime to Family Satisfaction and Cohesion. Paper presented to the Southwest Social Science Association, San Antonio, TX, March.
5. Lynd, R., and H. Lynd (1929). *Middletown*.
6. The Breakdown of the Family Meal. *Tufts University Diet and Nutrition Newsletter* (1991), 9 (5), pp. 3–5.
7. McIntosh (1996). *Sociologies of Food and Nutrition*, p. 93.
8. Cited in Whit, (1995). *Food and Society*, p. 147.
9. National Research Council (1945). Cited by Lowenberg, M., Socio-cultural Basis of Food Habits. *Food Technology*, 24, pp. 27–32.
10. On modernization and cuisine differentiation, see Goody, J. (1982). *Cooking, Cuisine, and Class: A Study in Comparative Sociology*. New York: Cambridge University Press; Mennel, S., Murcott, A., and A. Otterloo, (1992). The Sociology of Food: Eating, Diet, and Food. *Current Sociology*, 40, pp. 1–148.
11. Hegemony or hegemonic culture refers to exercising social control by controlling language, culture, and values.

12. McIntosh, E. (1995). *American Food Habits*, p. 112.
13. Gvion-Rosenberg, L. (1988). Cultural Pluralism or Culinary Hegemony, 1945–1987. Paper presented at the annual meeting of the American Sociological Association, Atlanta, Georgia, August.
14. Alba, R. (1990). *Ethnic Identity: The Transformation of White America*. New Haven, CT: Yale University Press.
15. Similar trends were observed in other industrial nations (for example, Japan). See Ashkenazi, M. (1991). From Tachi Soba to Naorai: Cultural Implications of the Japanese Meal. *Social Science Information*, 30, p. 296.
16. Guseman, P., and S. Sapp (1986). Regional Trends in U.S. Food Consumption: Population Scale, Compostition, and Income Effects. *Review of Regional Studies*, 1, pp. 1–24.
17. McIntosh, W. (1996). *Sociologies of Food and Nutrition*.
18. Kittler, P., and K. Sucher (2000). *Cultural Foods: Traditions and Trends*. Belmont, CA: Wadsworth.
19. Alba, (1990). *Ethnic Identity*.
20. Cited in Boyle, M., and G. Zyla (1996). *Personal Nutrition*, 3rd ed., p. 102.
21. Boyle and Zyla (1996). *Personal Nutrition*, pp. 104–109.
22. Apfel, I. (1998). Diversity Dollars and Sense. *Restaurants USA*, 18, pp. 22–26.
23. Boisseau, C. (March 23, 1992). Mexican Staple Creates a Multibillion-dollar Business. *Houston Chronicle*, p. C1.
24. Zelinski, W. (1987). You Are Where You Eat. *American Demographics*. 9, pp. 30–33; National Restaurant Association (1998). 1997 Menus: Old and New Share the Plate. *Restaurants USA*, 8, pp. 38–46.
25. Kittler and Sucher, (2000). *Cultural Foods*, p. 21.
26. Bourdeau, P. (1984). *Distinction: A Social Critique of the Judgement of Taste*. Cambridge MA: Harvard University Press.
27. McIntosh, (1996). *Sociologies of Food and Nutrition*, pp. 106–107.
28. Lamont, M. (1992). *Money, Manners, and Manners: The Culture of the French and American Upper-middle Class*. Chicago: University of Chicago Press.
29. Jerome, N. (1979). Changing Nutritional Styles in the Context of the Modern Family, in D. Hybovich, and M. Barnard (Eds.), *Family Health Care*, 2nd ed., New York: McGraw Hill.
30. Kucera B., and W. McIntosh (1991). Family Size as a Determinant of Children's Dietary Intake: A Dilution Model Approach. *Ecology of Food and Nutrition*, 25, pp. 1–12.
31. Sobal, J., and A. Stunkard (1989). Socioeconomic Status and Obesity: A Review of the Literature. 105, pp. 260–275.
32. Whit, (1995). *Food and Society*, pp. 104–106.
33. McIntosh, (1996), *Sociologies of Food and Nutrition*, p. 226; Thompson, B. (1994). *A Hunger So Wide and Deep: American Women Speak out on Eating Problems*. Minneapolis, MN: University of Minnesota Press.
34. Bordo, S. (1993). *Unbearable Weight: Feminism, Western Culture, and the Body*. Berkeley, CA: Unversity of California Press, p. 154.
35. Collier, J., and M. Rosaldo (1981). Politics and Gender in Simple Societies, in Ortner and Whitehead (Eds.), *Sexual Meanings*. London: Cambridge University Press. pp. 275–317; Fiddes, N., (1991). *Meat: A Natural Symbol*. London: Routledge, Ch. 3.

36. Kerr, Charles N., and M. Kerr, (1988); *Women, Food, and Families.* Manchester, UK: University of Manchester Press; DeVault, M. (1991). *Feeding the Family: The Social Organization of Caring as Gendered Work.* Chicago: The University of Chicago Press; McIntosh, W. (1996). *Sociologies of Food and Nutrition,* pp. 74–75; McIntosh, W., and M. Zey (1989). Women as Gatekeepers of Food Consumption: A Sociological Critique. *Food and Foodways,* 3, pp. 317–332.

37. American Medical Association (1992). *Physician Characteristics and Distribution in the United States.* Chicago: AMA.

38. Reskin, B., and H. Hartmann (1986). *Women's Work, Men's Work.* Washington, DC: National Academy Press; McIntosh (1996). *Sociologies of Food and Nutrition,* p. 79.

39. "Waitressing" attracted considerable attention by researchers. See Creighton, H. (1982). Tied by Double Apron Strings: Female Work Culture and Organization in a Restaurant. *Insurgent Sociologist,* 11, pp. 59–64; Hall, E. (1993). Waitering/waitressing; Engendering the Work of Table Service. *Gender and Society,* 7, pp.; 329–346; McIntosh, (1996). *Sociologies of Food and Nutrition,* pp. 80–84.

40. Leidner, R. (1993). *Fast Food, Fast Talk: Service Work and the Routinization of Everyday Life.* Berkeley, CA: University of California Press; Reiter, E., (1991). *Making Fast Food: From the Frying Pan into the Fryer.* Montreal: McGill-Queen's University Press; Ritzer, G. (2000). *The McDonaldization of Society.* New Century Edition. Thousand Oaks, CA: Pine Forge Press.

41. Hawkins, R. (1984). Employee Theft in the Restaurant Trade: Forms of Ripping Off by Waiters at Work, *Deviant Behavior,* 5, pp. 47–69; Paules, G. (1991). *Dishing It Out: Power and Resistance Among Waitresses in a New Jersey Restaurant.* Philadelphia, PA: Temple University Press.

42. Elias, N. (1939/1994). *The Civilizing Process.* Oxford, UK: Blackwell, cited in Ritzer,G. (2000). *Sociological Theory,* 5th ed., New York: McGraw-Hill. pp. 510–518.

43. Weber, M. (1921/1968). *Economy and Society.* Totowa, NJ: Bedminister; see also Ritzer, G. (2000). *McDonaldization of Society,* pp. 22–24.

44. Takaki, R. (1990). *Iron Cages: Race and Culture in Nineteenth Century America.* New York: Oxford University Press, p. ix.

45. Ritzer, G. (2000). *McDonaldization of Society,* pp. 11–15.

46. Ritzer, G. (1999). *Enchanting a Disenchanted World: Revolutionizing the Means of Consumption.* Thousand Oaks, CA: Pine Forge Press, p. 11.

47. Ritzer, G. (2000). *McDonaldization of Society,* pp. 15–16.

48. Ritzer, G. (2000). *McDonaldization of Society,* pp. 132–139.

49. Ritzer, (1999). *Enchanting a Disenchanted World,* pp. 172–176.

50. McIntosh, A. (1996). *Sociologies of Food and Nutrition,* p. 41; Dubish, J. (1981). You Are What You Eat: Religious Aspects of the Health Food Movement. In Lehmann, C., and J. Meyers (Eds.), (1993). *Magic, Witchcraft, and Religion: An Anthropological Study of the Supernatural,* Palo Alto, CA: Mayfield Publishing Company, pp. 69–77.

51. Giddens, A. (1991). *Modernity and Self Identity: Self and Society in the Late Modern Age.* Stanford, CA: Stanford University Press.

52. Dubish, cited in Lehmann and Meyers, *Magic, Witchcraft, and Religion,* pp. 73–74.

53. Dubish, citing Tom Robbins, *Even Cowgirls Get the Blues.* In Lehmann and Meyers, *Magic, Witchcraft, and Religion,* p. 69.

54. The relationship between the food reform movement (FRM) and professional dietitians is an ambivalent one, as we noted in Chapter 1. Dietitians, while accepting the broad outlines or dietary and culinary reforms, are quick to distance themselves from the self-styled "nutritionists" of the FRM. They note that the FRM does have its share of "snake-oil" salesmen, and flim-flamery. They are critical of the typical fast food fare, but also of things like macrobiotic vegetarian diets, demonstrably deficient in proteins and micronutrients.

55. Duewer, L., et al (1993). U.S. Poultry and Red Meat Consumption, Prices, Spreads, and Margins. *Agricultural Information Bulletin*, no. 684. Washington, DC: Department of Agriculture Economic Research Service.

56. These generalizations vary enormously by age, ethnicity, and social circumstances, but in general, support for the broad perspectives of the HFM increase with education.

57. Gardner and Halweil, (2000). Escaping Hunger, p. 35; Pagioli, S. (2000). The Slow Cities League, *The Morning Edition*, National Public Radio, September, 19; Darlington, T. (2000). Slow is Beautiful (and delicious). *Isthmus* (July 14), cited in *Utne Reader*, 102, pp 57–59, November.

58. Kantor, L. (1998). *A Dietary Assessment of the U.S. Food Supply*, Agricultural Economic Report No. 772, U.S. Department of Agriculture, Economic Research Service; see also Family and Nutrition Review (1999), 12 (2), pp. 51–54.

59. By contrast, the USDA spends only $333 million each year to educate people about nutrition. Gardner G., and B. Halweil (2000). Escaping Hunger, pp. 28–29.

60. Gardner and Halweil (2000). Escaping Hunger, p. 29; Hernandez, D., and E. Chaney (Eds.), (1998). *From Generation to Generation: The Health and Well-Being of Children in Immigrant Families*. Washington, DC: National Academy Press.

61. *New York Times* (2000a). A Novel Marketing Approach: Food Books Pitch Snacks to Toddlers, cited in *Omaha World Herald*, Sept 22, p. 13.

62. Gardner and Halweil, (2000). Escaping Hunger, pp. 26, 28.

63. *Los Angeles Times* (2000). Obesity Termed "Critical Public Health Problem," cited in *Omaha World Herald*, Wed., Oct. 4, p. 10.

64. *New York Times* (2000b). Kids Getting Fatter, but No One has Solutions. Cited in *Omaha World Herald*. October 22, pp. 13–14A.

65. *Los Angeles Times* (1998). Companies Work Overtime To Find a Weight-Loss Drug. Cited in *Omaha World Herald*, August 16, p. 5–A; *New York Times* (2000d). Science Asks Why People Eat, Eat, Eat. In *Omaha World Herald*, November 5, p. 9–A.

66. *New York Times* (2000d). Slimming Gimmicks Growing, cited in *Omaha World Herald*, October, 29. p. 2–A.

67. Gardner and Halweil, (2000). Escaping Hunger, p. 32.

68. Hill, J. *New York Times* (2000d). Researchers Revising Long-Held Stance on Chronic Dieting, in *Omaha World Herald*, October 18, p. 12.

69. Gardner and Halweil (2000). Escaping Hunger, p. 33.

70. *Dallas Morning News* (2001). Vending Study is Food for "Twinkie Tax" Effort, cited in *Omaha World Herald*, January 7, p. 9–A.

71. Gardner and Halweil (2000). Escaping Hunger, pp. 32–35.

CHAPTER SIX

1. Riche, M. (2000). America's Diversity and Growth: Signposts for the 21st Century, *Population Bulletin*, 55 (2), p. 5.
2. Laurent, B. (2000). In the America of 2100, Less Elbow Room. *Christian Science Monitor.* Jan. 21, p. 8.
3. Mamdani, M., (1972). *The Myth of Population Control.* London: Reeves and Turner.
4. Riley, N. (1997). Gender, Power, and Population Change. *Population Bulletin.* 52 (3), May.
5. Grist Magazine (August 10, 2000). Generation XL. *Grist Daily,* www.grist-magazine.com; Weeks, J. (1998). *Population: An Introduction to Concepts and Issues,* 7th ed. Belmont, CA: Wadsworth; Population Reference Bureau (2000). *2000 World Population Data Sheet.* Washington, DC: Population Reference Bureau. p. 2.
6. Riche, M. (2000). *America's Diversity and Growth,* p. 7.
7. Malthus, T. (1798). *An Essay on Population.* New York: Augustus Kelly, Bookseller.
8. Bender, W., and M. Smith (1997). Population, Food and Nutrition. *Population Bulletin,* 51 (4), p. 5; Lappe, F., J. Collins, and P. Rosset (1998). *World Hunger: Twelve Myths.* New York: Grove Press, p. 8.
9. Gardner, G. (1996). Preserving Agricultural Resources. In L. Stark (Ed.), *State of the World 1996.* New York: W. W. Norton, pp. 79–94.
10. Pimentel, D. (1998). Land Degradation and Environmental Issues. In G. Miller, *Living in the Environment,* 10th ed. Belmont, CA: Wadsworth, pp. 562–563.
11. John Steinbeck's novel, *The Grapes of Wrath,* chronicles tragic migration and hardship of displaced Great Plains farm families during the "dust bowl" and depression years.
12. Miller, G. (1998). *Living in the Environment,* pp. 552–555.
13. Miller, G. (1998), *Living in the Environment,* p. 555.
14. Pimentel, D., et al (1995). Environmental and Economic Costs of Soil Erosion and Conservation Benefits. *Science,* 267, pp. 1117–1123.
15. Livernash, R., and E. Rodenburg (1998). Population Change, Resources, and the Environment. *Population Bulletin,* 53 (1), pp. 20–21.
16. As of this writing, only preliminary reports were published. See summaries in Associated Press (2000), Report: 40% of Farmland "Seriously Degraded." *Omaha World Herald,* May 23, p. 2; Manning, A. (2000), Report Finds Much of World's Soil is "Seriously Degraded." Food Production Could be at Risk Across the Globe. *USA Today,* May 21, p. 5A; Independent Online (IOL) (May 5, 2000). Water for Food, www.iol.co.za.
17. Baylis, R. (July 21,1997). Water for Food. *Infoterra.* <Infoterra@cedar.univivie.ac.at>. Citing *New Scientist,* Jan 2, 1997.
18. Postel, S. (1995). Rivers Drying Up. *Worldwatch,* 8 (3), pp. 9–19; Postel, S. (1992). *The Last Oasis: Facing Water Scarcity.* New York: W. W. Norton.
19. Miller, G. (1998) *Living in the Environment,* pp. 503–504; Postel, S. (2000). Groundwater Depletion Widespread. In Brown, Renner, and Halwell (Eds.), *Vital Signs 2000: Environmental Trends that are Shaping Our Future.* New York: W. W. Norton, pp 122–123.

20. Miller, G. (1998) *Living in the Environment.* p. 504; Postel, S. (2000). Groundwater Depletion Widespread, p. 123.

21. Postal, S. (1993). The Politics of Water. *Worldwatch.* 6 (4) , pp. 10–18.

22. Gardner, G. (2000). Fish Harvest Down. In Brown, Renner, and Halwell (Eds), *Vital Signs 2000,* pp 40–41; Miller, G., (1998). *Living in the Environment,* p. 611.

23. *BBC News, Sci/Tech* (2000). Fish and Chips Under Threat. July 20, 6:20 G.M.T.

24. Gardner, G. (2000), Fish Harvest Down, p. 40.

25. Gardner, G. (2000). Fish Harvest Down, p 40.

26. Miller, G. (1998). *Living in the Environment,* p. 673; Miller, G. (1992). *Living in the Environment,* 7th ed. New York: W. W. Wadsworth, p. 374; Wilson, E. O. (1990). Threats to Biodiversity. In *Managing the Earth: Readings from Scientific American.* New York: W. H. Freeman.

27. Tuxill, J. (1998). Vertebrates Signal Biodiversity Loss. In L. Brown, M. Renner, and C. Flavin (Eds.), *Vital Signs 1998: The Environmental Trends that are Shaping Our Future.* New York: W. W. Norton. pp. 128–129.

28. Miller, K., et al. (1985). Issues on the Preservation of Biological Diversity, in Repetto, R. (Ed.), *The Global Possible: Resources, Development, and the New Century.* New Haven, CT: Yale University Press, pp. 337–362.

29. Nanbhan, G., and S. Buchmann (1997). Services Provided by Pollinators. In G. Daily (Ed.), *Nature's Services: Societal Dependence on Natural Ecosystems.* Washington, DC: Island Press. p. 141.

30. Sierra Club (1999). *America's Wasting Away: Public Health Threatened by Corporate Livestock Factories;* . The Turning Point Project (1999*). Crimes Against the Soil, the Air, and the Water.* www.turningpoint.org; see also Sierra Club (1999). *Corporate Hogs at the Public Trough: How Tax Dollars Help Bring Polluters Into Your Neighborhood.*

31. Allen, S. (2000). McDonald's Cleans Up Its Environmental Act. Associated Press, cited in *Omaha World Herald,* January 30, pp. 5–6.

32. Citizen Action (1992). *Water at risk: pesticides* [pamphlet]. Lincoln, NE; Miller (1998), *Living in the Environment,* pp. 625, 656.

33. See Livernash, R., and E. Rodenburg (1998). *Population Change.* pp. 32–33; Postel, S. (1994). Carrying Capacity: Earth's Bottom Line. In L. Starke (Ed.) (1999), *State of the World 1994.* New York: W.W. Norton, pp. 3–21; Brown, L., (1999). Grain Harvest Drops. In Brown, Renner, and Halweil (Eds.). *Vital Signs 1999: Environmental Trends that are Shaping Our Future.* New York: W. W. Norton, pp. 30–31.

34. Associated Press (2000) Report: 40% of Farmland "Seriously Degraded."; Independent Online (May 5, 2000), Water for Food; Bender, W. and M. Smith (1997). Population, Food and Nutrition, *Population Bulletin,* 51 (4), p. 13–14; Food and Agriculture Organization (1995). *Dimensions of Need: An Atlas of Food and Agriculture.* Santa Barbara, CA: ABC-CLIO.

35. Grist Magazine (November 16, 2000). Citing Jim Carlton in the *Wall Street Journal.* Grist @gristmagasine.com.

36. Brown, L. (1999). Overview: An Off the chart year. In Brown, Rennner and Halweil, *Vital Signs 1999,* pp. 18–19; Miller, G. (1998). *Living in the Environment,* pp. 596–597; Pimentel (1998), in Miller, G. (1998). *Living in the Environment,* p. 562–563.

37. Miller, G. (1998). *Living in the Environment,* p. 600.

38. Altieri, M. (1995). *Agroecology: The Science of Sustainable Agriculture.* Boulder, CO: Westview Press.

39. Nuttall, N. (2000). Sow Mixed Seeds for Bigger Harvest. London Times, August 17, www.the-times.co.uk.

40. Halweil, B. (2000). Where Have All the Farmers Gone?, pp. 21–22.

41. Brown, L., (2001). Eradicating Hunger: A Growing Challenge. In L. Brown, C. Flavin, and H. French (Eds.), *State of the World, 2001.* New York: W. W. Norton, p. 43.

42. Brown, L. (2001). Eradicating Hunger, p. 44.

43. Buttel, F. (2000). Ending Hunger in Developing Countries. *Contemporary Sociology,* 29 (2), pp. 14–15.

44. Young, E. (1997). *World Hunger.* London: Routledge, pp. 27, 30.

45. Associated Press (September 11, 2000). Report: As Fewer Families Go Hungry, Woes Linger, cited in *Omaha World Herald.* p. 4.; see also Poppendieck, J. (1998). *Sweet Charity.* New York: Viking; Young, E. (1997). *World Hunger.*

46. DeRose, L., E. Messer, and S. Millman (1998). *Who's Hungry?* pp. 36, 110–111; Food and Agriculture Organization (1998). *The State of Food and Agriculture.* Rome; Pinstrup-Andersen, P., R. Pandya-Lorch, and M. Rosengrant (1997). *The World Food Situation.* Washington, DC: International Food Policy Research Institute.

47. Buttel, F. (2000). Ending Hunger in Developing Countries. *Contemporary Sociology,* 29 (2), pp. 13–14. See also Lappe, F., Collins J., and P. Rosset (1998). *World Hunger: Twelve Myths.* New York: Grove Press; DeRose, Messer, and Millman (1998). Who's Hungry?; Young, E. (1997). *World Hunger.*

48. This way of conceptualizing the causes of hunger and the following is adapted from Buttel, F., (2000). Ending Hunger in Developing Countries.

49. For examples, see Simon J. (1981). *The Ultimate Resource.* Princeton, NJ: Princeton University Press; Eberstadt, N., (1995). Population, Food, and Income, In R. Baily, *The True State of the Planet,* New York: Free Press, pp. 7–47.

50. Field, J. (1993). *The Challenge of Famine.* West Hartford, CT: Kumarian Press.

51. Pinstrup-Anderson, P., et. al. (1997), *The World Food Situation.*

52. Buttel, F. (2000). Ending Hunger in Developing Countries, p. 19; about opposition to GE crops, see Busch, L., et al. (1991). *Plants, Power, and Profit.* Oxford, U.K.: Basil Blackwell; Lappe F., et al. (1998). *World Hunger: Twelve Myths.*

53. Brown, L. (1994). Who Will Feed China? *Worldwatch,* 7, (5), Sept./Oct.; Brown, L., and B. Halweil, (1998). China's Water Shortage Could Shake World Food Security. *Worldwatch* 11(4), July/Aug.; Brown, L. (1999). Feeding Nine Billion. In L. Starke (Ed.). *State of the World 1999.* New York: W. W. Norton, p. 128.

54. See Brown, L., et al. (1999) *Feeding Nine Billion;* World Commission on Environment and Development (1987). *Our Common Future.* New York: Oxford University Press.

55. Brown, L. (2001). Eradicating Hunger: A Growing Challenge. In L. Starke (Ed.), *State of the World 2001.* New York: W. W. Norton. p. 45.

56. Wright, T. (2000). Resisting Homelessness: Global, National, and Local Solutions. *Contemporary Sociology,* 29 (1), p. 31.

57. Wright, T. (2000). Resisting Homelessness, pp. 27–43.

58. Buttel, F. (2000). Ending Hunger in Developing Countries, pp. 16–17.

59. Sen, A., (1981). *Poverty and Famines.* New York: Oxford University Press; Dreze,

J., A. Sen, and A. Hussain (1995). *The Political Economy of Hunger.* New York: Oxford University Press.

60. DeRose, Messer, and Millman (1998). Who's Hungry?; Dreze et al. (1995). *The Political Economy of Hunger;* Lappe et al., (1998). *World Hunger: Twelve Myths,* Ch. 2.

61. Young (1997). *World Hunger,* Ch. 6.

62. Messer, E. (1998). Conclusions. In DeRose, Messer, and Millman (1998). Who's Hungry?, pp. 185–186.

63. Buttel, F.,(2000). Ending Hunger in Developing Countries; DeRose, Messer, and Millman, (1998), Who's Hungry?, pp. 185–187.

64. Buttel F. (2000). Ending Hunger in Developing Countries, p. 22.

65. DeRose, L. (1998), Food Poverty. In DeRose, Messer, and Millman (1998). Who's Hungry?.

66. Rosset, P. (1999). Multiple Functions and Benefits of Small Farm Agriculture in the Context of Global Trade Negotiations. *Policy Brief No.4.* Oakland CA: Institute for Food and Development Policy.

67. Leval, K. (1999). Top 10 Reasons to be Concerned About Where Agriculture Research Dollars Go. *Center for Rural Affairs Newsletter,* Feb.

68. Nelson, T. (1996). Closing the Nutrient Loop. *Worldwatch,* 9 (6), Nov./Dec., pp. 11, 13.

69. Lappe, F., et al. (1998). *World Hunger: Twelve Myths,* pp. 81–82.

70. Buttel, F. (2000). Ending Hunger in Developing Countries, p. 25; see also Krimsky S., and R. Wrubel (1996). *Agricultural Biotechnology and the Environment.* Urbana, IL: University of Illinois Press.

71. Henderson, E. (1998). Rebuilding Local Food Systems from the Grassroots Up. *Monthly Review,* 50 (3), pp. 112–124.

72. Buttel, F., (2000). Ending Hunger in Developing Countries, pp. 25–27.

CHAPTER SEVEN

1. Dower, N. (1996). Global Hunger: Moral Dilemmas, in Mepham, B., (Ed.). *Food Ethics.* London: Routledge, p. 9.

2. O'Neill, O. (1986). *The Faces of Hunger.* London: Allen and Unwin.

3. Singer, P. (1971). Famine, Affluence, and Morality. *Philosophy and Public Affairs.* Cited in Dower, N. (1996). *Global Hunger,* p. 11.

4. Fishkin, R. (1986). Theories of Justice in International Relations: The Limits of Liberal Theory. In A. Ellis (Ed.), *Ethics and International Relations.* Manchester: Manchester University Press.

5. Nussbaum, M., and A. Sen (1993). *The Quality of Life.* New York: Oxford University Press; Sen, A. (1998). The Living Standard. In D. Crocker and T. Linden, *Ethics of Consumption: Good Life, Justice, and Global Stewardship.* New York: Rowman and Littlefield, pp. 299–305; Nussbaum, M. (1998). *The Good as Discipline, the Good as Freedom.* In D. Crocker and T. Linden, *Ethics of Consumption,* pp. 317–324.

6. Crocker D., (1995). Hunger, Capability, and Development. In W. Aiken, and H. LaFollette (Eds.), *World Hunger and Moral Obligation.* 2nd ed. Upper Saddle River, NJ: Prentice Hall; Sen, A. (1999). *Development as Freedom.* New York: Knopf.

7. Shue, H. (1980). *Basic Rights: Subsistence, Affluence, and U.S. Foreign Policy.* Princeton, NJ: Princeton University Press.
8. Rawls, J. (1971). *A Theory of Justice.* Oxford: Oxford University Press.
9. Dower, N. (1996). *Global Hunger*, pp. 14–15.
10. Poppendieck, J. (1998a). Want Amid Plenty: From Hunger to Inequality. *Monthly Review,* 50 (3), p. 126.
11. Poppendieck, J. (1997). Hunger Amid Plenty: Six Strategies. Presented to the annual meeting of the *American Sociological Association*, San Francisco, CA, Aug., p. 1; Poppendieck, J. (1998b). *Sweet Charity: Emergency Food and the End of Entitlement.* New York: Viking Press, p.3.
12. Poppendieck, J. (1997). Hunger Amid Plenty, pp. 2–3.
13. Poppendieck, J. (1998b). *Sweet Charity*, pp. 25–26.
14. Food and Hunger Hotline (1995). Thirty Million Meals a Year: Emergency Food Programs in New York City. New York.
15. Second Harvest, (2000). *America's Second Harvest Update.* Chicago, IL: America's Second Harvest, p. 14.
16. Poppendieck, J. (1998b). *Sweet Charity*, pp. 8, 121–122.
17. The following section draws heavily from Poppendieck, J. (1997). Hunger Amid Plenty.
18. Cited in Poppendieck, J. (1997). Hunger Amid Plenty, p. 4.
19. Poppendieck, J. (1997). Hunger Amid Plenty, p. 104; Poppendieck, J. (1998b). *Sweet Charity*, p. 4.
20. Food Stamp Act of 1964, P. L. 88–525, sec 1.
21. Poppendieck, J. (1997). Hunger Amid Plenty.
22. Poppendieck, J. (1998b). *Sweet Charity*, Ch. 7.
23. Poppendieck, J. (1998a). Want Amid Plenty.
24. Buttel, F. (2000). Ending Hunger in Developing Countries, pp. 14–15.
25. Which has led some to quip that the emerging world economy is driven not so much by comparative advantage as by the comparative access to subsidies among nations.
26. Marsh, J. (1996). Food Aid and Trade. In B. Mepham (Ed.), *Food Ethics*, Ch. 2. New York: Routledge.
27. Individuals, of course, eat and thrive only in the short term!
28. Marsh, J (1996). Food Aid and Trade, p. 29.
29. Ritche, M. (1999). Free Trade versus Sustainable Agriculture. In D. Boucher (Ed.), *The Paradox of Plenty: Hunger in a Bountiful World.* Oakland, CA: Food First, p. 180.
30. Reibel, J., *Food Aid to India*, unpublished master's thesis. Cited in M. Ritche (1999). Free Trade, p. 180.
31. Cited in Ritche, M. (1999). Free Trade, p. 182.
32. Ritche, M. (1999). Free Trade, p. 182.
33. Rosset, P. (1999). Food and Justice in the New Millennium: Changing How We Think About Hunger. In D. Bourcher (Ed.). *The Paradox of Plenty*, pp. 330–336.
34. Brown, L. (2001). Eradicating Hunger: A Growing Challenge. In L. Starke (Ed.), *State of the World 2001.* New York: W. W. Norton, p. 45.

Photo Credits

Page 16: Pearson Education/PH College; page 33, Peter H. Buckley/Pearson Education/PH College; page 36, Eugene Gordon/Pearson Education/PH College; page 66, McMahon/Travel Montana's Home Page; page 70, Library of Congress; page 92 top, U.S. Department of Agriculture; page 92 bottom, Nova Scotia Department of Tourism and Culture; page 98, USDA/ARS/Agricultural Research Service; page 113 top, Stan Wakefield/Pearson Education/PH College; page 113 bottom, Ken Lax/Pearson Education/PH College; page 132, Laima Druskis/Pearson Education/PH College; page 136, U.S. Department of Agriculture; page 137, Marc Anderson/Pearson Education/PH College; page 140, Eugene Gordon/Pearson education/PH College; page 149, Michal Heron/Pearson Education/PH College; page 169, U.S. Department of Agriculture; page 185, Copyright WHO/J. Marquis; page 209, National Archives and Records Administration.

Index

of food, 69–70, 85, 111
  Engel's law, 124, 142
of obesity, 157
of soil erosion, 168
of transport, 109
Creutzfeldt-Jakob syndrome,
  125–126
Crocker, Betty, 85
Cro-Magnons, 32
Crosby, Alfred, 53, 55
Crusades, 49–50, 50–51
Cuba, 197, 224
cuisine(s)
  American, 74–76, 78,
    135–137, 139
  definition, 130
  edible and inedible foods,
    134
  ethnic, 72–75, 121,
    135–136, 138–139
  fusion, 140
  high- and lowbrow, 42, 43,
    137
  and identity, 4
  and immigration, 72–75
  protein sources, 134
  and reform movement, 154
  and social differentiation,
    135–137
cultural eutrophication, 176

dairy products, 59, 66, 67
  See also milk
Dalrymple, Oliver, 65
Davis, Matthew, 173
deficiencies
  diseases, 5, 15, 60
  mineral, 27, 60, 142
  and poverty, 5, 14, 142
  protein, 5, 10
  vitamins, 14, 15, 27, 60,
    99–100
Degler, Carl, 83
dehumanization, 145–146,
  147
dehydration
  as food process, 88, 91
  of people, 12–13
Delaney Clause, 22, 102
Delmonico's, 86
demographic transition,
  163–164
Department of Agriculture
  (USDA)
  and agribusiness, 118–120,
    119, 195
  dietary guidelines, 17, 104
  farm size studies, 126, 127
  and meat processors,
    116–117

organic foods, 153
and reform, 151
and research, 195
safety role, 120, 125
and soil, 167–168
developing nations. *See* Third
  World
Diamond, Jared, 35, 36
Dietary Guidelines, 104
Dietary Reference Intakes
  (DRIs), 16
diet foods, 104
dieting, 158, 159
dietitians, 20, 244 n.54
diet(s)
  African American, 85
  ancient Greek, 41
  definition, 130
  global trends, 124
  medieval, 45
  Native American, 53
  prehistoric, 33, 34
  Roman, 43
  See also American diet
difference principle, 205–206
diners, 87
dinner, 85, 135
diseases
  agriculture-associated, 35
  and agrochemicals, 21,
    177–178
  of crops, 174–175
  deficiency-related, 5, 15, 60
  food-born, 125–126
  medieval, 49
  and obesity, 157
  and oxidation, 28
  from *Pfiesteria*, 110
  trends, 106
distribution, 166, 186, 222
  See also transportation
Douglas, Mary, 96
Doyle, John, 99
drive-throughs, 103, 148
droughts, 82, 168
Dubish, Jill, 152
Dustbowl, 168

E. coli, 125
eating. *See* foodways
eating disorders, 47–48,
  143–144
eating out, 85–87
  See also restaurants
Ebers papyrus, 15
ecology
  and agrochemicals, 20–21
  agroecology, 182–183,
    197
  biodiversity, 174–175

CAFO effect, 110, 120,
  175–176
fisheries, 172–174
and food trade, 218
and genetic engineering,
  98–99
and globalization, 218
neo-Malthusianism,
  188–190
and refrigeration, 68
soil, 167–170, 182
water, 170–172
Website, 155
See also pollution
economy of scale, 126–128
edibility, 134–135
Edible Schoolyard, 155
education
  for farmers, 64, 199–200
  for nutrition, 156, 159–161
efficiency, 147
eggs, 105
Egyptians, ancient, 15, 37
elderly, 213
Elias, Norbert, 50, 146
elites, 141
endocrine disruptors, 21
energy
  measuring, 15
  in storage, 11
Engel's law, 124, 142
entitlement, 192, 193–194,
  205, 214
environment, toxic food, 5
Erdman, J. W., 104
ergotism, 49
Eskimos, 10
essential nutrients, 12
ethics, 202–206, 215–219
ethnic foods. *See* cuisine
ethnicity, 4, 138, 192
etiquette, 69, 132–133
Europe
  Eastern, 55
  Northern, 44, 49, 108
  Western, 27, 44, 153
  See also specific countries
European Union, 97, 108,
  126
evolution, 14, 32
extension programs, 64

fallowing, 45
families. *See* households
family farming
  in ancient times, 40–42
  decline, 94, 100–101
  productivity, 126–127
  survival, 110–111
  and USDA, 118